The Sixth Language

The

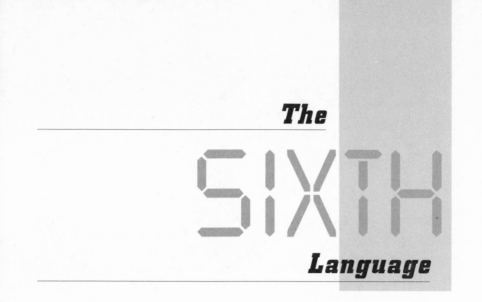

SIXTH

Language

Learning a Living in the Internet Age

Robert K. Logan

Published in 2000 by Stoddart Publishing Co. Limited
34 Lesmill Road, Toronto, Canada M3B 2T6
180 Varick Street, 9th Floor, New York, New York 10014

Distributed in Canada by:
General Distribution Services Ltd.
325 Humber College Blvd., Toronto, Ontario M9W 7C3
Tel. (416) 213-1919   Fax (416) 213-1917
Email cservice@genpub.com

Distributed in the United States by:
General Distribution Services Inc.
4500 Witmer Industrial Estates, Niagara Falls, New York 14305-1386
Toll-free Tel.1-800-805-1083   Toll-free Fax 1-800-481-6207
Email gdsinc@genpub.com

04   03   02   01   00   1   2   3   4   5

Canadian Cataloguing in Publication Data
Logan, Robert K., 1939–
The sixth language: learning a living in the Internet age
Includes bibliographical references and index.
ISBN 0-7737-6104-7
Internet (Computer network) — Social aspects.   2. Information society.   I. Title.
P96.T42L62 2000   303.48'33   C00-930082-1

U.S. Cataloging-in-Publication Data
(Library of Congress Standards)

Logan, Robert K., 1939–
The sixth language: learning a living in the Internet age / Robert Logan.
[368]p.: cm.
Includes bibliographic references and index.
Summary: The Internet as a new link in the linguistic chain and an evolution in human communication.
ISBN 0-7737-6104-7 (pbk.)
Communication and technology.   2. Educational technology.
3. Information society.   I. Title.
303.48/ 33 21 2000   CIP

Portions of this book were previously published in a book entitled *The Fifth Language* by Robert Logan, published by Stoddart Publishing in 1995.

Cover Design: Angel Guerra; Text Design: Kinetics Design & Illustration

THE CANADA COUNCIL | LE CONSEIL DES ARTS
FOR THE ARTS | DU CANADA
SINCE 1957 | DEPUIS 1957

We acknowledge for their financial support of our publishing program the Canada Council, the Ontario Arts Council, and the Government of Canada through the Book Publishing Industry Development Program (BPIDP).

Printed and bound in Canada

To my children,

Renee, David, Natalie, and Rebecca,

and their children, who will learn their livings

in the Internet age and the knowledge era

Contents

Acknowledgments

I wish to give thanks to Angel Guerra and Don Bastian, who were the first champions of this book. And to my editor, Sue Sumeraj, for her many helpful ideas and suggestions, as well as her careful copy editing.

I also wish to thank the many people whose ideas about work, learning, and life I have incorporated into this book. They include my children, Rebecca, Natalie, David, and Renee Logan, and my friends: Gaida Ansmits, Ann and Paul Beam, David Bell, David Bloomstone, Debra Brennan, Anthony Canali, Gilbert Cohen, Marnie and Derrick de Kerckhove, Alice Dong, Fred Eagleplume, Michael Edmunds, Howard Eisenberg, John Ford, Lois and Harley Frank, Judith Gabor, Barry Green, Bernard Hibbitts, Paul Kelly, Elena Lamberti, Diane and Bruce Laird, Michael Lax, Malcolm Lester, Paul Levinson, Jeff Long, Morley Markson, Eric McLuhan, Claire and Morris Miller, Pat and John Moffat, James Morrison, Issam Mousa, Leanna Pendergast, Mark Pizzolato, Larry Popofsky, Neil Postman, Peter Quattro, Elizabeth Reuthe, Mort Ritts, Irv Rosen, Val Ross, Ann Russell, Tony Schwartz, Ed Smits,

Al Sokolow, Norman Steinhart, Lou Stokes, Lance Strate, Marek Swinder, Judy Tang, Heidi and Alvin Toffler, Sara and Al Waxman, Michael Winton, Norman Winton, Bob Wong, Karen Zanutto, and Frank Zingrone.

I would like to single out Don Burril for his help in defining computer literacy and Patrick Michalak and Margaret Logan for their help in formulating the nine Internet marketing models in chapter 9. I am also grateful to the following people who helped enhance my understanding of knowledge management: Charles Armstrong, Verna Alee, Debra Amidon, Hubert Saint-Onge, Charles Savage, Patrick Sullivan, Elisabeth Sundrum, Karl Erik Sveiby, and Peter Vieser.

Finally I would like to thank the readers of *The Fifth Language*, the earlier version of this book, for their many suggestions and comments, which they sent to me via e-mail at logan@physics.utoronto.ca. I look forward to similar comments from the readers of *The Sixth Language*.

The Evolution of Language and Its Impact on Learning, Work, and Society in the Internet Age

Language is not the passive container or medium of human thought whose only function is to transmit and communicate our ideas and sentiments from one person to another. Language is, to borrow a phrase from Marshall McLuhan, a living vortex of power that shapes and transforms our thinking. Language is both a system of communications and an informatics tool. Without verbal language our mental life would be reduced to feelings, emotion, and the processing of our perceptions. Verbal language makes conceptualization, abstraction, and reflection possible. Our ability to use verbal language is what differentiates us from the rest of the animal kingdom. Other animals are capable of communicating with each other but the range of what they can express is limited to a small number of signals (less than 50). Human verbal language, on the other hand, is generative, so there are an infinite number of possible messages or meanings that we are capable of composing and communicating.

Language is a dynamic living organism that is constantly growing and evolving. As spoken language grows in terms of increased semantics and new syntactical forms, it also evolves into new forms of presentation and expression. In this book, I will develop the hypothesis that speech, writing, mathematics, science, computing, and the Internet form an evolutionary chain of languages. Two of the languages, mathematics and writing, emerged at exactly the same point in time — around 3100 BCE — followed approximately 1000 years later by science. Within my lifetime two languages have appeared in rapid succession: computing and the Internet, the fifth and sixth languages. I hope to demonstrate that computing and the Internet (which includes the World Wide Web) will play roles as important as those of the four languages that preceded them many years ago. I shall also discuss the rapid way in which we have moved from an industrial era economy some fifty years ago to one based on computers and information. We are now in the midst of still another transformation fueled by the Internet and the management of knowledge, which we must carefully distinguish from information. As we pass through the transition from the computer age to the Internet age and, at the same time, from the information age to the knowledge era, some of the observations in this book could take on new meanings and nuances. I encourage my readers to correspond with me and share their thoughts in this time of rapid change by e-mailing their comments to me at logan@physics.utoronto.ca.

The Origins of This Study

This study began as an attempt to understand how computers could best be used in the educational arena. My research, conducted at the Ontario Institute for Studies in Education (OISE) in Toronto, involved the classroom observation of the use of computers (Sullivan et al. 1986) and two theoretical studies (Logan et al. 1983; Logan 1986b) conducted for the Ontario Ministry of Education. My work in computer applications in education was carried out against the backdrop of work I had begun with Marshall McLuhan, in which we studied the effects of the phonetic alphabet and literacy on the development of deductive logic, abstract science, codified law, and monotheism (McLuhan and Logan 1977). My approach to understanding computers in education was therefore strongly flavored by the communications theories of McLuhan and the notion that the computer is a medium of communication. My own work in theoretical physics, on the other hand, which relied heavily on computers, made me equally sensitive to the information-processing aspect of computers. Therefore, at the very outset of my study to understand the impact of computers on education, I regarded the computer as both a communications medium and as a tool for processing information.

At the same time that I was considering the role of computers in education, I was also extending the work I had begun with McLuhan on the alphabet to include the role that other written notations played in the history of ideas. I was fascinated by the work of Denise Schmandt-Besserat (1992), who showed that the origins of writing and mathematical notation can be traced to the small clay tokens that were used for accounting purposes in the Middle East from 8000 to 3000 BCE. As a result of my consideration of her work, along with my own work on the alphabet effect (Logan 1986a), I recognized that all written forms of language — whether writing or mathematical notation — have both a communications and an informatics dimension, as do computers and the Internet. At this point I formulated the two main theses of this book:

- all forms of verbal language have both a communications and an informatics dimension that facilitates human thought; and
- speech, writing, mathematics, science, computing, and the Internet form an evolutionary chain of languages.

In studying the history of communications and information processing, I will demonstrate that each of these six forms of language has its own distinct semantics and syntax. Each evolved from its predecessors as new information-processing needs emerged that preceding languages could not deal with effectively. Each builds on the features of its predecessors, while adding a number of new information-processing elements of its own. Each new language eventually led to an information explosion and a new set of challenges that set the stage for the next level of development and the emergence of still another form of language, culminating in recent years in computing, the fifth language, and the Internet, the sixth language.

An understanding of the chain of events that led to the evolution of language and the emergence of the fifth and sixth languages, will foster a better understanding of the current impacts of computing and the Internet — and help predict some of the future effects. Two theoretical tools will help develop this understanding of how language evolves and new languages emerge. One is the communications theory or approach of Harold Innis and Marshall McLuhan, which is described in Chapter 2. A second is the dynamic systems approach, or Chaos Theory, as developed by Ilya Prigogine, which will be examined in the discussion of the evolution of language in Chapter 3. When evolutionary theories were first being developed, they tended to be linear, but in more recent times concepts such as co-evolution and emergence have come to the fore. Prigogine hypothesized that new levels of order emerge from chaos and that these new levels of order are, in fact, the new forms into which language evolves. Therefore new forms of language not only affect learning, work, social interactions, and knowledge structures, but they also feed forward and feed back: Old languages effect new languages; those new languages then affect the old languages. I originally elected to examine the role of computing in education within the context of communications theory and informatics. As I began to probe my subject more deeply, I realized that the focus of my study was not only the role of computers in education but the much larger topic of the relationship between language and learning or communication and cognition.

My insight that computing contained elements of both communication and informatics seemed to apply to all forms of language. The term "informatics" is generally used only within the context of computers. It is defined in *Webster's*, however, as "the science of obtaining and transmitting information," and hence is not strictly limited to computers. One can therefore consider the informatics of the oral tradition or of written texts as well as the informatics of mathematics and science.

These considerations led me to the realization that education should be basically concerned with the development of the skills associated with the use of all the modes of language — speech, writing, mathematics, science, computing, and the Internet. I saw that the informatics side of language connected to cognition and that my study overlapped three basic domains: cognition, and hence informatics; communication, and hence language; and education, or learning.

My study of the role of computers in education had suddenly expanded in what seemed like a hundred different directions, but at the same time it converged on my previous studies of the impact of written notations on the development of ideas and social institutions. I had begun my study to find optimal ways to use computers in education and found myself using the insights that the use of computers provided to try to understand the nature of cognition, language, workplace organization, social class, and education. I began to feel as though I was losing the focus of my study when I discovered that part of my task was to tie together these different domains, which computing seems so naturally to integrate. I also realized that understanding the relationship between technology and cognition could provide insights that might help us devise a plan of action for education for both the school system and the workplace that would make them more responsive to the needs of a knowledge-era economy.

The Four Facets of Computing and the Internet

Computing and the Internet are not just new technologies or new media of communication; rather, they are a radical new way to process and organize information and as such they represent two new forms of language. To fully understand computing and the Internet and their myriad impacts, we will study them from the perspectives of technology, communications, informatics, and language. In addition, we must also understand the relationships among these four aspects of computing and the Internet. How do technology, communications, informatics, and language affect one another's development or evolution? To what extent are they distinct categories and to what extent are they just four different facets of human thought and organization?

The Social Dimension

When we think of computing and the Internet we often think of them strictly in terms of technology, but there is another dimension to them, namely a socioeconomic one. All technologies have powerful effects on social, economic, and cultural life. The organization of work and of social-class structures are influenced by the evolution of technology, informatics, and language. Agriculture led to new forms of labor and its organization, to new settlements and a two-class social system of landowners and serfs. With the rise of the city-state and the advent of numeracy and literacy, there arose a third class — the middle class. The middle class, as I define it, is not made up of the middle-income earners, but rather of those who adopted literacy and learning as a lifestyle and a way to earn a living. The bourgeois values of the middle class that are disdained by many artists and members of the intelligentsia are, in fact, the values that prize learning and literacy and that led to the scientific, philosophical, and artistic achievements that have enriched our civilization. The middle class also led the Industrial Revolution and the current information revolution. An understanding of the role of social-class structure is another element in the development of an understanding of computing and the Internet, and their impact on education and work.

The Impact of Computing and the New Media on Learning and Work

"The future of work consists of learning a living in the automation age . . . Electric automation unites production, consumption and learning in an inextricable process . . . Paid learning is already becoming both the dominant employment and the source of new wealth in our society."

(McLUHAN 1964, 346–51)

Long before the advent of microcomputers, local area networks (LANs), and the Internet, Marshall McLuhan predicted that information technology would make dramatic changes in the structure of work and education. He was right. We are in the midst of a profound information revolution in which computer technology is changing the way we organize work and learn about our world. Knowledge, not capital, is the new source of wealth. Yet, paradoxically, our education system is in total crisis. Our schools are not working because they do not provide students with the type of training and education they require to cope with today's economic realities. But that is only one aspect of the problem. Despite significant unemployment, jobs go unfilled because of a lack of skilled personnel, and many who are employed are not properly trained to do their jobs effectively. There is a significant mismatch between the needs of the workplace and what the educational system is delivering. The root of the problem is that we do not have a proper understanding of the role of education in the knowledge era. We are still operating on a model of education that is a holdover from the industrial age. Computing, telecommunications, the Internet, and other forms of information technology have created a new environment and a whole new set of challenges.

One of the purposes of this book is to deal with the mismatches between school and learning, between education and work, and between computing and organizational structures inherited from the industrial age. It is about rethinking and reformulating the way we go about learning and preparing ourselves for work. It is a search for the new meaning of education. A cliché, perhaps, but a central question for a society in the midst of an information and knowledge revolution.

To conduct the search for the meaning of education and its relevancy to work we must examine the nature of cognition — or thinking — itself, and how it is affected by language, information technology, communication media, socioeconomic institutions, and social-class structures. If the information environment in which we live is an extension of our psyches, as McLuhan claimed, and it is undergoing rapid and profound change, then so too are the ways we think, process information, learn, organize and manage work, establish our values, set our goals, and formulate our aspirations. This book will examine all of these questions holistically. Not only must we question the relevancy of our education system, we must also examine our lifestyles. In the knowledge era, we can no longer compartmentalize our activities into education, work, and recreation as we did in the industrial era. This fragmentation no longer works because of the speed of technological change, plus the fact that work and the production of wealth are now knowledge-based. We can no longer divide work and learning. Life in the Internet age, or the knowledge era, only becomes meaningful when we integrate work, learning, and leisure time, whether we run a business, program a computer, or compose symphonies.

In describing the profound changes through which we are living, I have tried to strike a balance between optimism and pessimism. This is not a "technology gee whiz" book — the future is going to be automatically better, full of opportunities, and more satisfying. Nor is it a "doom-and-gloom" book, although for some caught in the avalanche of information, the future will be full of challenges. We face the possibility of electronic sweatshops, unemployment, and displacement. Computing and automation, for all their efficiencies, have increased the length of the work week, not reduced it. Many workers whose skills are overtaken by technology find themselves suddenly unemployed and, at a certain age, unemployable. This book tries to strike a balance between the service and disservice of information technology. It attempts to deal with reality as it is, not as the hyped reality of the techno-enthusiasts or the distorted reality of the technophobic and those displaced by technology. I hope the reader will gain an understanding of the current information revolution and, as a consequence, be able to take advantage of new opportunities rather than become a victim of the massive changes that are wiping out many traditional jobs and ways of handling information.

Why Our Schools Don't Work

Our schools are based on an industrial model, with a delivery system patterned on the factory. Millions of schoolchildren are taught the same content in the same linear sequential order, guided by a uniform curriculum dictated by a centralized bureaucracy at a municipal school board or state department (or provincial ministry) of education. Teachers continue to deliver an old style of book learning which does not take into account the nature of today's information-age economy or even some of the needs of day-to-day living. Students do not find enough relevancy in their schooling to take it seriously, which explains the high drop-out rate.

Not every aspect of the school system is a failure. Many students endure. Doctors, engineers, lawyers, and accountants continue to be trained. The success of our schools is limited, however. Today's education system serves yesterday's needs by training managers and technicians to fit into a hierarchically structured industrial organization that is rapidly disappearing. Two practices of the schools are counterproductive: The division of the curriculum into subject disciplines, which thereby encourage specialism, and too great a focus on content and not enough on process. Our school system must prepare individuals for the new demands of post-industrial society by providing them with both a knowledge base and a set of information-processing skills. It is unbelievable that many students graduate from university and/or high school with few or almost no computer skills at a time when computing is an indispensable part of life in the workplace for the majority of professions. This, to me, is a major indictment of our education system.

Even though the failure of the school system has been recognized for a number of years, little, if any, remedial action to make structural changes has taken place. This is due in part to the conservative nature of the education community. The main reason for the failure, however, is that contemporary education lacks a mission that is in tune with today's social and economic environment, which has evolved and changed at a much faster rate than our schools. It is not so much that the content of the curriculum is out of date as that the style of education is not suited to contemporary needs and challenges. Stop-gap measures such as adding computer science to the curriculum or using computers and the Net as teaching tools will not remedy the ills of education: "Schools have already spent billions on computers — 97% of the 110,000 elementary and secondary schools in the U.S. now have them. But scores on standardized tests in math and reading are no higher than they were in 1970. The history of technology in education has not been a stellar one" (*Business Week*, Nov. 11, 1991, 158). As seen in this quote, computers had penetrated nearly all schools by 1991. In the time since then, computers have become even more a part of school curriculum with the addition of the Internet, but one still hears the same complaints that their use has not yet resulted in increased learning. In fact, there has been a back-to-basics movement implemented in some jurisdictions, such as Ontario, where there is a greater emphasis placed on the skills associated with the use of writing and math.

Approaches that consider how computers and the Internet can be used to achieve present educational goals without considering how the entire educational enterprise should change are doomed to failure. The increased use of computers and the Net alone will not solve the problem. "The evidence of our neglect of philosophy as it applies to educational computing lies in the absence of a significant body of discourse on what computers ought to be used for in education . . . Where is the literature debating what the aims or goals of computer education should be? Such literature exists, but it is extremely meager" (Maddux 1988, 6).

The role of the microcomputer in the school and the workplace needs to take on a new meaning. From the classroom perspective, the computer is not a tool to automate teaching but an environment in which students can learn and develop their cognitive skills through exploration and discovery. In the world of work, the computer is not simply a tool to increase productivity; it creates a learning environment in which employees can continuously develop their information-processing and communication skills. Computers and the Net can facilitate a program of lifelong learning, another critical dimension in reformulating our thinking about education. Education must not stop once the student leaves school. It must become a lifelong process that integrates work and learning.

Integrating Work and Learning

If the key to survival in the knowledge era is to "learn a living" by integrating work and learning, then we must understand the relationship between education, work, and technology. Since knowledge workers and information technology are driving the changes in the information-age economy, the relationship between learning and work has to undergo radical change. Moreover, the rapid rate of technological change is forcing the integration of education and work. Schools that provide students with knowledge of the latest developments in their field but do not equip them with the skills to update that knowledge are failing their students. On the other hand, employers who ignore the role of training and education in their operations are equally derelict in their duties to both their employees and their organizations.

As the purpose of this book is to determine the most effective way to organize learning in our schools and in the workplace within the context of the new information environment of computers and the Internet, we must reformulate the relationship between schooling, education, and work. Schooling and education are no longer synonymous. In the model inherited from the industrial age, within which school-based and industrial-based educators have traditionally operated, learning and working are two separate activities that correspond to two distinct time periods in the life of an individual. In this model, basic learning takes place in the school years of childhood and early adulthood and determines to a large extent what kind of work will be pursued and how far the student will go in life. With the exception of those lucky few who have participated in a co-op program, the work undertaken by students during their school years is usually unrelated to their professional development and is undertaken solely to earn money. The focus of working life, on the other hand, is not about learning but about earning a living. Some time during this period is devoted to training or professional development, depending on the nature of one's job and the attitude of one's employer. But because the focus of a business organization is on the bottom line, the amount of resources and employee time devoted to learning is frequently quite limited. The concept of "just-in-time training" in which an employee is provided only with enough instruction to perform the tasks at hand is a perfect example of the minimal attention paid to education by most employers.

The separation of the domain of schooling and childhood from that of work and adulthood can be traced to the early days of the industrial age. Before this period, formal education was provided for a tiny minority of the population: the highly privileged members of the aristocracy or the bourgeoisie. For the vast majority, there was no formal schooling and precious little childhood. Children began to work as soon as they could perform chores that would contribute to their families' survival. Their only learning was an apprenticeship with their parents to learn a trade.

The industrialization of Europe led, beginning in England, to a system of formal education for the masses — and to the invention of the concept of childhood. At this time, a clear separation was made between learning — that is, school learning — and work or holding a job. This separation was almost complete except for the short training period just after a student left school, during which he learned the tricks of his trade. What he learned during this brief on-the-job apprenticeship would last a lifetime.

This model has endured, and still provides the foundation for our current education system and the induction of young people into the work force. But it is beginning to break down, primarily because the nature of work and the use of technology are changing. Perhaps more importantly, the rate of change is accelerating. Industrial-age schools were originally organized like factories and were mandated to mass-produce uniform and standardized graduates who could be easily integrated into the industrial system as both disciplined workers and consumers. The system worked because the methods and techniques of information processing, which were paper-and-pen-based, did not change within the time frame required to educate a young person. In fact, they did not change very much within the lifetime of an individual.

Now, because of the rate of change in technology, the idea of life-long learning is slowly gaining credence. Unfortunately, however, these technological changes have not led to any significant structural alterations to either the school system or the operation of the work-place. A great deal of lip service is paid to the idea, but neither schools nor industry seems willing or able to commit the resources needed to make lifelong education a reality. Whatever commitment is now being made to lifelong education is being made by individuals. The long-term solution to this mismatch will require a serious commitment by both the school system and industry, but it would immediately solve two major problems: the irrelevancy of schooling as a preparation for work, and the need to constantly upgrade skills because of the rapid changeover of technology.

Eleven Critical Questions

In order to achieve the goal of an integrated understanding of language, learning, and work, based on the recognition of the unity of communications, cognition, and education, I have formulated eleven basic questions that are critical for our study:

1. What are the relationships among language, communications, information, technology, and knowledge?
2. What are languages and how do they affect learning, work, and social interactions?

3. How does language evolve and new forms of language emerge?
4. How will computers and the Internet change our notions of what we mean by communication, information processing, language, learning, education, and work?
5. How is computing changing work patterns and the organization of social institutions?
6. How can computing be harnessed to inculcate students with the desire for lifelong learning?
7. How can work be organized to naturally promote learning?
8. How can education in the workplace be better organized to improve productivity so that learning becomes a lifelong activity and workers are properly trained to do their jobs?
9. How can computers and the Internet be used to achieve present educational goals?
10. How must present educational goals change to accommodate changes in the nature of work due to the widespread use of computers and the Net?
11. How can the school system be restructured so that the goals of education and the vocational needs of society in the Internet age or knowledge era can be better matched?

Only by addressing these questions can we make our schools and workplaces relevant to our needs and create an atmosphere conducive to lifelong learning. Because microcomputers and the Internet have been in use in the workplace and in schools for such a relatively short time, our understanding of these technologies is still primitive. Educators and managers have only begun to explore the possibilities offered by microcomputers and the Net. This book, however, addresses the many issues raised by the eleven questions above and provides a framework within which these issues may be addressed in the future, so that computers will affect education and work in a positive way. The study begins with an examination of the ideas of Harold Innis and Marshall McLuhan, who pioneered the study of the impact of communications media on social systems.

2

The Innis-McLuhan Communications Revolution:

The Method in the Madness of Marshall McLuhan

The pioneering work of the Canadian communications theorists Harold Innis and Marshall McLuhan provides cogent insights into the cognitive and social impacts of communications media and other information-processing technologies on work and education. The general theoretical framework of this book, including the notion that computers and the Internet are both media of communications and information-processing technologies, grew out of the organic way in which Innis and McLuhan treated communications and its relationship to technology.

Innis and McLuhan influenced a number of other fields, including commerce, politics, advertising, social sciences, and the arts. Their work was more concerned with the larger patterns of communication than with the meticulous analysis of detailed data. They made use of intuition and poetic insight and were given to speculation and generalization. Some have suggested that they were unsystematic in their approach and that they lacked a methodology. But although they did not articulate and separate their methodology and assumptions from their analyses, they nevertheless developed a systematic approach to media studies and communications theory that they employed consistently and coherently.

This chapter has four objectives. The first is to show that the work of Innis and McLuhan gave rise to a coherent school of thought — that of the Toronto School of Communications — with a systematic methodology and a common set of basic assumptions and presuppositions. The second is to articulate these assumptions, presuppositions, and methods based on the writings of Innis and McLuhan. The third objective is to update their approach by extending their methodology to include the most recent breakthroughs in communications and informatics due to microelectronics. Finally, the fourth objective is to develop a general framework for and specific insights into the ways in which the workplace and the education system can be reformed to meet the needs of the Internet age and the knowledge era. It is hoped that more practical work and educational models — models that make use of the benefits provided by new technologies — will emerge.

The Assumptions and Methods of the Toronto School of Communications

Harold Innis and Marshall McLuhan were, respectively, professors in the political economy and English departments at the University of Toronto, where they met, interacted, and influenced each other's work. McLuhan freely acknowledged the impact that Innis had on him. In the foreword to the 1972 edition of Innis's *Empire and Communications*, McLuhan wrote: "I am pleased to think of my own book *The Gutenberg Galaxy* as a footnote to the observations of Innis on the subject of the psychic and social consequences, first of writing and then of printing. Flattered by the attention that Innis had directed to some work of mine, I turned for the first time to his work. It was my good fortune to begin with *Minerva's Owl*. How exciting it was to encounter a writer whose every phrase invited prolonged meditation and exploration" (McLuhan 1972, ix).

Perhaps this quote explains why the work of Innis and McLuhan forms a coherent whole, exhibiting a unified purpose, set of assumptions, and methodology. Their work has inspired other scholars, many working in Toronto, to pursue similar lines of research in this tradition; hence the designation the Toronto School of Communications. That these two giants of communications both came from Canada may reflect the fact that, with the world's second-largest land mass and a relatively sparse population, Canada has always been challenged by the problems of transportation and communication.

In articulating the assumptions and methods of Innis and McLuhan, I have not attempted explicitly to separate the elements of their methodology from their basic assumptions. Innis, as an economic historian, and McLuhan, as a literary critic, developed their methodology intuitively, Innis through his concern with trade and commercial patterns in the economic world, and McLuhan by studying how writers affect their reading public. Rather than deducing their methods from a basic set of axioms, they arrived at their methodology inductively on the basis of their respective observations and experiences. The resulting methods and assumptions of their two independent approaches display an enormous number of parallels and contain a significant number of overlapping claims and conclusions. Innis turned to the study of communications per se toward the end of his career, whereas McLuhan pursued media studies almost from the outset of his academic life.

The order in which I have described their thoughts reflects my notion of a systematic presentation of their ideas. The ideas are presented sequentially, since this form of ordering lends itself to the written word. I can assure the reader from my own experience of working with McLuhan, however, that he never analyzed a problem sequentially and certainly not in the order presented here. All of the methods set out below were brought to bear simultaneously on whatever issue or challenge he was tackling.

Media as Living Vortices of Power

The unique element in the Innis-McLuhan approach to media studies, and hence the logical starting point for articulating their methodology, is their attitude toward the dynamic role that media and technology play in economic, political, social, and cultural environments. Rather than viewing media as passive conduits for carrying information or communicating ideas, the two theorists regarded media, as McLuhan put it, as "living vortices of power creating hidden environments (and effects) that act abrasively and destructively on older forms of culture" (McLuhan 1972, v). Computing, the Internet, and other information-processing technologies thus create the need for a re-evaluation of the workplace and of our education system: The older form of culture which the school system was intended to serve has been transformed by new technologies, and a new model for education and its relation to work must be found.

Media Create New Social Patterns and Restructure Perceptions

As "living vortices of power," media create new social patterns. Innis wrote that "a medium of communication has an important influence on the dissemination of knowledge over space and over time and it becomes necessary to study its characteristics in order to appraise its influence in its cultural setting" (Innis 1950, 33). Once the dominant media and technologies of a culture are known, one knows "the cause and shaping force of the entire structure [and] what the pattern of any culture [has] to be, both psychically and socially" (McLuhan 1972, xii).

Media not only have an impact on social patterns but also directly affect the psyche and the ways in which people think and learn. "The effects of technology do not occur at the level of opinions or concepts, but alter sense ratios or patterns of perception steadily and without any resistance" (McLuhan 1964, 18). A medium of communication creates a sensory bias, and hence a new cognitive style. Preliterate cultures existed in an acoustical world where all information was processed simultaneously in real time. Literate societies, on the other hand, developed a visual bias in their perceptions because literacy involves the use of the visual faculty in which information is processed in a linear sequential manner letter by letter or word by word. With the electronic dissemination of information, new sense ratios will emerge in which both the visual and the acoustical will come into play; the visual because of the continued use of abstract signs — the letters of the alphabet and/or numerals — and the acoustical because of the real-time simultaneity that instantaneous electronic communication makes possible.

"The Medium Is the Message"

Like most good aphorisms, McLuhan's famous dictum has more than one meaning. Two of its principal interpretations form an integral part of the philosophy of the Toronto School of Communications. One is the notion that, independent of its content, a medium has its own intrinsic effects on our perceptions, which are its unique message. "The message of any medium or technology is the change of scale or pace or pattern that it introduces into human affairs." McLuhan (1964, 8) cites the way the railway created "totally new kinds of cities and new kinds of work." What McLuhan writes about the railroad applies with equal force to the media of print, television, the microcomputer, and the Internet. "The medium is the message" because it is the "medium that shapes and controls the scale and form of human association and action" (McLuhan 1964, 9). The effects of a medium impose a new environment and set of sensibilities upon its users. For example, microcomputers in the classroom and the workplace affect social interactions because the display monitors encourage and facilitate sharing. The Internet, on the other hand, facilitates collaboration because of the ease with which people can instantaneously share ideas and information, even across large distances.

"The medium is the message" also carries the notion that a medium transforms its message or content. A movie shown on television or a play that is filmed affects its audience differently from the original. The classroom drill exercise in a workbook loses some of its tedium when it is programmed onto a microcomputer or accessed via a Web site.

"Media Analysis" versus "Content Analysis"

The aphorism "the medium is the message" has been subject to much misinterpretation, particularly by those who take it to mean that the content of a medium is to be totally disregarded and the only message is that of the medium itself. But McLuhan (1964,11) writes: "The latest approach to media study considers not only the 'content' but the medium and the cultural matrix within which the particular medium operates." This clearly indicates that McLuhan's intention was not to wholly ignore the content of a medium in analyzing its impacts. McLuhan, who enjoyed both hyperbole and paradox, was anxious, however, to shift the focus of analysis from that solely of content to one that also included the effects of a medium independent of its content. He believed that the study of communication patterns requires a balance between "media analysis" and "content analysis." The first step in using a new medium in an educational setting is to learn as much as possible about the medium itself. Once the medium and the skills required to use it are understood, one can then use the medium to acquire new knowledge. The actual content of a new computer-configured or Internet-based education system or workplace will not change that dramatically from the content of the past, but the style of delivery and the approach to that content will be radically different.

The Content of Any Medium Is Always Another Medium

The content of the telegraph is print, and the content of print is writing. The content of writing is speech, and the content of speech is thought (McLuhan 1964, 8). When a medium first appears, it uses the content of another medium exclusively for its content until its users have learned to exploit the new medium to develop new forms of expression.

Innis and McLuhan provide a number of historical examples to illustrate that the immediate content of a new medium is the content of an older one: "The narrow two- to three-inch column of the papyrus roll was continued in the early vellum manuscripts, which contained three or four columns to a page" (Innis 1950, 116). The press was first used to print ancient and medieval books rather than to produce new books. Printed books were often taken to a scribe to be copied and illustrated (Steinberg 1955). The first literature to appear in writing was transcriptions of material that had been composed orally, such as Homer's *Iliad*, the Hebrew Scriptures, and the Hindu Vedas. Only later did authors develop a prose style composed expressly for the written medium. A similar pattern developed with television. Movies and vaudeville were the first content of TV; only later were shows like Rowan and Martin's *Laugh In* or *Second City TV* (*SCTV*) crafted specifically to take advantage of the medium.

At first, the content of computers was print, mathematics, and scientific data. In the commercial world, computers were first used to perform complex calculations and manipulations of data. It is only in recent years that applications specifically designed for computers, like spreadsheets and relational databases, have emerged. Microcomputers were first employed in the classroom as electronic flash cards for drill and practice. It was only later that new educational applications such as word processing, simulations, and multimedia came to be used so that interactive learning tools could be created.

A similar dynamic holds for the Internet, whose first content was word-processed e-mail. In many ways the use of e-mail mirrors the use of faxes and "snail mail," particularly because many people still feel uncomfortable reading type onscreen. Look at the behavior of some senior executives: Rather than opening their own e-mail, they have an assistant print out the messages. They then respond to the e-mailed message by dictating a response, which the assistant types in and sends out over the Net. This is a clear example of McLuhan's notion that the content of a new medium is an older medium. The patterns of usage of e-mail, as we will explore later, are now changing so that an exchange of e-mail takes on the structure of a dialogue, and its content is more like a conversation than the formal exchange of memos.

It was only after the Internet had been in use a number of years that HTML (hypertext markup language) was developed and applied to the creation of World Wide Web sites in which graphics and text could be easily integrated and different pages could be linked with the click of a mouse. The development of tools like CGI scripting, which allows visitors to a Web site to leave information for the owners of the site, creates another dimension unique to the Web. Search engines designed to work on the Web have created an unparalleled information environment where users can find the exact information they need with no more effort than the click of a mouse and a mastery of some simple logic, or Boolean algebra. The growth of the Web in terms of the number of users, the amount of information available, and the variety of services available continues to astonish. The content of this new medium is older media: book stores and consumer goods stores; business-to-business products and services; apartment rentals, new home sales, and auction sales; software distribution; the content of CD-ROMs, radio shows, and even television shows (in a low density format but available whenever the viewer wishes to watch). The list continues to grow with the takeoff of e-commerce.

The Reversal of Cause and Effect

In the Innis-McLuhan approach, a medium or technology is studied by examining its effects not only on its direct users but on a society as a whole. One of the ways of understanding the effects of a technology is to consider the changes that would take place if that technology suddenly disappeared. With Innis and McLuhan, the notion of a one-to-one correspondence between cause and effect gives way to a "total-field-theory" approach where one and the same cause may have a wide diversity of predictable and characteristic effects (McLuhan 1972, ix). Rather than "matching one cause against another effect [Innis and McLuhan] went on making sense of the process released by the new structures of communication" (McLuhan 1972, x). Linear sequential cause and effect, brought into doubt by Hume's skepticism and discounted as a principle of causality by quantum mechanics, is replaced by an interplay of cause and effect. "Instead of asking which came first, the chicken or the egg, it suddenly seemed that a chicken was an egg's idea for getting more eggs" (McLuhan 1964, 12). A similar idea was developed in Richard Dawkins's *The Selfish Gene*. The notion that the gene is a mechanism to propagate the organism was reversed and evidence was presented to support the proposition that the organism is merely a mechanism for a gene to propagate more of its own kind (Dawkins 1976).

Reversal of cause and effect is the technique of the artist who begins with the effect he or she wants to create in an audience and invents a work of art that achieves that end. Reversal of cause and effect is one of the consequences of electronically configured information patterns and the need for the cybernetic feedback and feedforward of information: The speedup of information flow requires planners to have complete knowledge of all possible ultimate effects. An example of this "technique of discovery" — starting with the thing to be discovered and working backwards to reproduce the desired object — which was first understood and used in the nineteenth century, can be seen in the modern process of reverse engineering, whereby a competing firm takes a finished product and figures out how to manufacture it.

The reversal of cause and effect is the only way that we can reform the school system and develop a new model of education. We must work backwards from the desired effects if we wish to find a curriculum that will serve the needs of the Internet age.

Figure-Ground

The meaning of any "figure," whether it is a technology, an institution, a communication event, a text, or a body of ideas, cannot be determined if that figure is considered in isolation from the ground or environment in which it operates. The ground provides the context from which the full meaning or significance of a figure emerges. The concern with the relation of figure to ground explains the emphasis of the Toronto School on interface and pattern rather than on a fixed point of view.

The following examples illustrate the way in which context can transform the meaning of a figure: A smokestack belching smoke, once a symbol of industrial progress, is today a symbol of pollution; the steam locomotive, once the symbol of mechanical power, is now an art object and a focus of nostalgia; the suntan, once a sign of hard work in the fields, evolved into a symbol of affluence and holidaying, and is now becoming a symbol of reckless disregard for health concerns such as skin cancer.

The figure of the school, which has been slow to change, has taken on new meaning because of the radical changes in the information environment in which it operates. The school system, once considered an engine of social mobility and a fount of opportunity, is now regarded by many students as an obstacle or a prison in which one must do time until one is released into the real world as an adult. In order to succeed, the figures of the school and, for that matter, the workplace must change so that they are back in sync with the real world, a world that is undergoing continuous and rapid change due to the accelerated flow of information.

Interface and Pattern Rather Than a "Point of View"

A distinguishing characteristic of the Toronto School is the absence of the traditional methodology of orthodox scholarship whereby a particular "point of view" or hypothesis is articulated and all subsequent

From all of us with the Master of Arts in Communications and Technology program...

There are three things which inspire confidence
in the orator's own character –
the three, namely, that induce us to believe
a thing apart from any proof of it:
good sense, good moral character, and goodwill.

– **Aristotle, The Rhetoric**

Spring Institute 2003

observations are made to support or refute it. McLuhan (1977) describes his approach of working without a "point of view" as "observation minus ideas." A point of view ties one down to a single perspective and limits the richness of insight that one can develop. A point of view represents the visual bias of the written word rather than the simultaneous, all-at-once, acoustic flow of information characteristic of both the electric information age and the oral tradition. A point of view is equivalent to the "single vision of Newton."

McLuhan described how Innis articulated the alternative stance to adopting a point of view. "He changed his procedure from working with a 'point of view' to that of the generating of insights by the method of 'interface.' By contrast, a 'point of view' is merely a way of looking at something. But an insight is the sudden awareness of a complex process of interaction" (McLuhan 1972, viii). The point-of-view approach leads to classification, a left-brain process, whereas working with interface leads to pattern recognition, a right-brain process.

The point-of-view approach corresponds to what Thomas Kuhn (1972) calls "normal science." Once a revolutionary idea succeeds in describing a new set of data or phenomena, a new paradigm develops. This paradigm is imitated and articulated in as many areas of application as possible. The development of a new paradigm is "revolutionary science" and requires the lack of a point of view. "Normal science," or the articulation of the new paradigm, involves the adoption of the new paradigm as a point of view. The Toronto School attempts to operate in the revolutionary mode without a point of view.

The school system, on the other hand, operates by transmitting the paradigms of the past. It teaches by example and encourages the adoption of the point of view of others. This approach worked well during the industrial age when ideas were slow in changing. But in order to accommodate the rapid change characteristic of our times, we must train our young people to be innovative and open to new ideas, and not to rely necessarily on past points of view. The same applies to business, which also operates on the paradigms of the past but which must change to accommodate the new reality of microcomputing and connectivity.

The Service and Disservice of New Media

New media, including the institutions of schools and the corporation, and the mediums of the computer and the Internet, create both service and disservice. The new services of a medium are obvious since the purpose of any invention is to enhance or augment some activity of humankind. Each medium, however, is a "vortex of power" creating new environments and acting abrasively on older cultural forms. The potential for disservice and the destruction of cultural forms is enormous. One need only consider the effect of the speedup of information on the education system — where the curriculum is often obsolete by the time students leave school and enter into the work force — to see the destructive power of a new technology.

Consider the service and disservice of logic. Logic helped create a new scientific and rational way of thinking that led to many advances. However, the rational thought of the Greek philosophers, based on the technologies of the phonetic alphabet and deductive logic, also acted abrasively and destructively on the oral tradition. Indeed, Plato would have banned poets from his utopian Republic. The disservice of the rational approach did not extend merely to the destruction of the older order of the oral tradition. The excesses of being overly logical also impeded developments within the new order of thinking. Parmenides' arguments against the possibility of non-being on logical grounds inhibited the invention of zero by the ancient Greeks. The overly abstract approach of the Greek philosophers prevented the development of an empirical approach to science and likely delayed the scientific revolution. These examples illustrate that too much of a good thing can be a disservice.

The Internet provides another example of service and disservice. E-mail facilitates billions of communications each day between individuals across the planet as well as in the same office. E-mail allows a flow of ideas, information, and even dialogue without the frustrations of having to play telephone tag. E-mail provides control over space and time that allows us to increase the amount of communication we have with others in both business and social life.

On the disservice side, e-mail access results in an endless stream of useless, spammed messages and the unnecessary copies of communications between colleagues that clutter our mailboxes. Other negative side effects arise because e-mail speeds up the exchange of information, sometimes with disastrous effects. A Toronto lawyer and friend reports that a number of his clients have gotten into trouble by firing off e-mails without giving proper forethought to what they were saying; as a result, they compromised their positions. A hasty remark made in conversation or in an oral negotiation cannot usually be recorded and held against a person. A written response can be carefully vetted before being sent out. But e-mail encompasses the expectation of a rapid response time, and, while more casual than a formal letter, holds more accountability than a verbal gaffe.

Another disservice of e-mail in social interactions is that one tends to joke and banter in an e-mail the way one would in conversation but not in a written communication. Problems of misinterpretation can easily arise because e-mail does not provide the extra cues that spoken language carries as a result of tone, hand signals, body language, and facial gesture. (However, an attempt to overcome this problem has been developed by the use of emoticons to indicate emotional tone, such as the smiley :-) face used to indicate a jocular tone.)

The World Wide Web provides a valuable service because information can be rapidly self-published and disseminated with ease, at low cost, without being vetted by vested interests. The Web therefore provides independence to authors, who are sometimes censored by academic editors, book publishers, or professional interest groups such as doctors, lawyers, and psychologists. There is a great deal of misinformation and disinformation on the Web; hence, the prudent user must always be suspicious of the veracity of facts published in this way, and young children must be supervised. But one can find many examples of professionally vetted and published print information that is just as inaccurate and misleading as anything one finds on the Net.

A service of the Web is the unprecedented amount of information that can be so easily accessed, but this is tempered on the flip side by the disservice of the Web's information glut. While there are times when the precise information needed can be accessed with just a couple of clicks of the mouse, there are also moments when one feels as though finding an answer is like looking for a needle in a haystack. Other disservices of the Web include the "addiction" of some users to chat rooms, the prevalence of pornography, and the illegal dissemination of copyrighted material.

The Absence of a Moral Judgment

The Toronto School attempts to articulate the patterns of change that occur as new media create innovation and push out older forms without expressing a particular point of view or making a moral judgment. McLuhan held that "moral and emotional indignation was simply an indulgence on the part of those powerless to either act or to understand" (Marchand 1989, 121).

Because he described the power of electric technology and the threat that it posed to literacy, McLuhan was often accused of being an enemy of the book and an advocate of electronic media, a somewhat ironic epithet for one of the most widely read scholars of our time. McLuhan, in fact, was extremely critical of television and felt that its use by children should be carefully regulated by their parents. He was not passing judgment on the transition into the electric age of information, with its potential threat to literacy; rather, he was warning society of the powerful changes that electric forms of information were creating. Like the messenger of bad news who was killed by the king, he was attacked as though he were somehow responsible for encouraging the new phenomena. The same treatment is often directed at critics of the present-day school system.

Media Studies as Civil Defense against Media Fallout

"Is not the essence of education civil defense against media fallout?" (McLuhan 1962, 294 [Mentor ed.]). "What Innis indicates as a basis for social survival is nothing less than a reorganization of our perceptual lives and a recognition that the environments we witlessly or involuntarily create by our innovations are both services and disservices that make very heavy demands of our awareness and understanding" (McLuhan 1972, vii). It is only by studying various media and their effects that one can anticipate change and be prepared for it. "Control over change would seem to consist in moving not with it but ahead of it" (McLuhan 1964, 199). The school system and to some extent business, because of their intrinsically conservative nature, tend to move with change rather than ahead of it.

The Subliminal Effects of Media

The fish is unaware of the water in which it swims. It is blind to its environment — its medium. We, too, function and perceive reality in an information/communication environment that we take for granted. People do not realize that they live in a small village until they have been to a big city (Hall 1973). The fish only appreciates its medium once it has been forced out of the water.

Innis and McLuhan were aware of the "nemesis of creativity" which blinds a culture to its most significant inventions. "The Greek dramatists presented the idea of creativity as creating, also, its own kind of blindness, as in the case of Oedipus Rex, who solved the riddle of the Sphinx" (McLuhan 1964, 39). "It is one of the ironies of Western man that he has never felt any concern about inventions as a threat to his way of life. The fact is that, from the alphabet to the motorcar, Western man has been steadily refashioned in a slow technological explosion that was extended over 2500 years" (McLuhan 1964, 270). This time around we are being refashioned by a rapid explosion of information.

McLuhan (1964,17) describes the insensitivity to new media and technology as numbness: "The electric technology is within the gates, and we are numb, deaf, blind, and mute about its encounter with the Gutenberg technology." This numbness he attributes to the need to protect the psyche when it is suddenly exposed to the new "stress of pace" which a new medium creates. In the case of electric technology, McLuhan describes this numbness as a self-amputation of the nervous system, which becomes extended by the new medium. It is because of this self-induced numbness that the effects of media are often subliminal and hidden. Teachers continue to conduct their classes as though we were still in the midst of the industrial age. Businesses, even those in the information sector, such as IBM, conduct themselves along the patterns of the nineteenth century.

The Counterintuitive Effects of Media

The effects of media are complex because of the vast energies they release, the wide scope of their impact, and their subliminal natures. It is therefore understandable that, frequently, their impacts are counterintuitive. Henry Ford thought that by making the Model T affordable, Americans would be able to enjoy the countryside; instead, the automobile destroyed much of the countryside. The counter-intuitive effects of technology occur because their side effects over-whelm their intended or desired function. The increased access to information made possible by computers and the Internet has flipped into information overload because the approach to the use of these media is based on an industrial-age mentality and attitudes.

The Laws of the Media

McLuhan developed a set of rules that he called the Laws of the Media (LOM) for studying the effects of media or technologies (McLuhan and McLuhan 1988). LOM specifically illustrates the counterintuitive nature of technology's impacts. It consists of the following four laws:

1. Every medium or technology enhances some human function.
2. In doing so, it obsolesces some former medium or technology which was used to achieve the function earlier.
3. In achieving its function, the new medium or technology retrieves some older form from the past.
4. When pushed far enough, the new medium or technology flips or reverses into a complementary form.

To illustrate LOM, first consider the medium of money, which enhanced trade and commerce, obsolesced the barter system, retrieved the conspicuous consumption of hunting-and-gathering societies, and flipped into credit. Or consider the technology of the automobile, which enhanced transportation, obsolesced the horse and carriage, retrieved the knight in shining armor, and flipped into the traffic jam — the lack of mobility.

The laws apply with equal validity to all the artifacts of humankind, whether they are communication media, technological inventions, or scientific laws or principles. The term "obsolescence" used in this con-text requires some clarification because the word is often misinterpreted or interpreted too literally. The obsolescence of the barter system by money does not mean that the use of cash forever ended the straight exchange of commodities. It does mean, however, that cash transac-tions became the dominant mode of commercial exchange. Similarly, the obsolescence of the horse and carriage did not end forever this mode of transportation, which is still used as a tourist attraction in large cities and as a mode of transport in many third-world centers or among certain cultural groups. The automobile, however, has come to dominate traffic patterns.

This point becomes particularly important when considering the obsolescence of print by electric information. When McLuhan indicated that electricity had obsolesced print, defenders of the book pointed to statistics that showed an increase in the sale of books and the number of new titles available. They argued that the book had not been obsolesced but was alive and well. What these critics failed to grasp is that electric information has come to dominate print as the principal mode of distributing information and that information consumers spend far more time with electric media such as radio and television than they do with books. They also failed to take into account that the production of print material was also being more and more influenced by the electronic telecommunication, handling, and storage of information. When writing obsolesced the oral tradition, people did not suddenly stop talking to each other. But writing came to dominate the spoken word whenever a permanent record of information was desired or communication over distance was required.

A technology or medium does not disappear when it becomes obsolesced; it often becomes an art form or a source of nostalgia. The phenomena of antique reproductions and handcrafted utensils as art forms illustrates this idea. And in the age of supermarkets and slick packaging, a farmer's market becomes a source of intense nostalgia and a tourist attraction.

How do the Laws of the Media apply to computing? Information technologies enhance the individual's access to information, "retrieve" the generalist's approach to processing information, and hence obsolesce the specialist or the expert. Computing retrieves individual learning and hence obsolesces mass education. The computer, if pushed far enough, will flip into an information overload in which the quantity of information overwhelms the user and no pattern becomes discernible. The challenge facing schools and the workplace, therefore, is to provide context and relevance to information and "learning."

The Internet obeys a similar pattern of enhancing access to information, obsolescing the specialist, retrieving individual learning, and, possibly, flipping into information overload. The Laws of the Media can also help us to understand how the patterns of work, vis-a-vis personal contact and location, are changing as a result of the Net and the Web. The Net enhances access to information at the local level. The ability to satisfy one's information needs on a desktop is obsolescing the need to go into the office. The Net is retrieving the village or the homestead where one's needs are met locally or at home. Updating McLuhan's joke that asked "why does the executive drive downtown to use the telephone?" one could now ask "why do today's information workers drive to their offices to use the telephone, their computers, and the World Wide Web when they can access all three at home?"

This paradox of the contradiction between a physical workplace and a virtual work world underscores a real concern. If pushed far enough, Internet use could easily flip into social isolation. This potential development must be seriously entertained as we experience less and less human contact in our work spaces.

The Equivalence of Media and Technologies

As the Laws of the Media apply with equal validity to media and to tools, the distinction between technological inventions and media of communication is somewhat arbitrary. I use "technology" in its broadest sense to include not only hardware (machinery) but also all forms of communication and information processing, including speech, writing, mathematics, science, and computing. The term "technology" stems from the ancient Greek word *technologia*, which means a systematic treatment. The fact that computers are referred to as information technology supports my notion that the distinction between media and technology is an artificial one.

Media such as the book, the telephone, radio, and television differ from tools such as the hammer, the bulldozer, the airplane, and the light bulb, but there are also some very important overlaps. The most obvious is that all media function as tools serving our needs and all consist of some form of technology. One can also argue, however, that technologies become media, as seen in the case of a light bulb that is used to spell out advertising slogans. The road, the canal, and the railroad are also technologies that serve as media (grounds) for the automobile, the ship, and the train, respectively. The automobile, the ship, and the train have as their content passengers and freight. Moreover, the automobile functions as another kind of medium when it becomes a status symbol, a symbol of teenage rebellion, a symbol of a macho man's potency, or a haven for privacy. These meanings or functions of the automobile are often as important as its primary "message": mobility.

Technology as Extensions of the Body and Media as Extensions of the Psyche

From the Laws of the Media we discovered that technologies and media enhance human functions. Mechanical technologies serve to extend our physical bodies, while media of communication extend our psyches or nervous systems. So computing may be considered a form of "artificial intelligence" (AI). The confusion with the term "AI" arises when it is used to denote an independent intelligence separate from its human creators and users. Those who indulge in this futuristic fantasy forget that computers are only extensions of our own intelligence.

McLuhan (1964, 3) observed that mechanical technologies extended our bodies in space and that electric technologies extended our central nervous systems into what he termed "a global embrace, abolishing both space and time." The integrated nature of the total communications/technology environment is a consequence of this fact. "Since all media are extensions of ourselves, or translations of some part of us into various materials, any study of one medium helps us to understand all others" (McLuhan 1964, 139). Media therefore demand a holistic and multidisciplinary treatment if their impact on human interactions is to be properly understood. When considering the impact on education, we must consider how computers and the World Wide Web will change the nature of literature, mathematics, and science. When considering the impact on business, we must consider how computers and the Internet will integrate and align the processes of product design, manufacturing, distribution, marketing, and customer support.

If media are extensions of our psyches, the interconnectivity of the Internet means that its users will become extensions of each other's psyches. This parallels the way in which those that shared fire and the same hearth long ago became extensions of each other's psyches through the experiences they shared and the stories they told each other. With the Internet, the extension of our psyches has a global reach but, paradoxically, while we interact and share with correspondents all over the world, we need travel no farther than our desktop-based work stations.

The Flip: Humankind as an Extension of Its Technologies

"To behold, use or perceive any extension of ourselves in technological forms is necessarily to embrace it. By continuously embracing technologies, we relate ourselves to them as servo-mechanisms" (McLuhan 1964, 46). At first, technology serves as an extension of humankind and then suddenly a flip occurs and humankind is transformed into an extension of its technology. In terms of the Laws of the Media, the flip occurs in the following sequence: Technology enhances some function or extension of man, obsolesces some part of man's body, retrieves the gods in the sense that it provides us with the power to control nature, and, pushed far enough, flips into "machine in control of man" or "man as an extension of his technology."

To illustrate this point, consider whether alien beings monitoring activities on this planet would be able to immediately determine who was in control of the planet, cars or people. Indeed, it is difficult to determine whether people serve the automobile or the automobile serves people. Automobiles and people seem to receive equal attention. In terms of energy expenditures, the car, in fact, receives more kilocalories than people. Modern industrial humans spend 25 percent of their time providing themselves with transportation, compared with only 5 percent for members of hunting-and-gathering societies. The car has taken over modern life in terms of how we spend our time and how our urban and rural landscapes have been transformed by our need for mobility. We have become extensions of our cars, their servo-mechanisms.

The same argument can be made about computers and the Internet. Many of our institutions will have to change in order to accommodate the use of computer and Internet technology. We have no alternative, unless we wish to forgo the advantages that computers and the Internet provide. But we must use computers and the Internet wisely, recognizing what we give up when we submit to their tyranny.

History as the Laboratory of Media Studies

History is used as a dynamic tool in the study of media by the Toronto School. McLuhan (1972, xi) wrote: "[Innis] had discovered a means of using historical situations as a lab in which to test the character of technology in the shaping of cultures. Innis taught us how to use the bias of culture and communication as an instrument of research. By directing attention to the bias or distorting power of the dominant imagery and technology of any culture, he showed us how to understand cultures." McLuhan felt that an understanding of history was essential for understanding the future and the impact of new technologies. He often used the metaphor of the rearview mirror, a device by which we are able to determine what is about to overtake us from our past. Furthermore, according to McLuhan, history is not to be regarded as a series of events but rather as a dynamic process with a discernible pattern which repeats itself from culture to culture and from technology to technology.

Media as Staples

In *Empire and Communications,* Innis described socioeconomic and political systems in the context of their dominant forms of communication. He explained the difference between the imperialistic military bureaucracy of Rome and the conservative priestly bureaucracy of Babylon in terms of the materials upon which they wrote. The Babylonians used clay tablets, which provided a permanent written record of their culture and hence command over time. The Romans, on the other hand, wrote on an extremely portable medium, papyrus, which gave them command over space.

In their historical analyses, Innis and McLuhan regard technological media as staples or natural resources, exactly like wheat, cotton, or oil. Just as societies come into conflict over staples (wheat versus cattle in the American West) so, too, can conflicting media become a source of confrontation. The conflicts of the eighteenth and nineteenth centuries between oral cultures and industrialized society have given way in the twentieth century to the clash of mechanical or industrial forms of organization with electronic or post-industrial modes of operation in both the workplace and the school system. There is little doubt that not only have computers become staples of our economy but so too have the Internet and e-commerce which, as this book goes to press, are rapidly changing the ways consumers shop and businesses procure their supplies and services.

The Three Communication Ages of Humankind

McLuhan, building on the ideas of Innis, divided human history into three distinct periods based on the modes of sensibilities their media made available to them. The first era, that of the oral tradition, stretches from the time humankind first acquired speech to the beginnings of literacy 5000 years ago. The second era, the age of literacy, includes the period from the invention of writing to the discovery of electricity and its use in the form of the telegraph. The age of writing is further subdivided into three periods, the first beginning with the advent of written symbols, the second with the invention of the phonetic alphabet, and the last with the invention of the printing press. The third communication era, that of the electric flow of information, covers the period from the first use of the telegraph in 1844 to the present. "We live today in the Age of Information and Communication because electric media instantly and constantly create a total field of interacting events in which all men participate" (McLuhan 1964, 248).

Innis also divided history into periods in which different modes of communication dominated. He divided the age of literacy, however, by the nature of the medium upon which texts were written. "We can conveniently divide the history of the West into the writing and the printing periods. In the writing period we can note the importance of various media such as the clay tablet of Mesopotamia, the papyrus roll in the Egyptian and in the Graeco-Roman world, parchment codex in the late Graeco-Roman world and the early Middle Ages, and paper after its introduction in the Western world from China" (Innis 1972, 7).

During each of these three major communication eras, socioeconomic and cultural life was deeply affected by the dominant medium of communication. As each new mode of communication impacted on society, it dominated those that had preceded it, not obsolescing them, but dramatically changing their character and the uses to which they were put. Speech or the oral tradition naturally survived both literacy and electricity, but its function changed. It retained its dominance for conversation and everyday communication, but it was no longer used as the repository of a culture's traditions as it had been in Homer's time, nor as the means of spreading news from one village or country to another. The wandering minstrel who had conveyed information across both space and time was replaced by the written record, which spanned space through the courier and time through the library or archive. With writing, the spoken word took on new functions, sometimes becoming an art form in the guise of poetry or theater.

Writing underwent enormous changes with the advent of electricity. The modern newspaper, as McLuhan points out, is a product of the printing press and the telegraph. Electricity and the instantaneous flow of information changed the psychic environment of authors, causing them, in McLuhan's words (1964, vii), to "live mythically and in depth." As a result, writers became concerned with psychology, anthropology, and sociology. The psychological novel and stream-of-consciousness technique were born. Electricity produced another unexpected flip that affected the spoken word, namely, a revival of the oral tradition in the art, music, and literary worlds of the nineteenth and early twentieth centuries, as exemplified by jazz and the use of African masks in Cubism.

The structure of education also changed with the advent of each new mode of communication. With writing, education was transformed from the apprenticeship mode of learning on the job to formal schooling. The alphabet, abstract science, formal logic, and codified law gave rise to the academies of higher learning that appeared in ancient Babylon, Egypt, and Greece. The printing press gave rise to the modern school system of mass education and the assembly-line style of mass production. The mass media of radio, television, and telecommunications have shrunk the world to the dimensions of a global village.

Neither Harold Innis nor Marshall McLuhan lived long enough to see the two post-1980 revolutions of personal computing brought about by microcomputers and the World Wide Web made possible by the Internet. If they had had the opportunity to observe these two phenomena I believe they would have divided history into four distinct eras rather than the three they chose. I believe, like me, they would have added a fourth era by making a distinction between the era of the electric media of mass communication and the era of the *electronic* media of mainframes, microcomputers, and the Internet. While the dissemination of

electronic information parallels in some ways that of electric information, there is a very important difference: The users of electric media
are merely passive consumers of information whereas the users of
electronic media can interact with the information they access.

Writing, the Alphabet, and the Printing Press

McLuhan attributed the phonetic alphabet's power to its subliminal
effects. Of all the writing systems, the phonetic alphabet permits the
most economical transcription of speech into a written code. It also
provides its users with the model for abstraction, analysis, coding, and
decoding that came to characterize Western thought. The phonetic
alphabet introduced a double level of abstraction in writing. Words are
divided into the meaningless phonemic (sound) elements of which they
are composed and then these meaningless phonemic elements are
represented visually with equally meaningless signs, namely, the letters of the alphabet. This encourages abstraction, analysis (since each
word is broken down into its basic phonemes), coding (since spoken
words are coded by visual signs), and decoding (since those visual
signs are transformed back to spoken sounds through reading).

In an article entitled "Alphabet, Mother of Invention," McLuhan and
I (1977) indicated some of the cultural impacts that resulted from the
invention of phonetic writing. The Mesopotamian phonetic syllabary
inspired the organization of social mores into forms of codified law,
the most famous of which is the Hammurabic code. The impact on the
Hebrews of the alphabet that they borrowed from the Midianites
was immediate and dramatic. In addition to bringing writing to the
Hebrew children, Moses also brought them codified law, or the Ten
Commandments, as well as a more abstract and monotheistic concept
of God. These three developments occurred at the same time, as
symbolized in the Bible by the story of Moses receiving the Ten
Commandments on Mount Sinai: "He gave Moses, when He had made
an end to communing with him upon Mount Sinai, two tables of testi-
mony, two tables of stone, written with the finger of God" (Ex. 31:18).

The introduction of the phonetic alphabet into ancient Greek society
had an equally dramatic effect on that culture. Within 500 years of the
transmission of the alphabet from the Phoenicians, the Greeks developed the main intellectual concepts that have formed the foundation

of Western civilization. They created, for the first time in history, abstract science, formal logic, axiomatic geometry, rational philosophy, representational art, and individualism. While I am not suggesting a causal connection between these developments and the alphabet, I believe that the alphabet, by serving as a paradigm for classification, analysis, and codification, created the conditions that made these new ideas possible. Despite the superior achievements of the Chinese in technical matters, such as the inventions of silk, paper, gunpowder, metallurgy, porcelain, animal harnesses, and irrigation systems, to name a few, abstract science began in the West and not the East.

The most dramatic communications revolution to follow the introduction of the alphabet was the Gutenberg printing press. The revolutionary changes brought about by this technology have been documented by McLuhan in *The Gutenberg Galaxy*, a seminal work in which he shows the impact of print on such major cultural transformations as the rise of science, the Reformation, the Enlightenment, the rise of nationalism, and the Industrial Revolution. "The invention of typography confirmed and extended the new visual stress of applied knowledge providing the first uniformly repeatable 'commodity,' the first assembly-line, and the first mass production" (McLuhan 1962, 153).

Five Technological Breakthroughs
The effect of electricity is to speed up the process that it enhances, whether this be communication at a distance via telegraph, information storage via magnetic tapes, or information feedback via the thermostat. The impact of the speedup of information on each of the activities it affects is not always the same, however. McLuhan did not explicitly distinguish between the various phases of the electric information age; rather, he tended to treat all electric forms of information uniformly. He lumped together a number of separate and distinct breakthroughs, perhaps because each involved the electric speedup of information. "As technology changed, McLuhan did not appear interested in exploring the implications of the latest advances — not even the great technological wonder of the seventies, the microchip computer. For him, electronic technology was largely broadcasting — instantaneous, global communications" (Marchand 1989, 253).

Perhaps it was because of the integrative nature of electricity that McLuhan failed to distinguish between the various technological breakthroughs associated with the electric information age. Greater insights into each of these individual innovations can be achieved, however, by examining them separately, in much the same way that making a distinction between ideographic and phonetic writing or manuscript literacy and print also proved useful. A better understanding of the nature of contemporary information and communications systems and their impacts can be obtained, therefore, by distinguishing five separate technological breakthroughs (Logan 1982) that can be associated with the electrification of information. These are: (1) telecommunications; (2) information storage; (3) automation or cybernetics; (4) the general systems approach; and (5) microelectronics. This analysis represents an extension of the ideas of Innis and McLuhan to include computer and Internet technology within the framework of their approach to communications (Logan 1982).

The first electrification of information came in the form of telecommunications as represented by the telegraph, followed by the telephone, the microphone and loudspeaker, the radio, and finally television. The second breakthrough occurred with the electrification of information storage, first in the form of the phonograph record, then in the form of magnetic tape. The next development, automation, occurred as the computer and other cybernetic control devices provided the electric feedback of information. The fourth advance was the operations research or general systems approach to organizing human activities or projects and included the emergence of software on a par with hardware. The fifth breakthrough, microelectronics, entailed the miniaturization of the computer and a merger of hardware and software into a single integrated circuit imprinted on a silicon chip. Having identified the five breakthroughs that created the computer revolution, I will now examine each one in detail.

1. Telecommunications: Each of the communications and information breakthroughs brought about by the application of electricity has its roots in developments that occurred before the actual discovery of electricity. This is certainly true of the first application of electricity to communications, namely, the telegraph, whose predecessors include marathon runners, bonfires built along a chain of hills or mountains, semaphore, and the Pony Express. These forms of communication at a distance were obsolesced by the telegraph, telephone, and eventually, radio, television, telex, cable, satellites, and facsimile (fax).

An interesting footnote to the development of the telegraph is that the original purpose of this invention was to provide communications to control the railroad system; hence, the telegraph was not only the beginning of telecommunications but also one of the first electric cybernetic control devices. Only after it was installed along the railroad lines was its use as a telecommunications medium for the public realized.

2. Information storage: The information revolution is not solely a product of telecommunications and automation; the quantum jump in the storage of information that electric-configured devices permitted was another critical factor. The pre-electric roots of information storage extend to the very beginning of human communication, when information was stored in the mind and only later in books and libraries, the storehouses of print. Other forms of information storage include the photograph, the motion picture, and the phonograph record, all of which began as purely mechanical devices but were later electrified. "The phonograph, which owes its origin to the electrical telegraph and the telephone, had not manifested its basically electric form and function until the tape recorder released it from its mechanical trappings" (McLuhan 1964, 275). Electrification, however, did not in principle change the modes of information storage, but only affected the overall efficiency of these devices. The first true electrification of information storage occurred with magnetic tapes, which actually stored information in an electrical form rather than in a graphic, written, printed, or photographic manner. First used to store audio signals, magnetic tape was later upgraded to store video signals and to provide memory storage for computers. Other forms of electronic information storage for computers have since been developed using magnetic disks and bubble memory.

3. Automation: As with telecommunications, the roots of automation and the computer can be found in pre-electric mechanical devices. The first computers or computational devices were the abacus and the slide rule. Mechanical adding machines, representing the next level of sophistication in computation, were operated by turning a crank which activated a number of gears. The crank action of these machines was eventually electrified, but the actual computation remained mechanical until the development of the electronic computer. The first attempt at building a computer, made by Charles Babbage in the nineteenth century, involved a totally mechanical design. The Science Museum in London, England, still displays the computer that Arthur Porter built in 1933 using a Meccano set.

The development of electronics and the possibility of creating logic circuits permitted the construction of the first computers, beginning with the ENIAC in 1946. Other cybernetic control devices led to the automation of many manufacturing activities and control processes such as aircraft navigation. But the first cybernetic control devices were mechanical devices found in pre-electric factories. In essence, modern automation based on computers combines the principles of mechanical feedback with the flow of electric information. With electricity and electronics, the flow of information was greatly accelerated and control of information could be made much more intricate and accurate.

4. General systems theory: One side effect of the electronic communications revolution is general systems theory, or the operations research approach. The linear mode of thought characteristic of the industrial age collapsed with the introduction of electricity. The new speedup of information forced an integration of sources of data and knowledge that, during the industrial age, could be compartmentalized. The systems approach, in making the best use of computer hardware, led to the development of software to program tasks for the computer. As with the other breakthroughs, the general systems approach and software have pre-electric analogs. The ways in which preliterate hunting-and-gathering cultures maintained a balance with nature represents the origins of the general systems approach. The operations research approach was first deployed in military campaigns dating to Alexander the Great. Software was first employed in the form of programming cards for the Jacquard loom and later with the punched rolls of the player piano.

5. Microelectronics: The use of miniaturization as a strategy to enhance communication and information storage predates electricity and includes constructing models or plans as well as developing microfilms, microfiches, and other optical microforms. New patterns emerge and qualitative changes occur with each dramatic change in scale. The first computers built with vacuum tubes were large, clumsy, and extremely expensive. The history of computing has seen a steady reduction in their size. The invention of the transistors that replaced vacuum tubes resulted in more compact and practical computers. The development of transistors was key to the use of computers by large companies, government agencies, and educational institutions. It was the microchip, an integrated circuit etched on a tiny silicon chip, that led to microcomputers and the desktop- or personal-computer revolution. The recent emergence of laptop computers and now electronic notebooks is once again creating a dramatic change in the use of computers.

One important effect of miniaturization is portability. In fact, the original motivation to develop the microelectronic chip was portability: reducing the size of computers to facilitate space travel. The hand calculator is one of the spin-offs of the space program. Increased portability is one of the results of each communications revolution. Speech permitted us to take our experiences from one place to another. Tales and legends provided a means to store experiences and to move them through time. The written record provided an additional vehicle of portability across both space and time. As the materials upon which we wrote became progressively lighter, evolving from stone to clay tablet to animal parchment to papyrus scrolls to paper books, they also became more portable. Print increased portability, too, by permitting multiple copies of a book to be made cheaply and quickly. Books no longer had to be chained to a table in the monastery or the library, as circulating libraries came into existence. As the efficiency of printing increased and the costs of books decreased, readers could afford their own collections. Moreover, the disposable paperback book heralded a breakthrough in the dissemination of information through print.

Computers created a new level of portability. Information is easily transported from one computer to another through networking. Diskettes containing data can also be used to transport data or software routines from one site to another. With the introduction of laptops and notebooks it is possible to carry a computer wherever it is needed. Microelectronics or computer chips have also resulted in the design of customized computing devices for a large variety of equipment and machines ranging from the fuel injection systems of car engines to kitchen appliances.

Contemporary information processing and telecommunications devices have evolved through the integration of the above five technological breakthroughs. These technologies are compatible and reinforce one another's operations. Hybridizing them has produced hundreds of information-processing devices for a myriad of social, administrative, political, economical, and educational activities and institutions.

Of all the hybridized forms of information technology combining telecommunications and computing, the Internet, or the sixth language, is the most important (see Chapter 9 for a detailed discussion of the effects of the Internet and the World Wide Web). The Net integrates and aligns the computing power of users across the planet in both synchronous and asynchronous modes of communications. The Net and the Web embrace text, graphics, audio, and video and hence align and integrate all aspects of our perceptual sensorium and our cognitive competencies. When combined with face-to-face communication, this medium permits the highest level of sharing and collaboration the human race has ever been able to achieve. The quantitative change in what can be exchanged is so great that a qualitative change is taking place: We are making the transition from the information age to the knowledge era.

The Internet arose as a result of the hybridization of telecommunications and computing, but it also incorporates aspects of the other four breakthroughs delineated above. Hypertext and search engines automate the linkages to additional and desired information. Through the sharing of resources, Internet users pool the information storage capacities of their servers. As a result they have created an unprecedented amount of easily accessed data as well as a global switchboard connecting millions of users. The Internet supports a general systems approach on a global scale because of the communication linkages it makes possible. Web sites serve as models for the enterprises they represent, allowing managers to better see their organizations and hence better control and manage them. Finally, the Internet takes full advantage of microelectronics in the creation, storage, and distribution of information and knowledge.

New Information Patterns Emerge at the Speed of Light

Innis explained the space-time patterns of written communication and socioeconomic interactions in terms of the ease and speed with which written material or information could be transported. His notions are also valid for explaining the changes that occur with the electrification of information. McLuhan (1964, 352) noted, as did Einstein, that new information patterns emerge at the speed of light. "Today it is the instant speed of electric information that, for the first time, permits easy recognition of the patterns and the formal contours of change and development." McLuhan points out how the telegraph, "by providing a wide sweep of instant information," revealed weather patterns that had never been observed before. Information transmission at the speed of light is so nearly instantaneous that the barriers of distance are totally eliminated as far as the flow of information is concerned. "Many analysts have been misled by electric media because of the seeming ability of the media to extend man's spatial powers of organization. Electric media, however, abolish the spatial dimension, rather than enlarge it" (McLuhan 1964, 255).

McLuhan's insight about the speedup of information flow with electricity and telecommunications can be extended to the computer. The computer as an information-processing device repeats the same simpleminded calculations that a human thinker can perform but it can perform them automatically, faster, for longer time periods, and more accurately. The quantitative change created by the automation of information processing results in a qualitative change in which new patterns emerge because more data can be encompassed in a single stroke. The accuracy of the computer modeling that the Club of Rome commissioned to show the "Limits to Growth" is disputed by some, but the model did have the invaluable impact of making us more aware of many of the potential ecological disasters we face. This is a perfect example of the power of computers to provide new insights.

Fragmentation in the Age of Literacy

Before the age of literacy, the thought patterns and social forms of society were coherent, cohesive, and integrated. With writing, a fragmentation of social and psychic patterns began, reaching its zenith in the mechanical forms of the assembly line characteristic of the industrial age. This was particularly true of education, where knowledge was divided into specialized disciplines or subjects that were studied separately and taught by individuals who rarely communicated professionally with other scholars outside their own narrowly defined disciplines. Writing encouraged this fragmentation in two ways: through its direct influence, and through the printing press, which functioned as the precursor of mass production. Writing served as a paradigm for separation and fragmentation. It inspired the organization of information into sundry categories and enumerations.

"It has been suggested that writing was invented in Sumer to keep tallies and to make lists, and hence, was an outgrowth of mathematics" (Innis 1972, 26). This observation is further supported by the etymology of the Semitic root for writing, *spr*, which also means to count and to tell. One of the consequences of the closely linked arts of writing and enumeration was the creation of bureaucracies that assisted and gave rise to theocratic governments. "The beginning of the principle 'divide and rule' was evident in recognition of the religions of Babylon and Egypt and encouragement of the religion of the Hebrews at Jerusalem" (Innis 1950, 135). "Priestly bureaucracies" gave way to "military bureaucracies" and the principle of "divide and rule" was expanded to the principle of "divide and conquer." This led to centralized world states being fragmented into individual provinces.

The written word not only created a new geopolitical environment, it also transformed learning. A division was created between the knower or author and that individual's written knowledge. The divorce between the author and his or her writing permitted the objectivity necessary for scientific thought. "The literate man or society develops the tremendous power of acting in any matter with considerable detachment from the feelings or emotional involvement that a non-literate man or society could experience" (McLuhan 1964, 79). At the heart of the scientific method that writing encourages is the specialization and fragmentation of subjects, which can eventually flip into tunnel vision.

Phonetic writing with an alphabetic script reinforced the spirit of fragmentation that writing induced. Each word is subdivided into its basic sound values or phonemes, which are then represented by abstract meaningless visual signs. "The phonetic alphabet was a technical means of severing the spoken word from its aspect of sound and gesture" (McLuhan 1964, 193). The printing press continued to enhance the separation and fragmentation that the phonetic alphabet encouraged. Previously, print texts had to be read aloud to be deciphered and understood (McLuhan 1962, 103-5). Vocalizing written texts helped preserve elements of the oral tradition. "The lack of assistance to readers, or of aids to facilitate reference, in ancient books is very remarkable. The separation of words is practically unknown, except very rarely when an inverted comma or dot is used to mark a separation where some ambiguity might exist. Punctuation is often wholly absent, and is never full and systematic" (Kenyon 1937, 65). With the printing press, words are uniformly separated, punctuation is used systematically, texts are regularized, and spelling and grammar are standardized. Readers can read much more quickly and decipher the text silently for themselves. With the advent of silent reading from uniformly manufactured texts, the gap between the visual bias of literacy and the oral tradition widened. This further fragmented many aspects of social, economic, political, psychic, and spiritual life.

The modern scientific revolution, which began in the Renaissance and culminated in the breakthroughs of Newtonian mechanics, led directly to the Industrial Revolution, mass production, and the assembly line, all of which are based on segmentation and specialization of tasks. "The restructuring of work and association was shaped by the techniques of fragmentation, that is the essence of machine technology" (McLuhan 1964, 8). "The separation of function and the division of stages, spaces and tasks are characteristic of literate and visual society and of the Western world. These divisions tend to dissolve through the action of the instant and organic interrelations of electricity" (McLuhan 1964, 247).

The Global Village
A key element in McLuhan's historical overview of communications is that electric information moving at the velocity of light creates new patterns of communication and social interactions, which he describes as "an instant implosion" that reverses the specialism of the literate age and contracts the globe to a village in which "everybody lives in the utmost proximity created by our electric involvement in one another's lives" (McLuhan 1964, 35).

Electricity bringing information instantaneously from the four corners of the planet invests distant events with a personal dimension; it is as though they are occurring in one's own community. Communities across the globe become entwined in one another's affairs. Electrically based media transform the role of the individual in society; a social grid of highly independent individuals gives way to tribal patterns of intense involvement with one another and a return to elements of the oral tradition. McLuhan pushes Innis's notion of command over space when considering the impact of telecommunications in which information travels at the speed of light. The command over space reduces the entire globe to the dimensions of a village — a "global village."

"Electricity offers a means of getting in touch with every facet of being at once, like the brain itself. Electricity is only incidentally visual and auditory; it is primarily tactile" (McLuhan 1964, 249). Electricity keeps us in touch with one another whether we are in the same place or separated by physical distances, which electric signals can jump in an instant.

The introduction of electric information changed our view of work from that of a job to that of a role. A role becomes a way of life and gives more of an identity to an individual than a job. The reversal of mechanical forms by electricity has also affected the world of education and academe, although not to the extent that it has affected the commercial world. Today there is a more dedicated attempt to integrate studies and make sure that students are acquainted with a wider range of issues and disciplines than was the practice forty years ago. There is far more communication between disciplines, and some scholars now pursue interdisciplinary studies. Many universities now offer cross-disciplinary programs. The environmental movement has spawned the new interdisciplinary field of ecology. Other foci of study such as future studies, peace studies, native studies, women's studies, and black studies are examples of interdisciplinary fields that have appeared on university campuses to address the needs of students who have specific social and political concerns.

Of all the electronic-based information systems developed, perhaps none has contributed more to the creation of a global village than the World Wide Web. Information arrives on our desktop, taking essentially no more time to arrive from halfway around the globe than from a next-door neighbor's Web site. Not only has the time barrier been eliminated but so too has the cost barrier, once one has made the investment of a computer and paid for a link to the Internet. There is still not an equal, or for that matter, equitable distribution of communication and computing capabilities between the developed and the developing countries in our global village, but with the ongoing reduction in the cost of computing and communications, it can be hoped that these disparities will disappear in the not-too-distant future. What the Web and the Net do make possible for all societies is a more effective way to share information and knowledge across national borders.

Centralization versus Decentralization

In the literate age, centralized control was achieved by the technique of divide and conquer. This model of fragmentation, Innis and McLuhan contended, was a by-product of alphabetic literacy and was reinforced by the mechanical forms of industrialization that the printing press inspired. "Political organizations determined to an important extent by the limitations of armed force and characterized by centralized power emphasized the capital and left their impression on cultural activity. They provided a shelter for the development of communication facilities. Communication was subordinated to the demands of centralized power in religion and in political organization; it was characterized by the use of the eye rather than the ear. The scribe occupied a strategic position in centralized bureaucracies" (Innis 1950, 135). The pattern Innis described for literate society before the printing press applied with even greater force to print-dominated cultures, particularly once the Industrial Revolution commenced.

Centralized patterns of organization, which generally characterize political and religious institutions, extended during the industrial age to forms of work, particularly in manufacturing and distribution. This centralization reverses with the introduction of electricity: "Electric information provides instant data access equally to all members of the organization regardless of their hierarchical positions. For the external action of an organization this fact of instant information spells total decentralization" (McLuhan 1988, 67).

Industrial organization requires collecting staff and supplies at centralized locations for manufacturing and distribution. In electrically configured society, activity shifts from manufacturing material goods to processing information, which is a decentralized activity. The mode of organization is like that of the electric circuit: No point along a circuit (or a circle) may be regarded as the unique center of the circuit; each point is as central and essential as the next. The telephone, for example, places us at the center of a worldwide network of information. Computers linked by telephone lines and/or the Internet permit access to vast stores of knowledge from any point on earth. The microelectronic revolution, which has greatly reduced the cost of electronic equipment and increased portability through miniaturization, enhances this trend toward decentralization. There is little point in going to a centralized office to use information equipment that one can operate just as easily at home. One can network with others by telephone as easily from home as from the office.

Innis did not share McLuhan's notion that electricity decentralizes communication and other socioeconomic patterns. This divergence of views represents perhaps the most serious dichotomy between the two scholars. Innis saw radio as a force that promotes centralization. "The radio appealed to vast areas, overcame the division between classes in its escape from literacy, and favoured centralized bureaucracy" (Innis 1950, 82). McLuhan disagreed with this assessment. "A good example of this technological blindness (i.e., blindness to the effects of one's most significant forms of invention) in Innis himself was his mistake in regarding radio and electric technology as a further extension of the patterns of mechanical technology" (McLuhan 1972, xii).

Is McLuhan's critique of Innis fair? In terms of the centralized broadcast mode of operation of radio and television during the time that Innis and McLuhan were active, it is not. The centralized mode of operation of radio and television was dictated by the economics of a limited number of channels. The emergence of cable TV, fiber optics, communication satellites, pay TV, videotext, and, eventually, the information superhighway will vastly increase the number of channels and services available. This will lead to the decentralization of radio and television operations. Television regulatory agencies are already experiencing difficulties in regulating this once highly centralized industry because of the proliferation of new communication channels. McLuhan's critique is therefore valid in the long term because the present centralized broadcast mode of radio and television will not dominate these media forever. The way that cable TV has cut into the monopoly of the networks is a perfect illustration of this point.

The conflict between Innis and McLuhan over the issue of centralization is due to a difference in emphasis. Innis focused on the hardware aspects of electronic communication, which is, or has been, centralized, whereas McLuhan was more concerned with the software or information flow, which is decentralized. Consider the telephone system as an example. The hardware consists of the telephones, the wires connecting them, and the central switching stations. The software or information the system carries is provided by those who use the system to communicate with each other. The hardware may be centralized, as was dramatically demonstrated by General Wojciech Jaruzelsky when he pulled the plug on the telephone system during the suppression of the Solidarity movement in Poland in December 1981. The information flow on the telephone system is, on the other hand, decentralized. A phone call can be initiated from any point in the system. In the long run, not even centralized control of the communications hardware, the army, and the police can support a totalitarian regime, as the dramatic collapse of communism and other forms of dictatorship have demonstrated.

A similar centralization of hardware and decentralization of information is true of a computer network, in which there is a central computer and an information bank. A network of personalized microcomputers, or the Internet, the network of networks, on the other hand, is totally decentralized. The revolutionary effect of microcomputers on education will be a result of their decentralized grass-roots use and the fact that they can be networked through the Internet so that each user is at the center of a global network. Centralized mainframe computers, in use at least ten years before the introduction of microcomputers, had very little effect on schools.

Hardware versus Software

There has been a dramatic shift in economic activity from an almost total emphasis on hardware at the height of the industrial age to a focus on information and software products. The movement of information and the sharing and co-creation of knowledge is now the main source of wealth in the Internet age. These observations are easily confirmed: Look at employment levels in the different sectors of our economy. Before the Industrial Revolution, most workers were employed in agriculture. After the Industrial Revolution, the number in manufacturing soared, those in the service sector remained steady, and the number in agriculture declined dramatically to the present level of 5 percent of the North American work force. Today, the number of information handlers has grown dramatically to approximately 50 percent of the work force. Still more growth is expected. Those in manufacturing, currently 20 percent of the work force, will decline further as the full impact of robotization and automation transforms industrial activity.

Teachers and managers who were trained before the advent of computers and the Internet cannot fully comprehend the revolution through which we are passing because they view it through the eyes of a past era. The true integration of computing into education and the workplace will occur only when those who are now growing up with the technology become the teachers and managers of the future. Nevertheless, we, the members of the transitional generation who learned how to use computers and the Internet as adults, can make the transition from the industrial age to the computer age and the knowledge era easier by realizing that we must come to grips with a new phenomenon for which we were never trained.

Hybrid Systems

"The hybrid or the meeting of two media is a moment of truth and revelation from which new form is born" (McLuhan 1964, 55). Hybrid systems operate more efficiently than the individual components from which they emerge. Hence, the synergy they represent releases new forms of energy, creating additional "vortices of power." Electric systems, which favor integration, give rise naturally to hybrid systems.

The hybridization of the computer, the video screen (or CRT), and microelectronics has produced the low-cost personal computer and now the highly portable electronic notebook. The modem, which permits the marriage of the computer and the telephone system, instantaneously creates vast computer networks, such as the Internet, linking the databases of the world to the home or office. The marriage of the telephony system and computing created the Internet.

Societies Imitate Their Technologies

McLuhan observed that the fragmentation and centralization of industrial or mechanical society was reversed in the electric age of information to systems of integration and decentralization that retrieved some aspects of the social organization of preliterate society. These observations were based on the following set of assumptions:

1. The dominant tools or technologies of a society create patterns of usage which infiltrate or penetrate the social structures of a society.
2. These patterns change those structures.
3. Eventually, the social structures come to imitate or replay the patterns by which these dominant technologies are organized.

Communities alter their form to accommodate the technologies they use, which literally become extensions of themselves. The social structure so amended by a technology tends to reproduce new technological innovations in the same mold, thus reinforcing the existing pattern. "Once a new technology comes into a social milieu it cannot cease to penetrate that milieu until every institution is saturated" (McLuhan 1964, 177).

Eventually, the school system, one of the last institutions to make the transition, will succumb to the demands of the knowledge era. Educators and academics pride themselves on their ability to incorporate the latest in new ideas, which is true as far as their discussions and scholarly work are concerned. Unfortunately, this does not always translate into the way they organize the educational activities of their students.

There is an analogy between McLuhan's observation that societies imitate their technologies and Thomas Kuhn's notion (1972, 23–42) that once a new scientific theory scores a success, it serves as a paradigm for further scientific work, and every conceivable extension, articulation, and application of the original idea is developed. This process, which he calls "normal science," occurs with technology, as well. A technological breakthrough also serves as a paradigm which is extended, articulated, and applied in every conceivable way. For example, the idea of building things from repeatable fragmented identical elements began with the introduction of the phonetic alphabet. As we will see, the extension of this idea resulted in the development of codified law, monotheism, abstract science, and deductive logic. The articulation of the alphabetic paradigm of the repeatability of fragmented identical items in the hardware realm of mechanics created the printing press, the assembly line, mass production, and the general organizational principle of the industrial age.

The evolution of this fragmented, specialist, linear, sequential mode of organization came to an end with the introduction of electricity and its application to information systems. Slowly the patterns of industrial organization and social interaction reversed themselves as electricity reconfigured social structures. This development continues with the penetration of microelectronics or integrated circuits into organizational structures, which in turn will lead to a continuation of the integration and decentralization of social structures, along with a greater shift to software and hybrid systems.

In *The Third Wave*, Alvin Toffler discusses the possibility of being able to work at home by making use of an electronic workstation and increased communication with the outside world. This notion of an "electronic cottage" incorporates three major trends of economic life in the age of electric information:

1. the decentralization of economic activity;
2. the integration of work with home life and leisure activities; and
3. the replacement of a job with a role in society.

Break Boundaries

The boundaries between two technological orders and their subsequent social patterns have been described by Kenneth Boulding (1961) as "'break boundaries' at which [a] system suddenly changes into another or passes some point of no return in its dynamic processes."

Identifying break boundaries is one of the methods used by the Toronto School of Communications to understand the dynamics of social systems and their interactions with media of communication and information-processing technologies. The major break boundaries in communications and informatics are those associated with the introduction of ideographic writing, mathematics, phonetic writing, the phonetic alphabet, abstract science, the printing press, telecom-munications, automation, computers, magnetic storage of information, general systems theory, microelectronics, and the Internet. Each of these innovations created its own breaks in social patterns.

Acoustic versus Visual Space

The separation between the oral and literate traditions represents a break boundary for Innis and McLuhan. These two traditions are char-acterized by their respective oral and visual biases of communication and perception. McLuhan studied how the dominant mode of commu-nication in a culture created a sensory bias or grid by which the rest of the world was viewed. He created the notion of acoustic space and visual space, two worlds in which oral and literate society, respectively, lived. "Rural Africans live largely in a world of sound — a world loaded with direct personal significance for the hearer — whereas the Western European lives much more in a visual world which is on the whole indifferent to him" (McLuhan 1962, 28). McLuhan's observation is echoed by Innis (1950, 130): "The oral tradition implies the spirit but writing and printing are inherently materialistic." "The oral discussion inherently involves personal contact and a consideration for the feel-ings of others, and it is in sharp contrast with the cruelty of mechanized communication" (Innis 1950, 199).

Acoustic space not only includes the aural and the oral but also the tactile, and the interplay of these senses. It is a space characterized by direct contact with reality. Thought patterns within this world are con-crete and much use of metaphor and analogy is made. The visual world is one of abstraction and deductive logic. Geometry and science characterize visual space, whereas art and music are more represen-tative of acoustic space. As noted earlier, the perceptual bias of visual space is linear, sequential, rational, fragmented, causal, abstract, and specialized, whereas that of acoustic space is simultaneous, concrete, intuitive, all-embracing, mystical, inductive, and experiential. Visual space is characterized with patterns associated with the specialization of the left hemisphere of the brain, acoustic space with those of the right hemisphere.

The visual and oral biases of writing and speech, respectively, are obvious. The bias of electric communication is more difficult to identify.

Electric information patterns, however, reflect a number of the characteristics of oral communication, namely, integration, simultaneity, despecialization, decentralization, and less emphasis on hardware. The parallels between the oral tradition and electric information patterns led McLuhan (1962, 86) to the conclusion that the inherent bias of electric communication is oral. "A speed-up, such as occurs with electricity, may serve to restore a tribal pattern of intense involvement such as took place with the introduction of radio in Europe, and is now tending to happen as a result of TV in America. Specialist technologies detribalize. The non-specialist electric technology retribalizes" (McLuhan 1964, 24).

Multidisciplinarity versus Specialization

McLuhan recognized and valued a generalist and multidisciplinary approach. The depth and learning of the expert is valued as long as it does not exclude the learning and ideas of other experts. The tunnel vision of the specialist, however, is avoided. "The specialist is one who never makes small mistakes, while moving toward a grand fallacy" (McLuhan 1964, 124). The multidisciplinary approach is the only way to get at the large patterns of the interplay between a society and its technologies. It is an approach that blends naturally into the Innis-McLuhan style of scholarship. "Any subject taken to depth at once relates to other subjects" (McLuhan 1964, 347).

The effects of electric information patterns naturally reinforce the multidisciplinary approach of Innis and McLuhan. Electric technology "ends the old dichotomies between culture and technology, between art and commerce and between work and leisure" (McLuhan 1964, 35, 346).

Innis also found these dichotomies artificial and a barrier to meaningful scholarship. He described one of his essays as "a critical review, from the points of view of an historian, a philosopher and a sociologist, of the structural and moral changes produced in modern society by scientific and technological advance" (Innis 1950, 190). Innis and McLuhan adopted multidisciplinary approaches in order to deal with questions that were most relevant and meaningful to humankind. They saw overspecialization as a major stumbling block preventing scholars from dealing with pressing philosophical questions.

The Myth of Objectivity

Innis and McLuhan challenged many of the biases of visually oriented, left-brained specialists, including their belief in the existence of a single objective reality. "An interest in the bias of other civilizations may in itself suggest a bias of our own" (Innis 1950, 33). According to McLuhan, new media affect the sense ratios, or perceptions, of their users, and hence shift their perceptual realities, creating multitudes of realities. The objective reality of Einstein, who lived in the electric age, was quite different from that of Newton, as is reflected in the differences in their physics. Thomas Kuhn in *The Structure of Scientific Revolutions* articulates the process whereby objective realities shift each time the current phase of "normal science" is replaced by "revolutionary science." Jacques Lusseyran, who was blinded as a youth, criticizes the "myth of objectivity" in moving terms based on his own experience:

> When I came upon the myth of objectivity in certain modern thinkers, it made me angry. So there was only one world for these people, the same for everyone. From my own experience I knew very well that it was enough to take from a man a memory here, an association there, to deprive him of hearing or sight, for the world to undergo immediate transformation, and for another world, entirely different but entirely coherent, to be born. Another world? Not really. The same world rather, but seen from another angle, and counted in entirely new measures. When this happened, all the hierarchies they called objective were turned upside down, scattered to the four winds, not even theories but like whims.
>
> (LUSSEYRAN 1963, 112)

The User Is the Content

Operating under the "myth of objectivity," many scholars believe that they can analyze a text or work of art solely on the basis of its content, without any reference to the culture in which it is set, the intentions of the person who created it, or the attitudes of the audience for which it was intended. They also labor under the misconception that they can carefully disentangle their own cultural biases and read and analyze a text in a completely objective manner. The ambiguities of language or the author's intention are often ignored by these scholars. The text, play, movie, or art object is analyzed as a figure without a ground. What these scholars fail to understand is that they can never escape the bias of their language, their culture, and their particular form of scholarship.

Innis (1950, 132) warned us of this problem in *The Bias of Communication*: "We must all be aware of the extraordinary, perhaps insuperable, difficulty of assessing the quality of a culture of which we are a part or assessing the quality of a culture of which we are not a part. In using other cultures as mirrors in which we may see our own culture we are affected by the astigma of our own eyesight and the defect of the mirror, with the result that we are apt to see nothing in other cultures but the virtues of our own." Each reader or viewer brings his or her own experience to a medium and transforms the content according to his or her own need, which McLuhan expressed with his famous one-liner, "the user is the content."

Of all the media we have studied none exemplifies the notion of "the user is the content" more than the Internet, with the exception of the telephone, where the content of each conversation is literally that of the user. The same is equally true of e-mail where the users create their own content. The World Wide Web, like telephone and e-mail, also features two-way communication so that a well-designed Web site encourages input from the visitors. Those Web sites that become successful in drawing visitors make use of the input from visitors to build a site that better meets their needs. The Web site self-organizes through the interaction of the builders of the site and the users. Tools, such as WebTrends, that can track where the traffic to a site is coming from and which pages are most visited are another form of feedback from the users that helps to determine the content of the site.

Art as Radar and as an Early Warning System
One of the unique aspects of the Innis-McLuhan approach is the way that the insights and methods of artists are integrated into media studies. Not only is this a natural extension of the multidisciplinary approach, it is also a reflection of their belief in the superiority of artistic sensibility and its ability to detect currents of change before

they fully impact on a society. McLuhan was fond of quoting Wyndham Lewis, who wrote: "The artist is always engaged in writing a detailed history of the future because he is the only person aware of the nature of the present." McLuhan believed that the artist's insights were like radar or an early warning system that could pick up the social and cultural problems and challenges that new technologies created.

Just as Innis (1972, xi) had used "historical situations as a lab in which to test the character of technology in the shaping of cultures," so McLuhan used artistic insights — his own and those of others — as a lab in which to study the effects of technology. As a literary critic, he naturally was more concerned with the arts than was Innis, the economic historian. But Innis was no less an artist. "The artist is the man in any field, scientific or humanistic, who grasps the implications of his actions and of new knowledge in his own time. He is a man of integral awareness" (McLuhan 1964, 65).

There are critics who have dismissed the work of Innis and McLuhan as that of poets. As we see from the above definition of an artist, this is far from a negative criticism; rather, it is a vote of confidence. In terms of the language of the split brain, the integration of scholarship and art represents an attempt to integrate the left and right hemisphere patterns of knowing. Art education will be one of the important tools in helping our school system make the transition from the industrial age to the Internet age.

The Oral Tradition and Probes

One of the paradoxes of the Innis-McLuhan approach is that, while both men were extremely well-read scholars who wrote extensively, they were in many ways more a part of the oral tradition than the literary one. They were both excellent teachers whose lectures were a great source of delight and insight for their students. They were both masters of the spoken word more than of the written word. Both were criticized for their difficult prose. Innis admits his bias in an essay entitled "A Critical Review" (1950, 190): "My bias is with the oral tradition particularly as reflected in Greek civilization, and with the necessity of recapturing something of its spirit. For that purpose we should try to understand something of the importance of life or of the living tradition, which is peculiar to the oral as against the mechanized tradition."

McLuhan also confessed to a similar bias: "I have to engage in endless dialogue before I write. I want to talk a subject over and over" (Schickel 1965). He believed that in the age of electric information, the one-liner was the optimal mode of communication. McLuhan's memorable one-liners — the medium is the message, the global village, the Gutenberg Galaxy, the Mechanical Bride, and the user is the content — have enriched the English language.

Further evidence of McLuhan's bias toward the oral is his use of what he called "probes" for exploring new ideas in a way reminiscent of Plato's dialogues. McLuhan had no compunction about tossing out an untested or unfinished idea and playing with it to see what could be learned. He often remarked that "even if a probe is half true that is a lot of truth." His method was a very useful tool, but it confounded the academic establishment, which found inaccuracy difficult to condone even if it led to enlightened insights. McLuhan did not restrict his use of probes to discussions, but published them in his many books, a sin many academics could never forgive.

An Anti-academic Bias

The unorthodox methodology of Innis and McLuhan had an anti-academic bias built into it. The two theorists were highly critical of the academic approach to understanding the relationship between society and its media and technologies. Innis wrote: "Finally we must keep in mind the limited role of universities and recall the comment that 'the whole history of science is a history of the resistance of academics and universities to the progress of knowledge'" (Innis 1950, 194).

One of the specific critiques Innis and McLuhan made of academics is that they are too specialized, and hence unable to deal with the complexity and multidisciplinary aspects of communications. "In education the conventional division of the curriculum into subjects is already as outdated as the medieval trivium and quadrivium after the Renaissance" (McLuhan 1964, 124). Another of their concerns was that the human dimension of academic discussions or scholarship was often missing. "Perhaps we might end by a plea for consideration of the role of the oral tradition as a basis for a revival of effective vital discussion and in this for an appreciation on the part of universities of the fact that teachers and students are still living and human" (Innis 1950, 32).

Monopolies of Knowledge

One of the reasons that Innis was critical of universities is that they, like other literary-based institutions, represent what he called a "monopoly of knowledge." He writes: "A complex system of writing becomes the possession of a special class and tends to support aristocracies" (Innis 1950, 4). The academic style of writing, which avoids using vernacular expressions in an attempt to sound erudite, merely narrows the audience that can share its knowledge.

The first monopolies of knowledge were formed by the priestly bureaucracies of Babylon and Egypt. Secret learning societies in the ancient Greek and Roman world also maintained such monopolies. During the Middle Ages, "monopolies of knowledge controlled by monasteries were followed by monopolies of knowledge controlled by copyist guilds in the large cities" (Innis 1950, 53).

The printing press broke up these monopolies and enabled a new one to evolve. "Freedom of the press has been regarded as a great bulwark of our civilization and it would be dangerous to say that it has become the great bulwark of monopolies of the press" (Innis 1950, 139). "Even science with its emphasis on a common vernacular and on translations has come under the influence of monopolies of knowledge in patents, secret processes and military security measures" (Innis 1950, 129). It is probably the maintenance of a monopoly that makes the defenders of an old school of scientific thought so tenaciously defend their theories from the attack of the proponents of a new paradigm. Physicians are another group who have maintained a monopoly of knowledge, often mystifying patients with unnecessarily complex terminology and the use of Latin to write prescriptions.

As we have seen, there is a general trend for electricity to speed up the flow of information and decentralize its sources, which breaks up these monopolies and makes secrecy difficult. "Mechanization has emphasized complexity and confusion; it has been responsible for monopolies in the field of knowledge; and it becomes extremely important to any civilization, if it is not to succumb to the influence of this monopoly of knowledge, to make some critical survey and report. The conditions of the freedom of thought are in danger of being destroyed by science, technology, and the mechanization of knowledge, and with them, Western civilization" (Innis 1950, 32).

The fears that Innis expressed in 1950 have largely disappeared because automation and connectivity have led to open systems in which information is free to flow and small elites are no longer as able to control the creation of wealth. The Internet and the World Wide Web have played a prominent role in the breakdown of industrial era monopolies of knowledge by providing a medium whereby non-professionals have been able to share their experiences and network their knowledge. Web sites that act as electronic support groups have sprung up all over the Net, providing practical suggestions for those who have to cope with a variety of different medical, psychological, and social conditions. Rather than trained professionals observing the suffering of individuals second-hand and passing their observations on to a third party, those with first-hand experience are advising others of how they coped with and/or survived their particular challenges. While this process does not compromise the role of the trained professional, it has resulted, in many cases, in a more effective way of sharing tacit knowledge, and it has certainly broken down many monopolies of knowledge.

This new environment, in which individuals are more self-sufficient in obtaining their information needs, leads to new challenges, which will be explored in later chapters. For the moment, we turn to an examination of the evolution of language and the information systems that underlie our economic and political institutions and our education system.

3

Evolutionary Linguistics and the

Six Modes of Language

In the next two chapters I will attempt to explain the nature of language and the role it plays in all aspects of human activity. Specifically, I will address the following questions, formulated in Chapter 1:

- What are the relationships among language, communications, information, technology, and knowledge?
- What are languages and how do they affect learning, work, and social interactions?
- How does language evolve and new forms of language emerge?

The Six Modes of Language

The computer and the Internet are the most recent in a long series of techniques and technologies that organize human thought, for communicating, storing, retrieving, organizing, and processing information. The series includes spoken language, pictures, tallies, clay tokens, picture writing, logographic (pictographic or ideographic) writing, syllabaries, the alphabet, abstract numbers, numerals, mathematical signs (+,-,=), the concept of zero, geometry, mathematics, logic, abstract science, maps, graphs, charts, libraries, the printing press, encyclopedias, dictionaries, bookkeeping techniques, the scientific method, photography, the telegraph, the telephone, cinema, radio, audio recording, television, video recording, optical disks, computers, control theory, cybernetics, and the Internet.

Computing and the Internet, however, are more than just new technologies. They represent new forms of language if language is defined as a system for both communications and informatics. As I hypothesized in Chapter 1, computing and the Internet (which encompasses the World Wide Web) are part of an evolutionary chain of languages that also includes speech, writing, mathematics, and science. In order to establish the hypothesis, I will show that these six modes of language are distinct, each with its own semantics and syntax. Through historical analysis, I will demonstrate that each new mode of language evolved from the previous forms as new information-processing needs arose and that each new language subsumed the structures and elements of the earlier languages.

Exploring the origins and evolution of language helps us understand how it has affected the development of cognition, communication, and education. My definition of language as a medium for both communication and cognition corresponds to Lev Vygotsky's idea (1962) that language is a vehicle for "social intercourse" and "generalizing thought." Formal education may therefore be viewed as the learning of different languages. Before starting school, we begin to learn the oral form of our mother tongue. In school, we learn the written forms of the vernacular tongue and the language of mathematics — known colloquially as "the three Rs." Students then learn the language of science and, possibly, a foreign language. Vygotsky (1962, 109) claims that "the influence of scientific concepts on the development of the child is analogous to the effect of learning a foreign language, a process which is conscious and deliberate from the start." If that is the case, children ought to learn the languages of mathematics, science, and computing at the age when it is easiest for them to learn a new foreign language: when they are five to six years old.

With the advent of microcomputers and the Internet, education now includes the study of two new distinct languages, the fifth language of computing and the sixth language of the Internet. Essentially, education becomes the study of the six verbal languages of speech, writing, mathematics, science, computing, and the Internet. A comprehensive education must also include nonverbal languages and activities such as the visual arts, music, and physical education, but for this study I will focus on the integration of the six verbal languages and their impact on education and work. (Note, though, that, because of the way the World Wide Web integrates and aligns text and the art forms of graphics, video, and audio, any study of it cannot completely divorce verbal and nonverbal communications and languages.)

A New Concept of Language

The use of computers and the Internet to communicate and process information represents two new languages that educators must deal with as they have with the languages of mathematics and science. To understand the impact that computers and the Internet have on the way we organize information and work and educate our children, we must recognize not only that computing and the Internet are new forms of language, but also that they change our very notion of what defines or constitutes a language. Language is communication plus informatics. This definition may be unorthodox from a linguist's point of view, but it will prove extremely useful for a discussion of education.

Traditionally, the sole focus of linguists in defining language has been on communication. One example is Edward Sapir's definition of language (1921): "A purely human and non-instinctive method of communicating ideas, emotions, and desires by means of a system of voluntarily produced symbols." While it is true that the main function of language has been communication, that is not its only function; language also plays a key role in the processing of information, including its storage, retrieval, and organization. Language is a tool for developing new concepts and ideas; it is an open-ended system. Since writing, mathematics, science, computing, and the Internet permit the development of ideas that could never arise through the use of speech alone, we must consider these other modes as distinct, albeit related, languages.

While the information-processing aspects of language became more apparent with the introduction of writing, spoken language also served as a system to store, organize, and process information. Ernst Fisher suggests that human communication evolved differently from that of animals because our activities required that information be processed. "The development towards work [i.e., using tools to change one's environment] demands a system of new means of expression and communication that would go far beyond the few primitive signs known to the animal world. Animals have little to communicate with each other. Their language is instinctive: a rudimentary system of signs for danger, mating, etc. Only in work and through work do living beings have much to say to one another" (Fisher 1963, 23). At times, animals may communicate with other members of their species the way that humans do, but they cannot use language to conceptualize, to process information or to create new information.

Generalizing and extending Sapir's definition, I define language as: A purely human and non-instinctive method of communicating ideas, emotions, and desires as well as of processing, storing, retrieving, and organizing information by means of a system of voluntarily produced symbols. Given this definition of language, it is necessary to recognize that speech is not the only form of language. My suggestion that speech and writing, for instance, are two distinct but related forms or modes of language differs from the beliefs of traditional linguists, who consider speech as the primary form of language and writing as merely a system for transcribing or recording it. This tradition dates back to Aristotle: "The sounds . . . are symbols of ideas evoked in the soul and writing is a symbol of the sounds" (Bandle, Klingenberg, and Mauer 1958, 95).

Ferdinand de Saussure, one of the founders of the field of linguistics, formulated the modern attitude of linguistics toward writing when he wrote (1967): "Language and writing are two different systems of signs; the latter only exists for the purpose of representing the former . . . The subject matter of linguistics is not the connection between the written and spoken word, but only the latter, the spoken word is its subject." De Saussure's position was reinforced by another immensely influential linguist, Leonard Bloomfield, who wrote (1933, 21): "Writing is not language, but merely a way of recording language by means of visible marks."

The relationship between writing and language posited by de Saussure and Bloomfield is far too confining for an understanding of the implications of microcomputers and the Internet for the future of communication, work, and education. Their definitions are restricted to a model in which the sole purpose of language is communication. They do not take into account the information-processing capabilities of language, a key consideration for understanding the role of computers in society. These traditional linguists are mired in the industrial-age attitude of assigning only a single task to any activity. The definitions of Bloomfield and de Saussure have been re-evaluated by a modern generation of linguists who view language from the perspective of informatics, and hence understand the multi-tasking nature of language.

Michael Stubbs (1982) critiques Bloomfield's definition of writing as follows: "Writing is not merely a record . . . I know from personal experience that formulating ideas in written language changes those ideas and produces new ones." Joyce Hertzler (1965, 444) concurs: "People often find that their thoughts are clarified and systematized, and that necessary qualifications and extensions appear, when they subject them to the more rigorous test of exactness and completeness demanded by the written form." Frank Smith (1982, 204) agrees: "Ideas develop from interaction and dialogue . . . especially with one's own writing."

While it is true that written language is derived from spoken language, it is useful to regard them as two separate language modes because they process information so differently. The arguments that support the notion that writing is a separate mode of language can also be made for mathematics, science, computing, and the Internet. These four additional modes of language each have unique strategies for communicating, storing, retrieving, organizing, and processing information. I have therefore extended the notion of those linguists who consider speech and writing as separate modes of language to claim that speech, writing, mathematics, science, computing, and the Internet are six separate modes of language that are distinct but interdependent. They form an evolutionary sequence in which the later modes of language are derived from and incorporate elements of the earlier modes. They form a nested set of languages in which the later forms contain all of the elements of the earlier forms.

Speech, the first form of human language, is the basis of all other linguistic modes of communication and information processing. We can define spoken language as the sum of information uttered by human speakers. Only the nonverbal forms of human expression, such as music, dance, and the visual arts, do not derive directly from speech. A picture or a piece of music can describe a sunset non-linguistically, but a linguistic description is more amenable to information processing. The elements of text, namely, the words and the sentences, have meaning on their own. But non-linguistic elements, such as notes or brush strokes, make no sense outside of the context of a musical or graphic composition.

Written language, which is derived from speech, is defined as the sum of information that has been notated with visual signs. It differs from speech in that it involves a permanent record, whereas speech disappears immediately after it is uttered. I shall distinguish five different modes or forms of written language: writing (or literature), mathematics, abstract science, computing, and the Internet. Writing and mathematical notations were the first forms of written language; both grew out of the system of recording payments of agricultural tributes using clay accounting tokens in Sumer just over 5000 years ago. The language of science and its methodology emerged from writing and mathematics in ancient Greece some 2500 years ago. The methods and findings of science are expressed in the languages of writing and mathematics, but science may be regarded as a separate form of language because it has a unique way of systematically processing, storing, retrieving, and organizing information that is quite different from either literature or mathematics.

A little more than fifty years ago, another system for processing information emerged from science and mathematics in the form of computing, with its own unique cybernetically based and automated methods for processing and organizing information. Finally, the latest form of language emerged from computing and telecommunications in the form of the Internet and the World Wide Web. At first the Net was the private domain of the military and science communities. But with the release of Netscape in 1994, the Net and the Web entered the public domain of business, education, and the home user, and they have grown at a rate faster than any other medium in the history of human communication.

Whether these six modes of information processing and communication should be regarded as separate languages or whether they are merely six different aspects of the human capacity for languaging are questions I will not attempt to answer. For the purposes of this analysis, I will consider speech, writing, mathematics, science, computing, and the Internet as six distinct modes of language that form an evolutionary chain of development. What these modes of language share is a distinct method for the communication and processing of information, each of which changes our worldview. Just as Sapir argued that cultures dissect nature along the lines dictated by their native languages, so the six languages of information processing each provide a unique framework for viewing the world.

A Model for the Evolution of Thought from Language

In *Thought and Language*, Lev Vygotsky shows that language plays both a communication and an information-processing role. In his attempt to demonstrate the relationship between thought and language, Vygotsky posits three phases in a child's development of verbal thought: "social speech," "egocentric speech," and "inner speech."

The first form of speech — "social speech" — is purely for the purpose of communication and is nonintellectual. After using language as a tool for communication and social intercourse, children discover that language is also useful for facilitating their thought processes. They then begin to display a phenomenon known as "egocentric speech" in which they are basically talking to themselves. The child vocalizes but is not addressing anyone in particular. This form of speech, which commences at about age three, continues to about age seven, when it suddenly disappears and is replaced by "inner speech" — or thought. At first, egocentric speech does not differ greatly from social speech, but as the child matures, the speech takes on more and more of the aspects of inner speech.

Vygotsky's observations of children ages three to seven reveal that they resort to egocentric speech whenever they are confronted with a puzzling situation they need to think through. Vygotsky concludes that egocentric speech is basically the child thinking out loud, and that it naturally evolves into inner speech once the child realizes that vocalization is not necessary for problem solving or thinking. "We came to the conclusion that inner speech develops through a slow accumulation of functional and structural changes, that it branches off from the child's external speech simultaneously with the differentiation of the social and the egocentric functions of speech, and finally that the speech structures mastered by the child become the basic structures of his thinking" (Vygotsky 1962, 51).

Vygotsky's model is based on the notion that speech or language has two components: communications and informatics. Language in the form of social speech in children younger than age three is pure communication and social interaction. With egocentric and inner speech, language becomes a tool for processing information or assisting the child to think. The only difference between egocentric and inner speech is that the former, which appears first, is vocalized, and the latter is not. But both serve the same function. Once inner speech emerges and is used solely for the purposes of thought, egocentric speech disappears and vocalized speech is used exclusively for communication, except in times of stress, when even adults sometimes think out loud by talking to themselves.

Assuming that "ontogeny recapitulates philogeny," that is, that the development of the individual organism of a species follows the same path as the evolution of that species, we may conclude that a similar process occurred in the development of human speech and thought and that there existed a period in human society of purely nonverbal thought and nonintellectual speech. There then followed the integration of thought and verbal communication similar to that described for the child by Vygotsky. Speech took on both a communications and informatics role, although the communications role dominated at first. Admittedly, this conclusion is speculative, yet it does suggest a plausible model for the way in which the informatics aspects evolved from what was at first the purely communicative role of early human language.

The Evolution of the Six Modes of Language

The development of language is the one characteristic of *Homo sapiens* that distinguishes it from all other species. All species communicate, as the behavior of bees, birds, and primates demonstrates. No other species, however, has created such a perfect tool for abstract thinking as language. I believe that verbal language in the form of speech arose out of the need of pre-human hominids to conceptualize. The world of hominids became progressively more complex as they acquired the capability for tool making, for controlling fire, for the social intelligence needed to live in large groups to share the advantages of fire, for large-scale coordinated hunting, and for mimetic communication or signaling through gestures, hand signals, body language, and non-verbal vocalization.

The chaos that emerged with this complexity gave rise to a new level of order in the form of spoken language that represents, in terms of Prigogine's theories of chaos and complexity, a bifurcation, or branching, of human communication into two streams. The older non-verbal branch characterized hominid communication and the newer verbal branch, human speech. This split also represented a bifurcation of concept-based thought or conceptualization from the older percept-based thinking of hominids. I believe that all of the hominid skills itemized above, from tool making to mimetic communication, were percept based and that the emergence of concepts in the form of words increased the chances for survival of those hominids that could verbalize their thoughts and hence conceptualize. The first concepts were words that served as both metaphors and strange attractors for certain sets of percepts. The word "water" united all the experiences with water whether it was drunk, bathed in, or felt as rain.

The shift from percept- to concept-based thinking and from non-verbal to verbal language also represented the transition from pre-human hominids to full-blown human beings: *Homo sapiens sapiens*. The hominid brain was basically a percept processor; with language it bifurcated into the human mind, which could conceptualize and process abstract information. The mind is the brain plus language. This line of thought justifies one of the basic assumptions of this study: Language is not simply a communications system, but also an informatics tool. It also correlates with Vygotsky's hypothesis (1962) that the evolution of speech is connected to the use and manufacture of tools and the growth of the brain-case: "Biological evolution ties in with the growth of culture, since the use of language seems obviously associated with habitual tool use (limiting the use of gestures) and with increasing human intelligence."

The two principal uses of speech are for abstracting experience through conceptualization and communication. In preliterate societies speech was the medium for social interactions and a tool for the coordination of activities that require cooperation, such as hunting or food gathering. Spoken language evolved more complex functions and was used in the cultural apparatus of a society to tell tales and sing songs. Eventually, speech was used as a medium to record (or store) and retrieve cultural information in the form of poems, folktales, and folk songs. As stories became more complex, speech was used to organize the information stored in these formats. Organizational forms such as rhyme, rhythm, meter, and plot, in turn, became information tools which permitted larger amounts of data to be stored and successfully retrieved (Havelock 1963).

Eventually, however, speech and the human capacity for memorization encountered limits as to how much data could be recorded in this manner. Writing systems and numerical notations emerged, allowing the amount and type of data being stored to expand enormously. The invention of writing and mathematical notations also had a tremendous impact on the informatic capacity of human language and thought. Written records gave rise to new forms of classification, analysis, and other forms of information processing. The increase in information-processing capacity that mathematical notations make possible is easily confirmed by comparing the complexity of mathematical calculations that can be done with pencil and paper compared with calculations done solely in one's head.

The increase in the amount and sophistication of data that writing and mathematics made possible eventually gave rise to a new form of language and information processing — the language of science. Scientific activity, whether it is concrete or abstract, is confined to literate societies. Science is not just the gathering of new knowledge about nature, it also gives shape to that knowledge by organizing it systematically. It is a form of knowledge management. The effective storage and information processing that writing and mathematics made possible allowed scholars to gather and collect so much data that the only way to deal with the ensuing complexity and information overload was to develop a new mode of organization: the scientific method.

Science and the scientific method, however, also became tools for generating still more information-gathering activities. The information overload that modern science and the scientific method helped to generate led to the development of computers in the twentieth century as a way to help scientists cope with the enormous amounts of data they accumulated and the complex calculations they needed to execute.

Vygotsky's work shows how children discover that language, a medium of communication, can also be used as a tool to process information and solve problems. One can easily extend this notion backwards in time and conclude that at some point humans discovered that their system of vocalized verbal signals could be used internally, as a tool for thinking. But speech might have arisen first to make conceptual thinking possible, and only then was it used for communication purposes. A third possibility is that it emerged as a simultaneous tool for thinking and medium for communication.

The extension of speech and its concretization in the form of writing, mathematics, science, computing, and the Internet leveraged language as a tool for thinking and amplified its informatics capacity while preserving its communications function. The motivation for the emergence of new forms of language, however, seems to have been strictly the need for a greater informatics capacity, not increased communications.

Writing was first used not for communication but for the keeping of accounting records. For the period just after the emergence of writing, "few literary documents [were] excavated, although the same period has yielded tens of thousands of economic and administrative tablets and hundreds of votive inscriptions" (Kramer 1959). The very first words to be assigned a written form in the Sumerian language were the words for agricultural commodities that were collected as tribute by the priesthood who ran the irrigation system. They used writing to record who paid their taxes to the state. Written numerals were invented at the same time to keep track of the amounts of each commodity that were given in tribute.

The invention of writing and abstract numerals illustrates cyberneticist Ross Ashby's "theorem of requisite variety" (1957) as well as the notion that necessity is the mother of invention. According to Ashby, managers can control a system only if they can create a model of it that contains the requisite variety or complexity to accurately describe it. The priests running the irrigation system needed to collect tribute from farmers in order to feed the irrigation workers. They therefore needed to store and keep track of a complex set of data. Given that human memory has difficulty coping with more than seven, plus or minus two, elements at a time, the only way the priests could remember who had paid their tribute and who had not was to create permanent records of the tributes. It was only after the invention of writing for the purposes of economic control that writing was also used for the purposes of communication, and eventually, for other informatic applications such as the composition of stories or written poems.

The development of science was also motivated by purely informatic considerations. Abstract science permitted greater control of nature through better organization of information and the ability to make predictions. The scientific method provided scientists with the requisite variety to control a body of knowledge that the languages of writing and mathematics had not been able to manage.

The invention of computing is still another example of informatics driving the development of language. Without computing, natural and social scientists would not have been able to manage the information overload created by their disciplines. It was only after its initial application as an informatics device that computing was also used for communications; hence, its name in English is "computer" (as in calculator) and not "word processor," even though far more people use computers to process words than to compute or calculate numbers.

The Internet was also a response to an information overload. Computing increased the sheer number of messages that needed to be communicated as well as the number of people that needed to be communicated with. As the world shrunk to the dimensions of a global village, the number of people in the village with whom one wanted to communicate increased dramatically. This information overload, or traffic jam of messaging, gave rise to networking, client-server systems, and, finally, the Internet. The Internet, as opposed to client-server systems, was able to enfold the entire global community in a single electronic embrace. As is so often the case, a quantitative change created a qualitative change. As a result a new language emerged: the Internet, or the sixth language.

Starting with the ability to record ideas through writing and mathematical notation, human thought has become increasingly more complex. The need to model more complex phenomena has driven the development of the six modes of language. Consequently, each new mode of language is informatically more powerful than its predecessors, but at the same time a little less poetic (with the exception of the Net, which, because of its visual and audio elements is able to incorporate the arts and modes of artistic expression). In my model of the evolution of language, its information-processing capacity becomes more and more important as the complexity of human thought increases. It is essential to remember, however, that all forms of language possess a dual capacity for communication and information processing. Computers and the Internet are also communication devices and the spoken word has an informatics capacity. Both of these features of language must be addressed when we consider the nature of work and education.

The Semantics and Syntax of the Six Modes of Language

To strengthen the claim that writing, mathematics, science, computing, and the Internet may be regarded as languages in their own right and not just derivatives of speech, I will demonstrate that they qualify for this distinction solely on the basis of the criteria established by traditional linguists. According to two, Paivio and Begg (1981, 25), "semantics and syntax — meaning and grammatical patterning — are the indispensable core attributes of any human language." Semantics is the relationship between linguistic signals and their meaning or, in other words, a lexicon. "Naming is undoubtedly the most straightforward and dramatic example of such semantic behavior" (Paivio and Begg 1981, 25). Syntax is the structure or relationship among linguistic signals.

New modes of language evolved to model increasingly more complex phenomena, and hence, according to Ashby's theorem of requisite variety (1957), they required more complex structures to function. We therefore expect the semantics and syntax of new forms of language to retain the older structures and to add their own new unique elements to those structures. If writing, mathematics, science, computing, and the Internet are distinct modes of human language that deserve to be differentiated from speech, they must have distinct semantic and syntactic features above and beyond those of speech.

In the case of writing, the semantics of the written word are quite similar to those of the spoken word, although some constructions that are acceptable in oral language are not valid in prose, and vice versa. Oral contractions such as "don't" or "can't" are not widely used in formal prose writing.

As a rule, written vocabulary is considerably greater than oral vocabulary. We often use words in written communication that we would never use in oral discourse. Written signs, however, have an additional semantic feature above and beyond the spoken words they represent. They denote at the same time spoken sounds (phonemes), spoken syllables, and spoken words, and hence, carry a double level of abstraction: A written sign denotes a spoken word, which in turn denotes a concept from the real world. In logographic systems such as hieroglyphics, visual signs denote whole words. In syllabic systems, the visual signs represent syllables, and in phonetic alphabets, the letters represent phonemes. Words in the latter two systems are represented respectively by some combination of either syllables or letters, depending on the system.

It is at the syntactic level that written language begins to more radically distinguish itself from speech. Punctuation serves a function beyond semantically reproducing the natural pauses and reflections of speech; mainly, it provides a syntactic structure to language that is quite different from that of speech. Writing encourages a formal structuring of language consisting of sentences, paragraphs, sections, and chapters largely absent in spoken language. Analysis of the transcription of most oral discourse reveals that spoken language is not generally organized into grammatically correct sentences. In fact, the very term "grammar" betrays its association with writing through its etymology. The Greek term for "letter" (as in letters of the alphabet) is *gramma*. There are similar associations in other languages — *grammates* in the Latvian language means book. In short, grammar was not formalized before writing, just as there was no such thing as spelling before writing, and no uniform spelling before the printing press.

Grammars are not exact sets of rules. "Were a language ever completely 'grammatical' it would be a perfect engine of conceptual expression. Unfortunately, or rather luckily, no language is tyrannically consistent. All grammars leak" (Stubbs 1980, 39). Before writing, rigorous grammatical conventions were not necessary because any ambiguities could be resolved either by tone, facial expression, or dialogue. Listeners could always ask for an explanation if they did not understand what was said. With writing readers are basically on their own.

In addition to the formal distinctions between written and spoken language, there is also the empirical change of semantics and syntax that the storage features of writing encouraged. Within the semantic domain, there is a marked increase in abstract words and terminology as a language acquires a written form. A comparison between the lexicography of Homer (as found in the transcriptions of his orally composed poems) and that of the ancient Greek philosophers and playwrights of the fifth and fourth centuries BCE reveals the development of a new written vocabulary. The new lexicon of written words is rich in abstract terminology that appears in the language for the first time, and old words take on additional new abstract meanings (Havelock 1963).

Within the syntactic domain, the major structural change that comes with writing is the appearance of the prose system, which incorporates many more analytical features than the oral tradition. With writing, not only did visual syntactical elements appear, such as the spaces between words and the separations of sentences, paragraphs, and chapters, but the creation of permanent records through writing also gave rise to new syntactical elements such as charts, tabulations, tables of contents, and indexes.

In the language of mathematics, the semantic domain or lexicon consists primarily of precisely defined notations for numbers, such as 0, 1, 2, 100, 1/2, 0.4, and the square root of 2; mathematical operations such as +, −, x, and ÷; and logical relationships such as >, <, and =. Other semantic elements unique to mathematics are its definitions and axioms, such as those found in geometry, number theory, and other logical systems. The language of mathematics differs from natural language such as spoken English in that the semantic relationship between the signal — in this case, a visual sign like a numeral — and the phenomenon being represented as an abstract number is totally unambiguous. In written languages, there are often ambiguities between the written signal and the spoken word being denoted. With the exception of totally phonetic languages such as Spanish and Finnish, there are also ambiguities of pronunciation. George Bernard Shaw's famous example (Stubbs 1980, 51) of using "ghoti" to render the spoken word "fish" — taking "gh" from enough, "o" from women, and "ti" from nation — dramatically demonstrates the pronunciation ambiguities of the English alphabet.

The precision of the semantic conventions of mathematics also extends to the syntactic domain. The basic syntax of the language of mathematics is that of logic. Mathematical syntax, unlike that of spoken or written language, is totally unambiguous. The rules of grammar that govern speech and writing are subject to conflicting interpretations, while those of mathematics are not. The language of mathematics also introduces unique syntactical structures not found in natural languages, such as proofs, theorems, and lemmas.

The language of science includes the semantic elements of speech, writing, and mathematics, but it also introduces new semantic units unique unto itself. These include quantitative concepts such as mass, force, velocity, and mole; qualitative concepts such as organic/inorganic, animate/inanimate, solid/liquid/gas, and intelligence; and theoretical concepts such as inertia, entropy, valence, and natural selection. As in the language of mathematics, the semantics of science is characterized by precise and unambiguous definitions, even though much of the terminology that is employed corresponds to words that appear in everyday spoken language. In spoken English, mass can refer to either volume or weight. In physics, mass is precisely defined in terms of weight, but a careful distinction is made between mass and weight. An object's mass is universal, but its weight depends upon what planet or in what gravitational field it finds itself. A traveler in outer space might experience weightlessness but never masslessness.

As with its semantics, the syntax of science includes the structure of speech, writing, and mathematics. Science also introduces its own syntactical elements, however. The three most important elements — the ones which in a sense define the nature of science — are: (1) the scientific method; (2) the classification of information or data (taxonomy); and (3) the organization of knowledge, such as the grouping of scientific laws to form a scientific theory. The centrality of the classificatory and organizational structures is due to the fact that science is defined as organized knowledge. The scientific method, with its elements of observation, generalization, hypothesizing, experimental testing, and verification, defines the character of science. It qualifies science as a distinctive language rather than as a carefully organized scholarly activity such as history, which also makes use of organizational principles and other modes of language, namely, speech, writing, and mathematics.

The language of computing includes all of the semantic and syntactic elements of the earlier four modes of language. It also possesses its own semantic and syntactic elements by virtue of the activities of both its programmers and its end users. The semantics of the programming languages and end-user software programs specify computer inputs and outputs. The syntactic structures of programming languages and end-user software formalize the procedures for transforming inputs into outputs. These syntactic structures are basically unambiguous algorithms for ensuring the accuracy and the reliability of the computer's output. The syntactic structures that arise in a programming language or a relational database differ from the other language modes so that the user can take advantage of the computer's rapid information-processing speeds.

Although the Internet and the World Wide Web incorporate all of the semantic and syntactic elements of computing they also include their own unique elements in both categories. To clarify the relationship between the Web and the Net, the World Wide Web is one of many different elements of the Internet, which include its e-mail facilities, listservs, chat rooms, ftp facilities, Telnet facilities, Web pages, Web sites, intranets, extranets, portal sites, and e-commerce sites. Each of these facilities represents a semantic element of the sixth language of the Internet. Listservs are a way of distributing e-mails to a group of users who share an interest in a common topic, which allows an asynchronous e-mail dialogue to take place. A chat room is a place on the Internet where people can meet online to discuss a topic in real time. Ftp facilities allow files to be transferred from one computer to another through the medium of the Internet. The Telnet facility allows users to access their servers or home computers from anywhere in the world as long as they can find access to the Internet. Web pages are components of Web sites or intranets that integrate text, graphics, video, and audio. Web sites are publicly accessible collections of Web pages that can be found using a URL or Internet address. Intranets are private Web pages that can be accessed only by qualified users. Extranets are a collection of Web sites that can be accessed from a single Internet address. An e-commerce site is a Web site that allows commercial transactions to take place using credit cards or digital money.

The Internet also has a number of unique syntactic elements. One of the unique syntactic elements of the sixth language is hypertext, which makes it possible to link all Web sites and Web pages in cyberspace to form one huge global document. Another unique syntactic element is the Internet Protocol, which allows all of the computers connected to the Internet to form one huge global network and makes the Web, ftp, and Telnet all possible. McLuhan's prediction of a global village has been realized. Still another unique syntactic element of the Internet is the search engines, which increase access to knowledge and information and hence provide an extra level of communication that the other forms of verbal language cannot match. Search engines also help people to find each other and hence contribute to the creation of a global knowledge community.

4

An Evolutionary Chain of Languages:

From Speech to the Internet

The primary mode from which all the other modes of language derive is speech. Each of the other modes incorporates elements from its predecessors. Without speech, there would have been no writing and no mathematical notation; without writing and mathematics, there would have been no science. Without science, there would have been no computing, and without computing, no Internet.

The Internet incorporates all of the features of computing, which in turn incorporates the features of all the previous modes: speech, writing, mathematics, and science. Science incorporates speech, writing, and mathematics. Writing and mathematics arose at the same moment in history. They therefore only incorporated the features of speech, albeit different ones. It is worth tracing the history of the development of these six modes of language and detailing the history of human communication and information processing. The story begins with speech or the spoken word.

Speech

Speech, or spoken language, is the earliest and most basic form of human language. It is essential to all information processing and, perhaps, even to human thought itself. There are two schools of thought — one headed by Edward Sapir (1921) and Benjamin Whorf (1964) and the other by Lev Vygotsky (1962) — that claim that a spoken language determines the thought processes of its users and that thought arises from speech, not the other way around. Without fully subscribing to their theories, my analysis is, nevertheless, based on the premise that spoken language plays an essential role in all human information processing. Spoken language provides the categories with which we express our thoughts and ideas and organize our information.

Speech is most often regarded solely as an instrument of human communication. This is its primary function. The first uses of spoken language were for the purposes of communication. As this type of language evolved, however, its users discovered that verbal information could be recorded and stored through the mechanisms of poetry and song. This discovery gave rise to the oral tradition among preliterate people whereby vital information necessary for their survival, their identity, and their sense of history was recorded or stored in tales, epics, and legends. Oral language was used as a device for processing, storing, retrieving, and organizing information. The preservation or storage of information and knowledge in preliterate societies was achieved through the memorization of folktales or myths. These tales or legends were not merely entertaining stories told in an impromptu manner. They were, in fact, very carefully organized to provide listeners with the basic information required in their society. In his *Preface to Plato*, Eric Havelock refers to the storyteller as a "tribal encyclopedia." The information in the story was organized to facilitate its memorization as a way of preserving or storing it. As noted earlier, the use of rhyme, rhythm, meter, alliteration, plot, and other "literary" devices were used to aid the storyteller's memory. These techniques of information storage and organization, however, imposed a set of constraints on oral society, one which discouraged innovation and personal expression (Havelock 1963).

Writing and Mathematics

The origin of writing can be traced to the Sumerian culture at the end of the fourth millennium BCE. The writing systems that originated in Egypt, China, the Indus Valley, and Meso-America are independent, and their invention followed a different set of circumstances than those in Sumer.

Some people have argued that the idea of writing was transmitted from Sumer to Egypt and China, but this is speculative. This discussion focuses on the invention of writing in Mesopotamia because the Sumerians were not influenced by any other writing systems; their innovation grew out of the earlier notational schemes of tallies and clay accounting tokens.

Ironically, writing did not evolve from storytelling or the need to preserve oral tales and legends, but out of the need to enumerate and to make records of commercial transactions. Written records began with quantitative rather than qualitative data. "Writing was not a deliberate invention, but the incidental by-product of a strong sense of private property" (Speises, quoted in Meyers 1960). The transmission of the idea of writing to Egypt and China is assumed to have taken place along trade routes, which reinforces the notion that commercial, rather than cultural, activities stimulated the development of writing. This should not be surprising, since quantitative information is far more difficult to remember than verbal information. It is much easier to remember a story with a narrative and various characters or personalities than a set of numbers.

Tallies

The first form of human notation, tallies, were not written but were made either by making marks on an object — such as etching notches on a stick or a bone — or by collecting counters such as pebbles, grains, twigs, or shells. Tallies are based upon the principle of one-to-one correspondence, in which each item being enumerated is matched by a mark or a counter depending on the system (Schmandt-Besserat 1984a, 48-60). The number of identical marks or counters used for the tally was equal to the number of items being enumerated, such as the number of sheep in a flock, the number of animals killed in a hunt, or the number of full moons since the last meeting of two clans. The major limitation of tallies is that they record only the quantitative feature of the set of objects being enumerated, leaving the identification of the objects to context or to the memory of the enumerator. Tallies are, therefore, qualitatively nonspecific. They can satisfy only simple, low-technology cultures where only a few obvious items of daily life require accounting. They cannot be used, for example, to tally a complex set of commercial products.

The oldest form of tallies (and, hence, of human notation) currently identified are notched animal bones and antlers dating to about 15,000 BCE in the Middle East (Marshack 1964, 743; Schmandt-Besserat 1987, 44–48). These tallies show a series of notches or incised strokes in variable numbers, which can be interpreted as standing for collections of unknown items in a one-to-one correspondence. Marshack has proposed that some of the European Paleolithic tallies served to keep calendrical notations. Whatever the meaning of the Middle Eastern notched bones, it is clear that quantitative or numerical notation preceded written notation.

As primitive as they were, tallies produced an impact on the human mind at the cognitive level. They represent the first use of visual symbols to store, manipulate, and display information. In turn, they fostered abstract thought processes, as items of daily life came to be dealt with through the means of an abstract notation. Three deer, for instance, could be represented by three abstract marks. Tallies segmented reality. As a substitute for the deer, the marks isolated the deer from their context and abstracted them for scrutiny. Tallies also encouraged objectivity by separating the information from the knower, and at the same time displaying that information for all to use.

Tallies replaced verbal communication with objective nonverbal data removed and abstracted from their original context. Tallies created a new reality and set the stage for counting, mathematics, and accounting. As far as we know, they were the first artifacts to designate quantitative data nonverbally. Because the counters could be repeated infinitely, they increased the amount of data that could be handled by humans. Tallies provided a tool for organizing information and laid the foundation for the future development of other information-processing techniques.

Accounting Tokens

The next step in the development of notational technologies was clay accounting tokens. Denise Schmandt-Besserat's exhaustive study of tokens revealed that these clay artifacts, two to three centimeters long, were used for the enumeration and accounting of agricultural staples. Their use began in the prehistoric Middle East, circa 8000 BCE, at the very beginning of the agricultural age, which also had its roots in the Middle East. Each uniquely shaped token designated some measure of an agricultural commodity or product. The system, which started with twenty-four kinds of tokens, grew to 190 different types of tokens by 3300 BCE, just before the advent of writing and abstract numerals in Sumer. The shapes included spheres, disks, cones, tetrahedrons, biconoids, ovoids, cylinders, and triangles, which were further differentiated with incisions and punched marks. The tokens designated agricultural products and commodities such as measures of grains (barley, wheat, and emmer); jars of oil; livestock, primarily sheep and goats, differentiated by age, sex, and breed; wool, cloth, and different types of garments; measures of land expressed in terms of the amount of seed required to sow it; and service or labor (Schmandt-Besserat 1978).

Tokens and tallies share many characteristics, which suggests that the token system may have evolved from pebbles. Both tokens and tallies are palpable symbols that are easy to manipulate and are used in one-to-one correspondence with the objects being enumerated. Both fragment reality in that they abstract data from the context in which they are generated and from linguistic discourse; hence, they are not dependent on any particular spoken language. This helps explain the wide distribution of tokens throughout the ancient Middle East among people who spoke different dialects and languages. Today's use of Arabic numerals similarly spans many different cultures and linguistic groups.

Despite their similarities, tokens differed from pebbles and other tallies in very significant ways. Tokens were not randomly collected objects put to the secondary use of counting. They were man-made artifacts prepared specifically for the purpose of accounting. As opposed to a series of more or less identical counters such as grains or pebbles, tokens were molded into distinctive shapes that were easy to recognize and simple enough to be systematically reproduced. As opposed to unspecific tallies, each token shape stood for a specific commodity. In other words, tokens communicated both quantitative and qualitative information (Schmandt-Besserat 1987).

Tokens functioned as metaphors, translating words for economic concepts into a tactile medium. This was a radical change in data processing. While a group of pebbles could not be understood out of context, tokens became a reliable tool for data storage. Their meaning could be understood and translated unambiguously into speech by anyone initiated into the system. The tokens were a tool for data manipulation. Like tallies, they made possible the processing and retrieval of large amounts of data, but tokens had yet another advantage. They permitted a new dimension, that of diversification, which allowed many different commodities to be dealt with at once. As new commodities requiring enumeration arose, a newly shaped token could be created. The elements of an inventory consisting of different types of commodities could be manipulated simultaneously. As with tallies, the data could be easily laid out and displayed, and hence grasped both visually and physically. Tokens, however, could be organized and reorganized into different piles or more sophisticated patterns according to any number of possible categories, facilitating and enhancing classification. In a sense, the token system was the forerunner of the abacus, as well as spreadsheet analysis.

Tokens also had the potential of acting as a means of communication. While tallies could be used only as personal memory aids for items known to the enumerator alone, tokens were universal and systematized. A token came to represent the same product to individuals of entirely different communities speaking different languages and separated by great distances.

The main drawback was that the system became cumbersome. Although it was open and complete and could be expanded at will to convey new meanings, the creation of new shapes and new markings was bound to reach a stage of saturation or overburdening. This need for a new form of data processing eventually led to the invention of writing and abstract numerals.

The Cognitive Impact of the Token System

The token system changed the way people stored, manipulated, displayed, and communicated information and, in particular, it changed the way people counted. Tokens were a new tool for counting and computing. The unique feature of the counters was that they specifically designated the object being enumerated by the coding of qualitative information through a three-dimensional shape. Each token with its unique shape was used to enumerate one, and only one, object or commodity and no other. For example, ovoids could count only jars of oil. Tokens, in other words, merged the representation of the qualitative and quantitative features of a commodity. There was no token representing the abstract unit of "one." There were only tokens representing one unit or one measure of a specific commodity. When counting with tokens, it was not possible to separate the nature of the item counted from that of the quantity. Abstract counting was not possible with the token system; tokens did not represent abstract numbers.

There exists, in fact, no evidence for the use of abstract numbers at the time tokens first appeared, nor during the time of their major use and development from 8000 to 3100 BCE. Schmandt-Besserat's analysis (1984a, 1987) of notched bone (Marshack 1964) led her to the conclusion that these tallying devices were used exclusively in a non-mathematical, one-to-one correspondence mode. There does not seem to be the grouping of notches into sets corresponding to cardinal numbers such as 2, 3, 5, or 10. Analysis of the use of tokens has yielded a similar result, namely, that tokens were used to enumerate in one-to-one correspondence, like tallies, with the added feature that their distinctive shapes qualitatively designated the specific commodity being enumerated. Evidence for the way in which tokens were used comes from groups of tokens representing specific transactions found stored and bundled in clay envelopes. The analysis of these assemblages of tokens indicates that each enumeration of a product was tied to multiple repetitive occurrences of the tokens designating that product. That is, the tokens were used in one-to-one correspondence: n ovoids were used to designate n jars of oil. On the other hand, n jars of oil are never represented as a set of n tokens, each representing the abstract unit "one" tied to the ovoid token for a jar of oil.

The syntax of the tokens is such that they never functioned as adjectives modifying a noun. The syntactical structure of an abstract number, such as "three," acting as an adjective modifying a noun (or a noun phrase) such as "jar of oil" in the phrase "three jars of oil" does not appear before writing.

Given the lack of evidence for the use of abstract numbers with tallies and tokens, Schmandt-Besserat (1984a, 1987) postulated that tokens reflect a stage in the evolution of counting, before abstract numbers were used, known as concrete counting. Many historians of mathematics view the evolution of counting as having taken place in three main stages:

1. One-to-one correspondence, with no precise concepts of numbers.
2. Concrete counting, with the use of special numerical expressions for counting different specific classes of items.
3. Abstract counting, with abstract numbers that are universally applicable.

Schmandt-Besserat's analysis (1984a, 1987) of the archaeological data supports the claims of historians of mathematics and suggests that the use of tallies represented counting in a one-to-one correspondence with no specific concept of number. Tallies permitted people to count larger quantities of items than the vocabulary of enumeration that was available to them in their spoken language. Tokens acted as concrete numbers. As we have seen, they had meaning only as units of the commodity they designated and enumerated, and not as abstract absolute quantities. Concrete numbers, such as "a brace" of partridge or "a yoke" of oxen, like tokens, cannot be used to designate "two" as an abstract number and then be used to enumerate other objects. A brace of sandals is meaningless; one must instead refer to them as "a pair of sandals," that is, as a concrete number, or as "two sandals" where "two" operates as an abstract number. The invention of tokens made it possible for enumeration to become specific and for "concrete counting" to develop.

The dominant technologies of a culture, whether they are informational, mechanical, or economic, are interrelated and follow a similar pattern of evolution, reinforcing each other until a new level of technological innovation or breakthrough arises and new social patterns emerge.

The history of information processing in the Middle East during the period 15,000–3000 BCE is one of major breakthroughs followed by long periods of stability. The breakthroughs — tallies, tokens, and writing — may be viewed as "break boundaries" between radically different economic and social systems. The tally system was in use for thousands of years by hunting-and-gathering societies. It remained static, not undergoing any significant morphological or functional changes as long as hunting and gathering was the economic base of the culture. It is not a coincidence that the token system, a major elaboration and significant modification of the tally system and a breakthrough in information processing, emerges around 8000 BCE, just as agriculture is emerging as the economic base for a new form of society.

The token system became a stable technology of information processing for the next 5000 years until another major shift in economic life occurred, namely, the urbanization of Sumer at Uruk between 3350 and 3100 BCE (Kramer 1956). With urbanization, tokens began to evolve new forms and applications. Clay tokens were used to record the payment of tributes and taxes to those who maintained and administered the irrigation system upon which all agriculture depended. Tokens became an administrative tool that allowed political and economic control of the agricultural countryside by urban centers of commerce and trade. Cognitive breakthroughs and advances associated with these innovations resulted in a chain reaction in which new information-processing techniques arose, including abstract numeration, logographic writing, and phonetic coding.

The new advances in the technology of information, such as tallies, tokens, abstract numerals, and writing, did not occur in isolation. Rather, new information forms emerged as changes took place in the social and economic environment. The cognitive foundations of the previous level of information technology served as a starting point for satisfying the new information demands of a changed environment. For example, the tally system was transformed into the token system by the demands for new accounting procedures required by the new agricultural lifestyle. Similarly, urban life brought with it pressures for a more complex accounting system as the number of items to be enumerated and the number of social interactions to be taken into account dramatically increased. These demands manifested themselves in a spurt of creative activity in which the simple token system was articulated and expanded, and new structures were added, which eventually led to the invention of writing and abstract numbers. An overview of this complex process of innovation, described below, can be obtained from Table 1 (pages 92–93), which shows the stages through which the use of tokens passed — along with the cognitive processes associated with them.

Complex Tokens, Envelopes, and Impressed Logograms

Changes in the way quantitative information was processed can be attributed to changes in the socioeconomic system of its users. The token system during the long purely agricultural period from 8000 to 3350 BCE remained remarkably stable with the appearance of a limited number of plain or simple tokens corresponding to basic agricultural commodities of the time, such as wheat and sheep. Between 3350 and 3100 BCE, the token system underwent a metamorphosis that can be attributed to the pressures of urbanization. With the rise of urban life and, in particular, the monumental temple complexes such as Eanna at Uruk, the largest economic institution of its time, there suddenly appear in the ruins, along with "other administrative material such as seals and sealings" (Schmandt-Besserat 1988a), complex tokens representing a number of finished manufactured products, no doubt produced in the urban workshops of Uruk and other population centers. The great majority of tokens from this period are found in the temple precincts, indicating that they were associated with a coercive taxation and redistribution system of a strong central government. This interpretation of the token findings is reinforced by Sumerian reliefs of the period showing citizens delivering their goods to the temple (Kramer 1956).

Another important development in the token system occurred with the appearance of clay envelopes, which functioned as containers to hold a number of plain tokens. It is presumed that the envelopes were used to consolidate all of the tokens employed in a single transaction.

The surfaces of the envelopes were marked with the seals of the individuals involved in the transaction, and hence the envelope served as
a receipt or contract (Schmandt-Besserat 1984b, 47). The envelopes
had the disadvantage, however, of masking their contents because
of the opacity of their clay surfaces. The problem was overcome by
impressing the tokens to be contained in the envelope onto the wet
surface of the envelope. This technique revealed the contents without
the necessity of breaking the envelope and also had the unexpected
and certainly unplanned side effect of creating the first logograms
(Schmandt-Besserat 1987).

A logogram is a two-dimensional visual sign that abstractly represents the written form of a single word. Egyptian hieroglyphics and
Chinese characters are examples of logograms. Two different types
of logograms can be distinguished: pictograms, which represent the
words they designate pictorially; and ideograms, which represent
the ideas of the words they designate. A logogram can also simply
represent the word symbolically. The system of writing that makes use
of logograms is called logographic writing.

The initial purpose of token impression was to reveal the contents
of an envelope, not to substitute token impressions for tokens. But
that is precisely what happened. Approximately fifty years later, it was
realized that the actual tokens contained within an envelope were
totally redundant and their use was dropped. The curved envelopes
quickly evolved into flat two-dimensional tablets with the impressions
of tokens upon their upper surfaces. The evolution of envelopes into
tablets represents a major breakthrough in information processing.
The flat tablet became the prototype of all two-dimensional writing
surfaces, including the pages of a book and the CRT video display of
a computer.

It is important to note that the impressed logogram, semantically,
was no different from a three-dimensional token. The logograms were
two-dimensional negative imprints of the three-dimensional tokens.
They were immediately recognizable to the users of the token system
because they shared the same outline and bore the same markings as
the actual tokens. In fact, the first tablets are not true writing but merely
the permanent records of an accounting system based on tokens, in
which the tokens themselves were actually discarded once their

imprints had been made. From the point of view of function or informational content, impressed logograms on clay tablets operated exactly the same way as the three-dimensional token system. The medium changed, however, and the way that information was displayed changed radically from a collection of palpable three-dimensional clay objects to abstract symbols arrayed in two-dimensional patterns on the flat surface of a clay tablet. The shift from three-dimensional artifacts to logograms triggered a chain reaction that resulted in the invention of logographic writing, phonetic coding, and abstract numerals.

Preparing the Way for Numerals and Writing

The manufacture and manipulation of tokens and impressed signs promoted the development of hand-eye coordination and the fine motor skills essential for writing. More importantly, tallies, and especially tokens, introduced the visual bias that characterizes written notation. Tokens stressed the importance of uniformity. They were the first class of artifacts whose uniformity of shape was key to their function. Tokens were used as repeatable symbols in much the same way that numerals and the letters of the alphabet are. The visual bias created by the use of uniform and repeatable tokens increased when the tokens were used to imprint the outer surfaces of clay envelopes and, later, the impressed tablets. The pattern of token markings arranged in neatly spaced lines within a two-dimensional array permitted the user (or reader) to encompass the whole field of data in a single glance.

Tallies, tokens, and impressed signs also paved the way to writing and abstract numerals on the cognitive level. Each of these methods of record keeping can be regarded as phases in the development of abstract notation. Impressed token markings increased the level of abstraction. The two-dimensional format of the impressed tablets was more abstract than three-dimensional tokens, in that the negative impression of the tokens could not be grasped in the hand and manipulated like three-dimensional tokens. The loss of volume, concreteness, and tactility removed the symbols one step further from the physical three-dimensional reality for which they stood. The display of information within a two-dimensional array, however, permitted the user to see the information in a new light. By being able to observe more data at a single glance, the user of the tablet system began to think more globally about the data. More abstract patterns of classifying and analyzing the data became possible. If the medium is the message, then the message of the two-dimensional display of information on tablets was that of abstraction, classification, analysis, uniformity, repeatability, and the power of the visual.

I believe that the development of tallies, tokens, impressed signs, numerals, and writing were phases in the development of metaphorical (visual) thinking and that the earlier notational forms created a perceptual and cognitive environment conducive to the invention of writing. To summarize how tallies, tokens, and impressed signs led to numerals and writing, let me iterate the many features that abstract numbers and writing shared with previous record-keeping devices (tallies, tokens, impressed envelopes, and impressed tablets).

Each system employed metaphors and symbols and hence abstracted information by fragmenting reality from its representation in a sign system, thus creating an artificial medium for the expression and notation of ideas in which the basic elements were easily manipulated. Each system consisted of uniform elements, which were used in a repeatable fashion within the context of a linear two-dimensional array (truer of later stages of the token system), and thus produced a visual bias that required good hand-eye coordination for their creation and use. The application of these systems promoted objectivity, and hence standardized uniform measures and a system of economic and political control.

The Advent of Writing and Abstract Numerals

Once tokens were used to produce two-dimensional impressed signs, a series of rapid but fundamental changes took place that transformed the token-based notational system for "concrete numbers." There emerged two notational systems, one for abstract numerals and one for written words. Abstract numerals were built out of the two impressed token signs for the small and large measure of wheat, the "ban" which came to represent the number 1 and the "bariga" which represented 10. The second notational system was a full-fledged writing system for transcribing the words of spoken language into visual signs incised on the clay surface of a tablet with the sharp end

Breakpoints in the History of Information Processing with Tallies and Tokens

Table 1

TIME FRAME	MORPHOLOGY	ASSOCIATED COGNITIVE ADVANCE OR NEW COMMUNICATION CAPABILITY
15,000–8000 BCE	TALLIES Notched sticks, etched bones, pebbles, shells	ENUMERATION: ONE-TO-ONE CORRESPONDENCE
8000–3400 BCE	SIMPLE TOKENS Three-dimensional clay objects	CONCRETE COUNTING AND NUMBERS Record keeping and data storage Information or data processing Primitive sign and symbol capability Classification — control — centralization
3400–3250 BCE (Urbanization at Uruk)	COMPLEX TOKENS Greater variety of three-dimensional clay objects • Multiplication of shapes • Incisions and punctuations • Perforations	SIGN AND SYMBOL ARTICULATION — METAPHOR Abstracting classes through common shapes but differentiating subjects Complex classification Complex data processing and record keeping Specialization

Date	Stage	Description	Significance
3250–3150 BCE	TOKEN-IMPRESSED ENVELOPES	Clay containers of tokens whose outside surfaces have been impressed with the tokens that are contained inside	**ABSTRACTING THREE-DIMENSIONAL ARTIFACTS INTO TWO-DIMENSIONAL SIGNS** Primitive set theory or chunking of data More abstract symbolization — visual metaphor Translation of tactile into visual
3150–3100 BCE	IMPRESSED TABLETS	Two-dimensional clay tablets upon which token forms have been impressed	**GREATER ABSTRACT SYMBOLIZATION** Token no longer physically present Ability to work in a totally two-dimensional medium
3100 BCE	INCISED TABLETS	Two-dimensional clay tablets upon which • signs that replicate the shapes of tokens have been incised, • ban and bariga tokens have been impressed, • new incised signs have been added.	**ADVENT OF WRITING AND ABSTRACT NUMERALS** Logographic writing Abstract numerals Phonetic writing

of a stylus. The shapes of the original impressed token signs were imitated in the new incised format and formed the first vocabulary or lexicon of the new written language. Words other than those for commercial commodities emerged based on the principle of representing words pictographically or ideographically. Paradoxically, the very first incised signs did not represent the words pictorially, but represented the shape that the accounting token corresponding to that word made when impressed into a clay tablet. Writing began as an extremely abstract symbol system.

The transformation that took place circa 3100 BCE was far more than a change of form from impressed tokens to incised signs. It was a change of concept. Instead of signs that fused qualitative and quantitative information, there were two separate types of notation: one verbal and one numerical. Incised signs were used to transcribe spoken words or qualitative information — that is, they rendered spoken language in a written form. The two former impressed logograms, the ban and the bariga, were used to express abstract numbers. With the emergence of two notational forms, a qualitative one with written words and a quantitative one with abstract numerals, the language of the written word and the language of mathematics emerged as two separate and distinct systems for recording information. The transformation that led from impressed logograms to incised pictographic writing and abstract numerals involved the following five major changes:

1. The transition from token impressions to incised signs: The two-dimensional impressions of tokens onto clay tablets inspired the emergence of a new form of signs. The new incised signs took the form of small designs traced with the sharp end of a reed stylus on the surface of a clay tablet while the clay was still wet. The designs mimicked the shape and form of the token impressions. The stylus was pressed lightly onto the clay surface to produce the number of short strokes necessary to draw a sign. Circa 3100 BCE, the practice of imprinting the clay tokens was dropped completely, with the exception of the signs for the two grain measures, which continued to be impressed.

How did this technique for creating signs arise? One possible motivation for the use of incised signs rather than impressed tokens is that the former technique allowed the creation of new signs for words that had no corresponding tokens. Still another reason is that there could be no confusion with the old notational system. The sign for a ban of wheat repeated twice followed by a jar of oil sign can only be read as two jars of oil if the jar of oil sign is incised. If the jar of oil sign had been impressed, however, the three signs could possibly have been misinterpreted as a tablet from the old system and read as two bans of wheat and a jar of oil. By using incised signs for the words and impressed signs for the numbers, the new tablets could never be confused with the older tablets consisting of impressed signs only.

The transition between impressed and incised signs was rapid, a matter of only fifty years, or two generations. The commodities signs that had been produced by impressing the corresponding token into the clay were now rendered with a stylus by sketching the token's outline and repeating its markings. Each of the incised logograms in this new written language became a visual metaphor or a pictographic symbol of the former tokens. The critical empirical evidence supporting this hypothesis for the invention of writing is the existence of a one-to-one morphological correspondence between the first pictographs representing the most usual Sumerian commodities, such as grain, livestock, oil, and textiles, and the three-dimensional tokens used to represent these goods before writing.

2. An increase in the repertory of signs — pictography and ideography: The representation of tokens by an incised sign on the tablets led to the idea that any concept could be conveyed by an incised sign. The use of the stylus, in other words, led to the invention of new pictographic and ideographic signs completely unrelated to the tokens and designating new concepts unrelated to agricultural commodities.

3. New semantic and syntactic values of the symbol system: Not only did the incised signs differ from the impressed logograms morphologically, but also semantically and syntactically. The impressed logogram for a sheep carried the meaning of "one sheep" and functioned as a modified noun (that is, a concrete number) in which both quality and number were denoted. The incised logogram was, on the other hand, a more abstract symbol which denoted an unmodified noun and hence stood for "sheep." A separate symbol was required to denote the number of sheep even if it was only one.

4. Signs to express sounds — phonetic writing: Pictography was unable to satisfy one particular need of the Sumerian scribes: It could not render an individual's name. The capability of pictograms or ideograms did not allow for a representation of each individual by a miniature portrait. Sumerian ingenuity provided the solution. Names were expressed phonetically. Logograms, used to write an individual's name, were read phonetically as the sound of the word they represented in Sumerian. The sign for oil was read as the sound "i" (long e) and the sign for arrow was read "ti." When associated together in rebus fashion, as the Sumerians would have done it, the two signs spell "E.T." — the name of a cinema hero from outer space.

5. Signs to express plurality — numerals: The first written numerals representing abstract numbers appear at exactly the same time as incised logographic writing (Schmandt-Besserat 1984*a*, 56). The actual signs to represent numerals were made by impressing different combinations of the cone and sphere tokens representing, respectively, the small and large measure of wheat, the ban and the bariga. These numerals still retained the visual metaphor of the one-to-one correspondence with a pile of pebbles. The number 3 was represented by the impression of three cones (or three wedges) and the number 4 by four cones (or four wedges). The new element of abstraction in notation was the use of a new sign, the circle, that is, the impression of the sphere, for the number 10. This created an economy of notation since 43, for example, could be represented as four circles and three wedges instead of forty-three wedges. This system was more efficient than the older system of tallying. It was an early and primitive predecessor of the system of Roman numerals, which would represent 23, for instance, as two Xs and three Is, or XXIII. The two impressed logograms used to represent the abstract numbers 1 and 10 still retained their function as "concrete numbers" for grain. It was left to the scribe to decide, according to the context, whether the wedge was the numeral 1 or a ban of grain, and whether a circle was the numeral 10, or a bariga of grain.

The Bifurcations of Impressed Logograms

As we have seen, both logographic writing and the notation for abstract numbers arose 5000 years ago from clay accounting tokens, which in turn first made their appearance 8000 years ago. The token system underwent a linear sequence of development and enrichment from 8000 to 3100 BCE that consists of the following steps or stages:

1. plain tokens;
2. complex tokens;
3. tokens in clay envelopes;
4. impressed logographs on clay envelopes containing tokens; and
5. impressed logographs on clay tablets.

None of these changes represents a bifurcation, but they do represent either an increase in the variety and number of tokens or a morphological change of the tokens, that is, a change in their physical form. The meaning or function of a three-dimensional token circa 8000 BCE, and an impressed logogram created by pressing a token into wet clay circa 3100 BCE, were the same. During the above five steps, neither writing nor abstract numerals emerged. The next development in notational technology was profound and followed shortly after the introduction of the two-dimensional clay tablet. The impressed logograms on clay tablets not only underwent semantic and morphological variations but were subject to a series of Prigoginian bifurcations, discussed below.

The two logograms for the small and large measure of grain, the ban and the bariga, remained unchanged morphologically. They continued to serve as "concrete counters" for the two measures of grain, but they also took on a second semantic function: They came to represent the abstract numbers 1 and 10, respectively. At the same time that this transition took place, incised logograms also came into being. All of the existing impressed logograms, other than the ban and the bariga logograms, ceased to function as "concrete counters"; they changed both morphologically and semantically. Each impressed logogram — with the exception of the two grain signs — was replaced by incised signs that graphically resembled the older impressed logograms they were replacing. Similarly, the signs no longer functioned as "concrete numbers" but as logograms designating single spoken words or phrases. In addition to the transformation of the old impressed signs into incised signs, other incised signs began to appear, designating concepts that had not been part of the original token vocabulary, which consisted of approximately 190 agricultural commodities and manufactured goods.

Some fifty years after their introduction, incised signs took on a second semantic function. As well as ideographically or pictographically coding a single word, they also phonetically coded those phonemes and words that had the same pronunciation as the word they represented ideographically or pictographically. The incised sign for an arrow, ti, also represented its homonym, life, which was also pronounced "ti."

The sudden explosion of semantic function in 3100 BCE marks the beginning of literacy and numeracy. To understand the interplay of the cognitive elements that contributed to this development, a more sophisticated model is required. The work of Ilya Prigogine and his theories of bifurcation and social amplification illuminate the process that took place in Sumer 5000 years ago.

From his studies of chemical systems, Prigogine developed the notion that out of the chaos of a system there spontaneously arises a new level of order as a bifurcation from an older form of organization gives rise to a new form of organization. A bifurcation, as the etymology of the word suggests, is the splitting of a stream of development into two branches. With a bifurcation the older form of organization remains, but a new form of organization evolves from it, retaining some of its properties unchanged, transforming other elements into new structures, and suppressing other elements so that they appear only as vestigial reminders of earlier structures with little or no structural role. Biological evolution, for example, can be thought of as a series of bifurcations. The evolution of language represents another example. Before spoken language, communication between hominids consisted of hand signals, facial gestures, body language, and nonverbal vocalizations.

All of these elements have been incorporated into spoken language and still play an important role in communication. Some scholars claim that 90 percent of the communication of spoken language is still nonverbal and that the way things are said is more important than what is actually said. When spoken language evolved into a transcribed form of language, the vestigial elements of speech, namely, vocalization, gesture, hand signal, and body language, were abstracted away and written communication became purely conceptual, based on the literal meaning of the words. With mathematics and science further abstractions took place; all of the ambiguities of verbal language were removed to create instruments for numerical calculations and analysis, respectively. I hypothesize that the emergence of writing and mathematics represents an evolution of spoken language that can be modeled in terms of Prigogenian bifurcations, in which new levels of order emerge from the chaos of the information loads that developed when speech could no longer handle the complexity of large-scale agricultural activity.

The emergence of the complex notational structures of the numerals and writing that suddenly appeared in 3100 BCE can be described as a series of bifurcations involving the two-dimensional "concrete counter" logograms, of which impressions were made by pressing the original three-dimensional tokens from which they were derived into a wet clay tablet. The emergence of abstract numerals and writing can be described in terms of the following three separate bifurcations:

Bifurcation 1: the split of two-dimensional impressed logographic signs into two morphologically and semantically distinct sets of signs — the incised signs and the impressed signs in which incised signs are used exclusively for verbal notation or writing and impressed signs used exclusively for accounting and numerical notation;

Bifurcation 2: the split of the impressed logograms for the ban and the bariga into two semantic functions — the old one as "concrete numbers" for small and large measures of grain and the new one as the "abstract numbers" for 1 and 10, respectively; and

Bifurcation 3: the split of the semantic function of the incised signs, in which they are used not only to code spoken words ideographically or pictographically, but also phonetically.

It is impossible from the archaeological data (Schmandt-Besserat 1979, 27–40; Schmandt-Besserat 1988*b*, 1–175) to give the exact dates of the above bifurcations. Logic dictates that Bifurcation 3 must have occurred sometime after Bifurcation 1, since the incised signs would have had to have been established as logograms designating a word

with a particular sound before they could have been used to phonetically code the homonyms of that word. Empirical evidence supports
this conclusion: Fewer examples of the phonetic use of the incised
signs are found compared with their more concrete use as logograms.

The relative timing of Bifurcations 1 and 2 can be determined by a
process of elimination and a linguistic analysis of the archaeological
data. As illustrated in Table 2, there are only three logical possibilities
for the relative timing of Bifurcations 1 and 2:

   (i) Bifurcation 1 occurred before Bifurcation 2;
  (ii) Bifurcation 1 occurred at the same time as Bifurcation 2; or
 (iii) Bifurcation 1 occurred after Bifurcation 2.

The fact that impressed logograms functioning as "abstract numbers" did not appear before the existence of incised signs — and when
they did appear, they were always used to modify an incised sign —
indicates that Bifurcation 2 did not occur before Bifurcation 1. There
are no cases where the ban and the bariga signs are used to modify an
impressed token logogram such as the jar of oil or the sheep sign.

The absence of any tablets in which incised signs are repeated
many times to function as "concrete numbers" in the way tokens or
impressed-token logograms functioned indicates, on the other hand,
that Bifurcation 1 did not occur before Bifurcation 2. This leaves only
one possible conclusion: Bifurcations 1 and 2 occurred at precisely
the same time; hence, Model B in Table 2 best explains the data. It
would seem that the emergence of abstract numerals and that of ideographic writing were tied to each other and occurred at the same point
in history.

Each of the three bifurcations represents the birth of a new form of
semantic or numerical expression in which a new abstract branch
splits off from an older, more concrete one.

Bifurcation 1 represents the emergence of true writing using an
ideographic or pictographic coding scheme in which each word is
uniquely represented by a visual sign, that is, the written form of the
word. Bifurcation 1 also involved the splitting of abstract logograms,
each designating a single word, from impressed logograms or "concrete numbers" that designated both a quantity and a quality. The

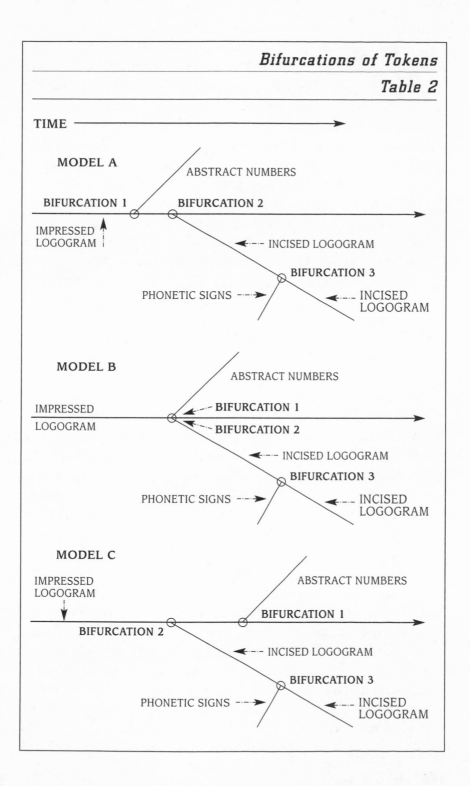

Bifurcations of Tokens
Table 2

incised logogram abstracts away from the impressed logogram the sense of number, leaving a purely qualitative system of notation; hence, the beginning of true writing, which is capable of coding a spoken language into written signs.

Bifurcation 2 represents the emergence of a notation for "abstract numbers," which eventually evolved into our present system of Hindu-Arabic numerals. It also involved the splitting of "abstract numbers" from "concrete numbers," and hence the creation of a purely "quantitative notation" in which the quantity being notated is totally independent of the nature (or quality) of the objects being enumerated.

Bifurcation 3 took place within the confines of verbal writing and represents the separation of logographic and phonetic coding. These two systems of coding, which emerged within fifty years of the beginning of true writing, also exhausted all of the known possible techniques for coding spoken language into written signs. (Exceptions such as the Morse code or the electronic binary coding of information with computers represent a form of coding in which written language and not spoken language is coded.)

Bifurcations 1 and 2, which occurred at the same moment in history, represent the original split between the quantitative and qualitative modes of notation and analysis that exists today. Bifurcations 1 and 2 reversed the 5000-year-old trend that had been established with tokens, of combining quantitative and qualitative description and analysis. The separation permitted a specialization of notations, and, therefore, techniques of analysis that led to many other advances. This split also had an impact at the subliminal level and set the pattern of information processing. It contributed to a cognitive style of analysis in which the quantitative and qualitative are carefully distinguished and are treated separately. The Western characteristic of specialization had its roots in Bifurcations 1 and 2, and thus began some 5000 years ago.

In addition to specialization, the three bifurcations led to other Western characteristics of abstract thought. Western thought patterns, as compared with those of the East, are abstract and deductive rather than concrete and analogical. As shown in Table 3, each of the bifurcations involves a transition from a less abstract to a more abstract notational element:

Bifurcation 1: from token impressions to ideographic writing;
Bifurcation 2: from "concrete numbers" to "abstract numbers"; and
Bifurcation 3: from ideographic coding to phonetic coding.

The "concrete counters," whether in the form of tokens or impressed logograms, coded information by analogy: quantitatively, by one-to-one correspondence, and qualitatively, by pictographic symbols. Abstract numbers and phonetic signs code information using logical algorithms, and promoted the abstract logical thought of Western civilization that was the heir to the token system. With this in mind, the origin of Western thought can be dated to circa 3100 BCE, when, in Sumer, abstract numerals, ideographic writing, and phonetic coding emerged, setting the pattern for all subsequent intellectual developments that were derived from these systems of notation (McLuhan and Logan 1977, 373–83; Logan 1986a).

The Evolution of Phonetic Writing Systems

Phonetic Syllabaries

At first, only names and monosyllabic words were rendered phonetically. Later, phonetic signs for certain commonly used syllables developed so that polysyllabic words could be rendered phonetically, and a set of syllabic signs came into existence. The Sumerian writing system eventually evolved into a mixture of ideograms and phonetic syllabic signs. When the Sumerians, who spoke a non-Semitic language, were conquered by the Semitic-speaking Akkadians, circa 2300 BCE, the conquerors used the Sumerian writing system to transcribe their own spoken language. The ideographic signs retained the same meaning but were pronounced according to Akkadian speech. The phonetic signs, however, retained their Sumerian pronunciation and became more abstract because their sound was meaningless to Akkadian speakers. The Akkadian writing system shifted to a much greater extent to phoneticization, until eventually there was a finite, but complete, set of phonetic syllabic signs capable of rendering all the spoken sounds of the Akkadian language. The logographic signs, with a few exceptions, began to disappear. Eventually, the writing system was reformed to a system of only sixty syllabic signs.

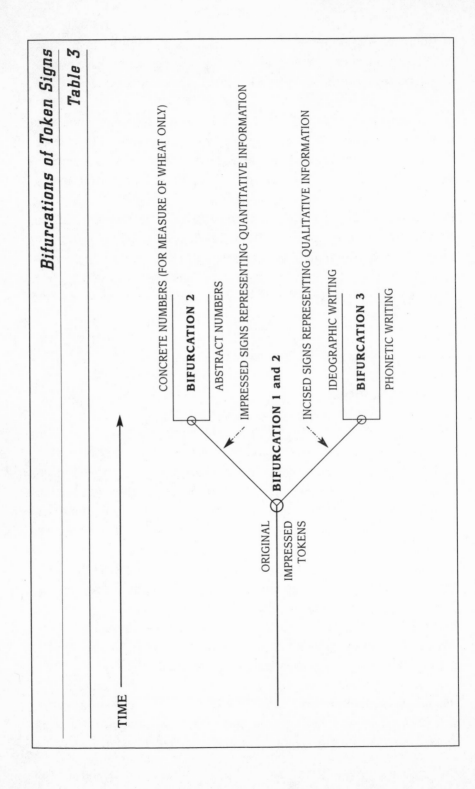

Bifurcations of Token Signs

Table 3

TIME →

ORIGINAL IMPRESSED TOKENS

BIFURCATION 1 and 2

IMPRESSED SIGNS REPRESENTING QUANTITATIVE INFORMATION

CONCRETE NUMBERS (FOR MEASURE OF WHEAT ONLY)

BIFURCATION 2

ABSTRACT NUMBERS

INCISED SIGNS REPRESENTING QUALITATIVE INFORMATION

IDEOGRAPHIC WRITING

BIFURCATION 3

PHONETIC WRITING

The reform in the writing system during the reign of Hammurabi, circa 1750 BCE, was accompanied by reforms of the system of weights and measures and by the establishment of a legal code throughout the Hammurabic empire. The reformed syllabic writing system and the other accompanying reforms represented another breakpoint in information processing. They were brought about by the pressures for the uniformity and regularity required to govern an empire consisting of many different city-states and ethnic groups.

The Phonetic Alphabet

The next stage in the evolution of notational systems was the invention of the phonetic alphabet. The phonetic principles that emerged in the transition from impressed to incised logograms and that were employed to create syllabaries were used to code the individual phonemes of a spoken language. This development took place in two stages. In stage one, the Canaanites (or Proto-Phoenicians) developed a writing system with only twenty-two signs, one for each of the consonants of their spoken language. The absence of a system for coding the vowels did not present major difficulties because in Semitic languages the consonants determine the root word. The function of the interior vowels is to provide grammatical information such as tense (as is the case with the English words *sang, sing, song,* and *sung*).

The actual invention of the alphabet by the Canaanites is thought to have resulted from a borrowing of a subsection of the Egyptian writing system in which a set of twenty-two uni-consonantal signs were used to phonetically render proper names. The use of the Egyptian uni-consonantal signs paralleled the first use of phonetic signs by the Sumerians. The sound value of the letters of the Canaanite alphabet (or the Egyptian signs) is the same sound as the initial consonant of the spoken word that the sign designates pictographically. For example, the second letter of the Semitic alphabet, "beit," which means house, was represented originally by a picture of a house, □, and had the sound value of the letter B.

The Addition of Vowels

The second stage in the development of a fully phonetic alphabet occurred when the Greeks borrowed the Phoenician alphabet and transformed it to suit their language. They added three new consonants to accommodate the special sounds of their language. Their major breakthrough, however, was to create signs for the vowels by transforming the aspirant consonants of the Phoenician alphabet, not required for Greek pronunciation, into the vowels of the Greek language. For example, "h" became an "e." It would have been impossible to render Greek or any other Indo-European language with an alphabet consisting solely of consonants. Imagine trying to distinguish "idea" from "duo" without vowels, or the following group of words from each other: *bat, bait, beat, bet, boat, bout,* and *but.*

With the addition of vowels, the Semitic alphabet was transformed by the Greeks into a totally phonetic alphabet capable of translating every spoken word of the Greek language into a unique combination of letters and every combination of letters into a unique pronunciation. No system of writing has ever surpassed the totally phonetic alphabet for its capacity to represent any spoken language unambiguously with a minimum number of visual signs. Subsequently, the phonetic alphabet was borrowed and transformed by many different cultures and became the writing system for hundreds of languages, particularly those of Europe, western Asia, and northern Africa, but not necessarily limited to those areas.

Writing and the Alphabet Effect: A New Mode of Information Processing

Writing goes beyond the mere transcription of spoken language. Although writing is a medium whose content is spoken language, its uses differ from those of speech. It organizes and stores information quite differently than speech; in effect, it is a different form of language. Written language has evolved in ways quite different from speech. The rules for the construction of speech and prose are quite different. Prose is not recorded speech but a much more formal organization of information. The closest form of writing to speech is poetry, which is meant to be heard. Prose is not meant to be heard and, in fact, the most efficient form of accessing the information contained in prose writing is to read it silently.

The epic poems of Homer provide a unique opportunity to compare the oral and the written forms of language. The poems were composed and presented orally long before they were transcribed in their present form "sometime between 700 and 550 BCE" (Havelock 1978, 3). Before their transcription, there was no particular order in which the various episodes were presented by the bard who performed them. Once the verses were committed to writing, however, they became objectified, an artifact that could be studied and scanned visually, their components compared, and then edited into some temporal order, as is the case with Homer's verses. "The story pieces are sorted out and numbered so as to achieve the effect of a single overall time sequence which moves forward but with interruptions, flashbacks, and digression to an appointed end. Thus arose the arrangement of our present text . . . this arrangement being the work of the eye, not the ear, a work achievable only when the various portions of the soundtrack had been alphabetized" (Havelock 1978, 19).

The very act of transcribing an oral composition requires an ordering. The text becomes a physical artifact that can be "looked at, reflected upon, modified, looked at repeatedly, shown to others, etc." (Havelock 1978). The medium helps determine the mode of organization: "Due to the transitory character of the acoustic medium, spoken language is organized by continuity, connectivity, and integration . . . in addition to intonation. By contrast, because of the visual medium, written language is organized by discreteness, and segmentation" (Ludwig 1983, 39).

The objectification of information, or the separation of the knower from the knowledge that writing permitted, encouraged abstraction, systematization, and the objectivity of scientific thought. Phonetic writing, particularly alphabetic writing, encouraged classification and codification of information. Alphabetizing provided a natural way of ordering verbal information. It is interesting to note that the order of the letters of the alphabet never changed despite the fact that it was passed from one culture to another and adopted by so many different languages. The names and shapes of the letters changed but not the order of their presentation when the alphabet is recited as "abcdef."

The use of the alphabet as a writing code promoted and encouraged the skills of analysis, coding, decoding, and classification. Each spoken word to be transcribed had to be broken down into its phonemic components, each of which was then represented by a unique letter of the alphabet. The impact of information processing due to alphabetic writing was enormous because it introduced a new level of abstraction, analysis, and classification into Western thinking. At the same time that the Hebrews adopted alphabetic writing, they codified their law in the form of the Ten Commandments and introduced, for the first time in the history of humankind, monotheism and the notion of a prime mover or first cause.

The Greeks also made enormous intellectual strides shortly after their adoption of the Phoenician alphabet and its modification to include vowels. They were the first culture to develop deductive logic, abstract science, and rational philosophy. The Hebrews and the Greeks were also the first societies to write fairly objective histories of their own nations.

While none of these intellectual developments can be causally linked, Marshall McLuhan and I postulated (1977) that the use of phonetic writing systems created an environment conducive to the development of codified law, monotheism, abstract science, deductive logic, objective history, and individualism. All of these cultural innovations occurred primarily between 2000 and 500 BCE in the closely linked cultures found between the Tigris-Euphrates river system and the Aegean Sea. The introduction of the phonetic alphabet represents a break boundary because of the tremendous intellectual and cultural fallout that followed from its use (Logan 1986a).

Zero and the Place Number System

One of the themes of this chapter has been the way in which one notational system influences the development of another through a process of evolution. We have also seen that although the notation systems for writing and abstract numerals are independent, they arose together from impressed token logograms. Without abstract numerals, there might not have been writing, and without writing, there might not have been abstract numerals. The two systems of notation share a number of features. Writing employs a basic set of visual signs (for example, a set of logograms, a syllabary, or an alphabet) to transcribe or record the sounds of a spoken language into an array of visual signs. The language of mathematics also notates numbers and mathematical operations with a set of visual signs. For example, the operation of addition is represented with the + sign. At first, writing and mathematical notation were used to store the verbal or mathematical utterances of spoken language. As their use expanded, however, literature and mathematics emerged as languages in themselves, with their own peculiar techniques for processing, retrieving, and organizing information quite distinct from that of speech.

The cross-pollination between the two systems of notation continued, as writing evolved its more sophisticated phonetic elements. The alphabet influenced quantitative analysis because it stimulated an analytic and rational approach to the organization of qualitative information. This led to the development of abstract science and deductive logic by the ancient Greeks. In turn, logic and science stimulated the need for exact and precise quantitative analysis and measurement. This led to axiomatic geometry, the elements of Euclid, the quantitative astronomy of Ptolemy and Aristarchus, the Pythagorean obsession with numbers, the mechanics of Archimedes, and the botanical and biological classification schemes of Aristotle.

The Semitic alphabet stimulated quantitative analysis directly by becoming the basis of a number system in which each letter was assigned a numerical value. The first nine letters represented 1 through 9, and the next nine letters represented 10, 20, . . . through 90. There were also letters for 100 and 1000. Any number between 1 and 100 could be represented by a maximum of two letters. For example, 18 would be written as חי where (ח) is 8 and (י) is 10. The Semitic number system was not a place number system in that 81 was not written (יח) but rather as (עא) where (א) is 1 and (ע) is 80. The system was a forerunner of the place number system in that it contained one of the essential features for such a system; namely, that all numbers between 1 and 9 had their own unique ideographic signs. The element lacking from the alphabetic number system (which the Greeks and Hindus also employed with their alphabets) that prevented it from serving as a place number system was the concept of zero and the zero symbol.

The place number system and the concept of zero were inventions of Hindu mathematicians as early as 200 BCE. The Hindu writing system at the time was alphabetic, as was their number system. Once the Hindu mathematicians developed the notion of zero, or *sunya*, as they called it, they quickly devised a place number system.

Sunya means "leave a place" in Sanskrit and indicates that the zero or sunya concept arose from recording abacus calculations. If the results of a calculation was 503, this could not be written as "5" "3" because it would be read as either 53 or 530, but if instead the result was written as "5" "leave a place" "3", the number being designated would be interpreted properly as 5 hundreds, no tens, and 3 units. "Leave a place," or sunya, soon evolved into the abstract number of zero, 0.

The Arabs used the Hindu system and transmitted it to Europe, where it arrived in the fifteenth century. The Arabs had translated sunya, or "leave a place," into the Arabic *sifr*, or cipher, the name we still use for zero as well as the name for the whole place number system itself. Our present-day term "zero" derives from the shortened version of the Latin term for cipher, *zepharino*. The place number system brought with it many advances in mathematics, including simple algorithms for arithmetic, negative numbers, algebra, and the concept of the infinite and the infinitesimal, and hence, calculus.

One of the mysteries associated with the invention of the place number system is why the Greeks, the inventors of vowels, who made such great advances in geometry and logic, did not discover zero. The explanation lies in the Greeks' overly strict adherence to logic, which led Parmenides to the conclusion that non-being (and hence, nothing) could not "be" because it was a logical contradiction. The Hindus, on the other hand, had no such inhibition about non-zero. In fact, they were positively inclined to the concept of non-being since it constituted their notion of nirvana (Logan 1986*a*; Logan 1979, 16).

The Language of Mathematics

Numeric notation, like writing, grew out of the system for recording the payment of tributes with clay tokens. The language of mathematics grew out of spoken language and the need for a mathematical notation for enumeration. The mathematical statements expressed in the numerals and the signs for mathematical operations can always be translated into spoken language or writing. For example, the equation 1 + 2 = 3 may be spoken or written as, "One plus two is three." The language of mathematics may be regarded as a medium whose content is the mathematical concepts of spoken language, namely, abstract numbers and mathematical operations, such as addition, subtraction, multiplication, and division. Once a mathematical language or notation emerged, however, it took on an existence of its own and evolved in ways quite different from either speech or writing due to the unique methods of processing information that its use stimulated.

A mathematics notation allowed abstract mathematical operations that could never have been carried out in a person's head to emerge. The notation became a tool of investigation and invention. It suggested ways of generalizing results, and thus led to new concepts. The concept of and notation for zero provides a good example. In addition to the place number system, the concept of zero, originally notated as a dot and then later as a small circle, resulted in a number of new mathematical ideas. Not long after introducing zero, the Hindu mathematicians invented negative numbers which they notated by placing a dot above a number (Logan 1986a; Logan 1979). For example, $\dot{3}$ represented minus three or three below zero, which the notation literally suggests, as the 3 sits under the zero sign.

The zero sign, sunya — "leave a place" — was also used to represent the unknown. This allowed the development of algebra because the mathematician was able to "leave a place" for the unknown and deal with it as though it were also a number. Here, we see clearly how the existence of a notation (for zero, in this case) allowed the ideas of negative numbers and algebra to develop. The notation for zero caused mathematicians to think of zero as a number like 1 or 2, and hence to consider mathematical operations with this number such as addition, subtraction, multiplication, and division. The addition or subtraction of zero leads to no change and multiplication by zero yields zero, but the division of a number by zero leads to an interesting result: infinity, another new concept or invention of the Hindu mathematicians. The idea of infinity led them also to the notion of the infinitesimal, a concept that was an essential element in the development of calculus (Logan 1986a; Logan 1979).

The Impact of Quantitative and Qualitative Notation and Analysis
There is no way short of speculation to determine how the idea for numerals and writing arose from the impressed token logograms. Because of the difficulty of establishing causal relations among cognitive

processes, even when historical data are readily available, it is difficult to determine how qualitative and quantitative notational systems influenced each other's development. It is evident, however, that the new level of abstraction that pictographic writing established created an environment conducive to the development of abstract numbers and vice versa. It is clear from Schmandt-Besserat's work that the processes of literacy and numeracy are more closely linked than is commonly acknowledged. Numbers and phonetic writing emerged from a single progenitor, the clay token, in which both quantitative and qualitative information had been merged. The separation of this information into two distinct streams of written words on the one hand, and numerals on the other, opened new avenues of abstract thought and information processing. Ideographic and phonetic writing represented the first means of supplementing and extending verbal language. Numerals representing abstract numbers made possible new techniques of quantitative analysis. Both these developments mark the beginning of objective learning or the separation of the knower from the knowledge (Schmandt-Besserat 1985, 149–54).

The quantitative (from the Latin *quantus* — how great) and the qualitative (from the Latin *qualis* — of what kind) are two key categories of Western thinking that have, from the philosophical thoughts of the ancient Greeks to contemporary social science, been regarded as distinct and independent modes of analysis. The common origin of quantitative and qualitative notation from clay tokens argues against the notion that these two categories form a dichotomy. The fact that the two forms of notation emerged at the same point in history indicates the cognitive power that the interplay between the quantitative and qualitative can release.

Other breakthroughs in information processing can be associated with this interplay. The letters of the alphabet were used to notate abstract numerals until the Hindus, under the influence of alphabetic literacy, invented zero and developed the cipher system (Logan 1986*a*; Logan 1979). It is not an accident that zero and the place number system were the invention of mathematicians who used the alphabet. The place number system and the alphabet share a number of features that contribute to their abstract nature:

1. Each system contains a small number of elements: twenty-six letters (for the English alphabet) and ten numerals.
2. They form a complete set so that the total set of possible spoken words can be represented alphabetically, and any number, no matter how large or small, can be expressed in terms of some combination of the ten numerals.
3. The individual elements of the two systems, the letters and the numerals, are atomic — that is, they are identical and repeatable.
4. The values (sound or numerical) of the aggregate elements (words or numbers) of the system depend not only on their atomistic components (the letters or numerals of which they are composed) but also on their order or syntax. In other words, both the letters and their order determine a word, and the numerals and their order determine a number. For example, ON is not the same as NO, nor is 18 the same as 81.

These similarities in the two systems illustrate two points: the alphabet was probably a stimulus to the development of the place number system; and quantitative and qualitative notational schemes are not all that different and require many of the same fundamental cognitive skills.

The common origin and emergence of quantitative and qualitative notation is only one of the indicators of the overlap of these two categories. An abstract number denotes the quantity of objects in a set, but it can also describe a quality of the set. In addition to their numerical values, the abstract numbers 1, 2, or 3 also denote the qualities of oneness, twoness, or threeness. For example, in the saying "Two's company and three's a crowd," the numbers 2 and 3 are abstract numbers and yet also describe qualities. The relationships described are quite independent of the actual 2 or 3 individuals who constitute "company" or the "crowd."

Abstract numbers themselves possess both quantitative and qualitative features. The difference between the abstract numbers 3 and 4 is quantitative in the sense that 4 is one more than 3, but the difference is not purely quantitative; it is also qualitative in that 3 is a prime number and 4 is not, but rather a perfect square. Another overlap of the two categories of letters and numerals is the way in which their use is combined for the purposes of creating classification schemes; for example, the call numbers for library books and license plates where letters and numbers are used together.

The link or overlap we have established both empirically and theoretically between the qualitative and the quantitative is confirmed etymologically when the terms used for the profession of writing or numerical accounting are examined. In ancient Babylonian or Hebrew, the term for one who writes and one who counts is identical, namely *spr* (Demsky 1972). There is a similar overlap of meaning of these words in English. A "teller" is one who counts or tells, and the expression "to give an account" can mean either to provide a narrative or an enumeration depending on the context in which the word is used. One finds a similar overlap in other languages. In German, the word *zahlen* has a double meaning denoting either counting or telling.

Numeracy, the ability to conduct mathematical calculations, is a cognitive skill that emerged as a result of the development of quantitative notation. Although there are individuals who can do calculations in their head without using notated figures, the origin of these calculational techniques required the existence of numerals. While literacy and numeracy are quite distinct cognitive skills, it is obvious that there is a strong overlap between them. The claim that some individuals are gifted with words but not numbers or vice versa has little basis in our understanding of the origins of these skills. Marked differences in an individual's literate and numerate skills could be due to a disparity in interest rather than intrinsic abilities. Historical research has indicated that literate and numerate skills are related and associated with each other. Split-brain research supports this hypothesis, as both the literate and the numerate activities seem to be concentrated in the left hemisphere of the brain.

The importance of these observations for contemporary education is not obvious. The observations do indicate, however, that current instruction in primary school of reading and writing, on the one hand, and mathematics on the other, requires greater integration. Drawing parallels between the two notational systems could certainly help students to understand the abstract nature of the alphabet and the place number system. It might help those who are strong in math but weak in reading, or vice versa, to use their strengths with one notational system to better understand the other. These suggestions are purely speculative but certainly worthy of further examination and research. The use of the computer in education might provide exactly the correct environment for such an integration as the computer treats all abstract notation in more or less the same manner. In fact, the computer may be regarded as a device for the manipulation of abstract symbols, whether they are alphabetic or numerical.

The Advent of Abstract Science

Abstract science is the systematic organization of knowledge that the languages of writing and mathematics gave rise to. It is a language in its own right because it possesses unique semantic and syntactic elements including its special vocabulary, analytic tools, classification schemes, and employment of the scientific method.

The fact that abstract science with its special way of organizing information arose in an intensely literate and numerate environment is not an accident. Writing provided a number of the basic tools of classification and analysis required for scientific thinking. It also provided an environment conducive to innovation. "A technological society can only exist where there is a fair amount of literacy. For oral habits of mind emphasize memory and training . . . [and this] suggests an inability to deal with new and hitherto inexperienced situations. Given the flexibility and scope of the written word . . . it is not surprising to find that the human mind is freed to deal with events and situations in a more innovative and complex manner" (Hershbell 1978, 90). Just as context and plot aid oral memory, the categories, methodology, theories, and generalizations of science play a similar role. They provide a context or a schema that aids the memory and allows an individual to consider more data with a single sweep of the mind. Just as the cognitive structures due to writing "impose an organization that can be used to guide the retrieval process" (J.R. Anderson 1980, 218), the cognitive structures of science perform a similar role.

Further evidence for the link between mathematics, writing, and science is that the vanguard of Sumerian science was the teachers in the scribal schools. "Within its [the school's] walls flourished the scholar-scientist, the man who studied whatever theological, zoological, mineralogical, geographical, mathematical, grammatical, and linguistic knowledge was current in his day, and who in some cases added to the knowledge" (Kramer 1959, 2).

Both writing and the existence of a system of mathematical notation were essential ingredients in the development of abstract science. But science as an organized body of knowledge and a methodology goes far beyond writing and mathematics as a unique system for processing, storing, retrieving, organizing, and communicating information. Science is not just knowledge about nature but rather knowledge organized in a special way so that results can be generalized and new information can emerge or be easily collected from the existing knowledge base. The language of science is constructed in such a way that it is conducive to classification. For example, the categories that Aristotle created were the beginning of scientific language. "The theory of categories is partly a theory of language and partly a theory about reality . . . Aristotle did not think of the structure of language as mirroring the structure of reality. But he did believe that there are specific items of language and reality the consideration of which forms the crucial link between the two" (Moravcsik 1967).

Because science organizes information in a unique way, I consider it a language quite distinct from speech, writing, and mathematics. If science is regarded as a medium, then writing and mathematical notation are its content, as are its observational data, categories, hypotheses, and theories. Writing and mathematical notation play a special role in that they are the media through which science is reported. Spoken language is also a part of science in that it facilitates communication among scientists.

Developing an understanding of nature and applying that knowledge to practical affairs has been a universal feature of all societies since the beginning of time. There developed within the framework of Western civilization, beginning with the ancient Babylonians, Egyptians, and Greeks, a more systematic and abstract approach to scientific inquiry, which we shall label abstract or theoretical science. Abstract science is characterized by the use of deductive logic, mathematics, a systematic organization of information using appropriate classification schemes, and a methodology for formulating and testing hypotheses — the scientific method.

Understanding the historical roots of abstract science is important for a number of reasons: First, abstract science represents a way in which both the qualitative and quantitative modes of analysis merge through science's use of the languages of speech, writing, and mathematics to study and describe nature; second, abstract science has developed into a language itself because of the unique way that it processes, stores, retrieves, organizes, and communicates information; and third, abstract science has provided one of the essential ingredients for the development of still another language, computing.

The roots of abstract science may be traced to the origins of literacy and numeracy in Mesopotamia. The existence of a writing system led naturally to a more formal system of classification. The first classification schemes were nothing more than a compilation of lists of plants, fish, rivers, city-states, and rulers, prepared by the teachers in Sumerian scribal schools to teach reading and writing. The emergence of codified law and phonetic writing in Mesopotamia also contributed to a spirit of classification that later influenced the development of Greek science. The Mesopotamian notation for numbers and the need for quantitative analysis that commerce inspired led to the development of arithmetic, an essential ingredient for abstract science.

Another essential element in the origin of science was Egyptian geometry. Because of the annual flooding of the Nile River, and the need to measure land area before and after the flood, the Egyptians made a number of empirical discoveries that formed the foundation of geometry. The first Greek scientists, beginning with Thales, formalized Egyptian geometry by proving a number of empirically derived theorems from a set of first principles, or axioms. They extended and generalized the Egyptian results and so developed not only axiomatic geometry but deductive logic, another essential ingredient of abstract science.

Deductive logic led to the notion of causality and a "first mover." The pre-Socratic philosophers attempted to explain all natural phenomena in terms of first principles. Thales, for example, believed all things to be derived from water. For Anaximander, the first principle was the neutral substance Apieron from which opposites emerged. Anaximenes described all of nature in terms of air, while Heraclitus used fire as his first principle. The ancient Greek philosophers might have derived the idea of a unifying principle guiding the universe from the Hebrews' notion of one God, Jahweh, the creator of the universe. The Hebrews developed a notion of causation and the prime cause which they attributed to Jahweh.

> In fact, the name Jahweh incorporates the notion of causing to come into being. "The enigmatic formula in Ex. 3:14, which in the Biblical Hebrew means 'I am what I am,' if transposed into the form in the third person required by the causative Jahweh, can only become 'Jahweh asher jihweh (later jihyeh), 'He Causes to Be What Comes into Existence.'" The Hebrew notion of causation did not develop along the logical scientific lines of the Greeks. Rather, they incorporated it into their unique sense of history, with its promise of the future, the Promised Land, and their role as the Chosen People.
>
> (ALBRIGHT 1957, 87)

The phonetic alphabet with which the Greeks transcribed their spoken language provided them with a model for the abstraction, analysis, and classification essential for formulating abstract science. The written word, as transformed by the printing press, also played a key role in the development of modern science as a result of the superior storage and organization of information that print made possible.

The most convincing argument for the importance of writing and numeracy to the origin of science, however, is the simple empirical evidence that all breakthroughs in abstract science have occurred in literate and numerate cultures. As a result of their careful observations, many preliterate societies developed a good understanding of many aspects of nature, such as the medicinal properties of plants or the behavior and habits of animals. What distinguishes their knowledge of nature from abstract science is the way in which they organized their information. Abstract science leads to new discoveries because it organizes information in a systematic way. The organizational structures of abstract science naturally pose questions to the scientist that stimulate the process of discovery. Whereas preliterate cultures are content to describe nature as they encounter it, and limit their studies of nature to that which is immediately practical to them, abstract scientists will go out of their way to perform experiments to test the universality of their organizational structures. The ancient Greeks saw little practical consequence in their first studies of amber, but they pursued their investigations for their own sake, and what they discovered eventually contributed to our present understanding of electricity.

Science as a mode of language, and hence as a system of information processing, has led to a series of breakthroughs in our understanding of nature on a large number of fronts, including astronomy, physics, chemistry, biology, and medicine. It has also had a major impact in social fields through the social sciences and the fields of information and computer science. Science as a language has been influential in practical endeavors through the various fields of engineering it has spawned and through the Industrial Revolution, for which modern science acted as a model or paradigm.

Thomas Kuhn (1972) explains how the information-processing techniques of science are propagated through the articulation of its paradigms. Kuhn's model of science and how it changes can be used to show the transition from one regime of information processing to another. When speech could no longer handle the information-processing needs of agricultural society, visual notational systems were introduced, and these led to abstract numerals and ideographic writing. This paradigm was repeatedly articulated, which, in the domain of writing, led to phonetic coding, syllabaries, and finally to the phonetic alphabet. In the field of mathematics, the notation of abstract numbers led to signs representing arithmetic operations, zero, the place number system, algebraic notation, vectors, tensors, and calculus. When the information-processing capabilities of mathematics and writing were no longer sufficient, abstract science with its methodology of generalizing, hypothesizing, and testing arose to fill the gap.

Finally, when science outgrew its information-processing capabilities, computers were developed, bringing contemporary society to its present level of information processing. The paradigm of the mainframe computer as an automated number-cruncher has already undergone a number of articulations resulting in the minicomputer, the microcomputer, the electronic notebook, the hand calculator, and a host of software applications among which word processing, spreadsheets, databases, accounting packages, multimedia, and desktop publishing are the most popular.

The Advent of Computing

The computer may be regarded simply as a device for the automated processing, storing, retrieving, organizing, and communicating of information. It basically manipulates abstract symbols, whether they are words, numbers, equations, or databases. Computers change inputs into outputs in a systematic, reliable, and relatively rapid manner. The operations of the computer are closer to its French name, *ordinateur*, or "that which orders," than its English name, which better describes its humble origins as an automatic calculator. To understand its implications, however, it is useful to define computing as a language in the way speech, literature, mathematics, and science are defined as language.

By defining computing as a language I am making a distinction between the computer, which is a human-built hardware artifact, and the processes and skills needed to use this hardware to organize and communicate information. It is the organizing and communicating of information and ideas which is the language of computing and the computer which is the medium. The same parallel holds for speech, writing, and mathematics. The medium of speech consists of the vocal cords, the tongue of the speaker, the air to transmit sound waves, and the ear to receive them. For writing and math the medium is the pen, the ink, the hands that write, and the eyes that read. The language in these three examples are the spoken words, written words, and mathematical symbols that organize and communicate information, ideas, and thoughts.

The language of computing may be considered to include all of the information resident in computers, as well as all of the information and techniques needed to operate computers. The information resident in computers may be regarded as the content of the language of computing, and includes spoken language, written language (literature), mathematics, and science. The techniques for using computers may be seen as the grammar of the language of computing. The reason that computing may be considered as another level of language is that its strategies for processing and communicating information are very different from that of the other modes.

Just as literacy and numeracy were essential for the development of abstract science, so in turn was modern science essential for the development of computers. Modern science provided the necessary technical ingredients such as electronics, circuitry, the magnetic storage of information, mathematics, logic, Boolean algebra, solid state physics, and telemetry. Science also provided the motivation to design computers because progress in a number of fields required computational techniques for calculating complex mathematical problems that could not be solved using standard numerical techniques. The computer, with its ability to perform large numbers of simple calculations at high speed, provided the solution to these problems. Complex calculations could be broken down into a large number of smaller and simpler problems using the techniques of numerical analysis. The solutions to the simpler problems could be calculated by developing algorithmic procedures, which in turn could be automated. This methodology is the basic principle behind the computer-based solutions of the complex mathematical problems that arise in the domain of science, as well as governmental administration (for example, collecting taxes and tabulating census results) and big business (for example, maintaining airline schedules or financial records).

The Advent of the Internet

Originally, the Internet was organized by the American military and was designed to provide a backup communications system if the United States lost large blocks of its normal communications system due to nuclear attack by the Russians. As a result, the Internet was designed without a central switching system or headquarters. It is a distributed network where each of the computers on the Internet contributes to its communication and distribution capability. The Internet makes use of the infrastructure of the telephone companies, and more recently the cable companies, but it is not operated by any telephone company or other form of central administration. It is the world's largest self-policing community of individuals and organizations operating without any centralized regulating authority. The lack of a regulating authority or an agency to vet its content has implications for the role the Internet plays in society, particularly in the education of the young. This is an issue I will address in Chapter 9.

The Internet may be regarded simply as a global network of computer users and servers that are linked using the TC/ICP protocol and the infrastructure of telecommunication lines that span the planet. The Internet permits the sharing of information in both synchronous and asynchronous modes in a variety of formats including text, graphics, video, and audio. As its ramifications are studied, however, it becomes clear that the Internet is a language in the same way that speech, literature, mathematics, science, and computing are languages. Once again, a distinction must be made between the hardware artifacts of the computers, servers, routers, and telecommunications links that compose the medium of the Internet and the process of organizing and communicating information that is the language of the Internet.

The language of the Internet may be considered to include all of the information resident in computers across the planet that can be accessed by the Internet, as well as all of the information and techniques needed to operate the Internet. One may consider local dialects of the Internet to be all the information contained on local intranets that are only accessible to a closed group of users, as well as all of the information and techniques needed to operate the intranet. The information resident in the Net may be regarded as the content of the language of the Net, and includes text, graphic, video and audio. The techniques for using the Net may be seen as the grammar or syntax of the language of the Net and include the TC/ICP protocol, browsers such as Netscape and Explorer, and markup languages such as HTML for hypertext and XML for e-commerce applications. The reason that the Net (or intranets) may be considered another level of language is that its strategies for processing and communicating information are very different from that of the other five modes of language. Although the language of computing is absolutely necessary for the development of the Internet, the way in which the Internet has developed and been used is completely different from the development and use of non-networked computers. The Internet is a hybrid medium of computing and telecommunications.

Language: Cognitive, Technical, and Social Interplay

Upon those that step twice into the same river different waters flow.

(HERACLITUS)

The evolution of the six languages suggests a model or theory for the development of communication and information-processing systems, based on the idea that all innovations have a cognitive, social, and technological component. They are the three basic dimensions of the process of cultural change.

Our notion of technology should not be limited to hardware inventions, but rather, as the Greek word *tekhne*, meaning "skill" or "art," indicates, should incorporate all human tools. These include the physical tools used to organize the material world, the conceptual and cognitive tools used to organize information, and the socioeconomic tools or institutions used to structure or organize society. Examples of physical tools include pottery, the plow, and the steam engine. Examples of conceptual tools include spoken language, the alphabet, the number system, scientific laws, and mathematical algorithms. Socioeconomic tools or institutions include tribal organization, priesthoods, the family, markets, and bureaucracies. But not every technological tool belongs exclusively to one class. Some tools, like the clay tablet, the printing press, and the computer, have both a physical and a conceptual component. This division is tacit in the terminology that distinguishes between the hardware and software components of a computer. The school is another example of a mixed system: The bricks and mortar are physical, the curriculum is conceptual, and the administration is socioeconomic.

Every technological tool (whether physical, conceptual, socioeconomic, or mixed) involves new ways of organizing information and hence requires new cognitive skills. And, vice versa, each cognitive breakthrough manifests itself in terms of one or more new tools or organizing principles: the airplane; Einstein's Theory of Relativity; the Magna Carta.

The six languages which have been under discussion may be considered as basically conceptual technological tools, but each one requires one or more physical artifacts. The development of speech required the evolution of a biological artifact, namely, the *Homo sapiens* speech apparatus, consisting of an enlarged pharynx, a specialized larynx, greater muscular control over the tongue, and the use of the pharynx, the mouth, and the nasal cavity as sound resonators. With all the other forms of language, the physical artifacts are man-made tools. For writing and mathematics, the first artifacts were simply a clay tablet and a wooden stylus. With the passage of time, other physical artifacts were used, including parchment, papyrus, paper, ink, pens, lead, pencils, the compass, the ruler, the protractor, the printing press, and the typewriter.

At first, the physical artifacts of abstract science were the same as those for writing and mathematics. But as science became increasingly more empirical and experimental, the physical tools of science came to include the instruments of experimentation and observation. Examples include the astrolabe, the telescope, the pendulum, the inclined plane, the microscope, the test tube, the Petri dish, the Faraday disk, nuclear reactors, and particle accelerators.

The physical artifacts of computing were at first mechanical calculators, which were eventually replaced by electric and electronic components such as electro-mechanical relays, vacuum tubes, transistors, integrated circuit silicon chips, and magnetic memory devices such as tape drives and disk drives, monitors, and printers. The conceptual components of the language of computing are the operating systems, the software programs, and all of the theoretical ideas that led to computers, including Charles Babbage's original model of a mechanical computer circa 1835.

The physical artifacts of the Internet are the computers in the network, the routers, and the telecommunications infrastructure that make the linkages possible. The conceptual components of the language of the Internet are the protocols, TC/ICP, the browsers, HTML, XML, Java script, CGI script, and new tools that continue to emerge to serve this medium which appears to be poised to penetrate all aspects of human activity.

In tracing the development of the six modes of language, I have noted how each new development, including the very origin of speech, resulted from the interplay of the cognitive or conceptual tools, physical technology, and socioeconomic factors at work in the culture. It is believed that speech developed in order to provide a level of control over and coordination of the tools that erect toolmaking proto–*Homo sapiens* began to manufacture and implement. "Philip Lieberman (Lieberman 1975) has claimed that there are similarities between the cognitive patterns — roughly, the mental maps or plans — which underlie the chipping of stone tools of the sort made during the Paleolithic period, and the syntactic structure of human language" (Hickerson 1980, 25).

Cognitive tools and physical technology are two resources at the disposal of human innovators, and the needs or demands of society are often the motivating force. Necessity is the mother of invention, yet invention does not occur in a vacuum. All of the previous innovations in a culture provide the resources, both cognitive and physical, for the next level of innovation. The previous innovations also contribute to changes within the socioeconomic system that give rise to new social demands. Each new invention, technological innovation, or discovery gives rise to new technical capabilities, new cognitive abilities, and new social conditions. These then interact with the existing economic, political, social, cultural, technical, and cognitive realities of the culture to set the stage for the next round of innovation. Thus, technological change in our model is part of an ongoing iterative process. It began with the inception of *Homo sapiens*, and continues to this day at an ever-quickening pace.

The history of ideas has the appearance of a linear evolution of technical change. Periods of technological stasis are punctuated by moments of violent technological change and breakthroughs. This gives rise to a picture of the "great moments" in the history of technology in which "great individuals" charged with genius make earth-shattering breakthroughs. These innovations are slowly digested by the rest of society until the next genius comes along to once again "shake things up" and start a new process of change.

In fact, between explosions of creative energy, a ferment of activity takes place, quietly at the cognitive level of individuals, and within the dynamics of the socioeconomic interactions of society. Change is at work not only within these two spheres but also at the interface, where a subtle tension between the two arises, from which change flows. As Heraclitus explained, during a period of great technological change in

Greece when the impact of alphabetic literacy was first being felt, "All things happen by strife and necessity." It is the cross-impact back and forth among the technical, cognitive, and socioeconomic spheres that gives rise to technological innovation.

This model was at work in the developments that led from the tallies of hunters and gatherers, to the token system of Neolithic Middle Eastern culture, to the emergence of writing and abstract numerals with the urbanization of Sumerian society at Uruk circa 3100 BCE. The Middle Eastern token system grew out of the economic and social needs to enumerate commodities and keep a record of transactions. The need for a notational scheme arose because quantitative information is more difficult to retain in one's memory than verbal information. We know that the storytellers of preliterate societies were able to commit elaborate stories to memory, but there is no evidence to support the retention of quantitative data.

The use of the token system in ancient Sumer allowed administrators to control the flow of wealth and to build a centrally controlled communal irrigation system. This led to greater wealth, the rise of urban centers, the specialization of skills, the proliferation of the variety of goods, and the need for the capability to handle more complex transactions involving a greater variety of commodities and merchandise. This chain of events gave rise to complex tokens, clay envelopes, impressed logograms, and finally abstract numbers and writing. Each development in the chain of events accelerated the rate of discovery and increased the variety of information the system could store, organize, and process. Phonetic writing allowed still more sophisticated information processing, and hence greater control of society by central authorities. The government that arose made use of the new tool of writing to establish legal codes and the increased mathematical abilities to establish standard weights and measures. The centralized government also established and subsidized the scribal schools needed to train government clerks, and hence supported the scholarly activities and research of the teachers, which laid the foundations for scientific thought.

The developments leading to the invention of the alphabet by the Canaanites, its transfer to Greece by the Phoenicians, and the addition to it of vowels were a result of the commerce that took place among the Egyptians, the Semitic tribes of the Levant, and the Greeks. Each of the breakthroughs in information storage and processing, such as the invention of numerals, writing, tablets, syllabaries, the alphabet, and papyrus, permitted the storage of more and more information. This resulted in the need for even more sophisticated information-processing techniques. The adoption and adaptation by the ancient Greeks of the phonetic alphabet led to the advent of abstract science, rational philosophy, deductive logic, axiomatic geometry, objective history, representational democracy, and individualism. While the intellectual ferment was not directly tied to the commercial and administrative activities of the society, a number of links existed: The philosophers who developed new ideas were intimately involved in the practical affairs of state; a number of the pre-Socratic philosophers such as Heraclitus were legislators in their community; Anaxagoras owned an olive press and was a successful merchant; Aristotle was a tutor to Alexander the Great; Archimedes used his mechanical talents to build war engines; the library and museum at Alexandria was state-subsidized, and flourished partly because of the successful commercial production of papyrus.

The Roman era, which continued the tradition of Greek learning, was even more oriented toward the practical application of knowledge. The Romans did not advance abstract thinking as much as the Greeks, but they were responsible for the transmission of the fruits of Greek thinking and its application in the world of commerce and civic administration. Roman engineering and architecture were disseminated throughout Europe by their conquering armies. The collapse of the Roman empire resulted in the collapse of literacy and book learning. At the practical level, however, advances in the development of technology continued once order was restored. By the time of the late Middle Ages, mechanics and other practical arts were quite sophisticated.

Modern science emerged in the Renaissance as a marriage of the empirical spirit fostered by mechanics and the return to Greek scholarship and an interest in abstract science. The growth of modern science, engineering, and industrialism, beginning with the Industrial Revolution, is a perfect illustration of the model in which the interplay of the cognitive, technical, and socioeconomic environments results in a chain of innovations, inventions, and conceptual breakthroughs. The economic growth of this period and the institutions of capitalism, mercantilism, and nationalism gave rise to conditions that encouraged technological and conceptual breakthroughs. The spirit of uniformity and specialization that infused the industrial system, scientific activities, and social institutions also characterized information processing and communication. The printing press, dictionaries, and encyclopedias also reinforced the pattern of uniformity and specialization.

The success of the information-processing patterns of the industrial and scientific era, however, created new problems and challenges. The complexity of the numerical calculations required for further progress could no longer be handled by the available technology. As commercial and government administrative procedures became more data-intensive, the need to automate simple information-processing procedures became more critical. It was this environment that motivated the invention of computers. Once the technology of computers was available, information scientists started working on new information-processing techniques rather than just automating the pre-computer techniques of the past. These new techniques addressed the problems of complexity and overspecialization. The general systems approach — or cybernetics — grew out of the need to control systems that had grown too complex to be handled by the information-processing techniques of the scientific era.

The scientific method succeeds by breaking down a system into its basic components and then narrowing the focus to one of those components so that a critical mass of research can produce a breakthrough or new paradigm. That paradigm is then articulated and applied in as many domains as possible (Kuhn 1972). Science analyzes systems into their basic components and deals with them one at a time in a linear fashion. This reductionist methodology creates a bias which sometimes makes it difficult for scientifically trained personnel to deal with a complex system such as the eco-sphere, where the interactions of all of the components are so critical to understanding the overall operation of the whole.

The techniques of cybernetics, based in part on the technical capabilities that computers make possible, allow an integrated systemic approach to emerge: the non-linear impacts of each of the subsystems on each other are taken into account. The Internet reinforces and amplifies cybernetic principles and techniques by integrating and aligning the contents of computers linked on an enterprise-wide level or even a global scale. The techniques of computers and cybernetics would never have occurred unless the complexity fostered by science had emerged. This parallels the rise of science as a way to deal with the complexity of the information collected with written and numerical notation. Whenever an information-processing system leads to information overload, it can be handled only by a new level of information processing.

Accompanying each breakthrough in information processing, there has been a major shift in education, as well as in the patterns of social organization and work. The global village that the Internet makes possible is becoming a cybernetically configured village and a global knowledge network, at least for that segment of the world with access to computers and telephony. A large percentage of the world's information and knowledge assets — or information on where to find them — are suddenly instantaneously available, a mere click of a mouse away. The Net also allows the feedforward and feedback of information on a global scale. The following chapter examines the emergence of these new patterns and shows how the evolution of education, work, and social class parallels the evolution of language and information processing.

5

Why There Are Schools and a Middle Class:

The History of Education and Social Class

Each step in the evolution of language affects the way a society sees the world and its economy. With the introduction of each new medium of communication or information processing, the education system, social-class structures, and the organization of work have been transformed. I expect this pattern to repeat itself in our society as a result of the introduction into the workplace and the school system of microcomputer systems in the late seventies and the Internet in the mid-nineties. To provide a perspective on the dimension and nature of the changes that microcomputers and the Internet will bring, this chapter will examine the role that communications and technology have played historically in the origin and evolution of education systems, social-class structures, and work patterns.

These three aspects of social organization — education, social class, and work — are not independent of each other. The purpose of an education system is to train individuals to assume a productive role in society. The educational infrastructure of a society also influences the economic development of the society as a whole, hence the link between work and education. The tie-in with social-class structure occurs because social class is a function of the way that work is organized in society and strongly correlates with the educational level of individuals and their families.

The institution of the school or formal education is such an intrinsic part of our culture, we take its existence for granted. We do not realize that schools, as opposed to education, are a relatively recent development. Schools were first organized only 5000 years ago in Sumer, shortly after the invention of writing. The objective of these first schools was to train young people to become scribes. Education, as opposed to schooling, did not start with the advent of writing, but can be traced to preliterate society. Preliterate education, however, is as different from formal schooling as oral communication is from written communication. Education and schooling are not the same, although the overlap during the industrial age was almost total. In the knowledge era, education will once again be quite distinct from schooling. It will, however, be closely tied to work (as it was in oral societies) to the ongoing use of information technology, and to the process of lifelong learning.

In order to understand how social-class structures might affect the organization of education in the Internet age, it is essential to examine how class structures have affected education in the past and, in turn, how education affected class structures. Class structure is not determined by how much a group earns, but by how they earn a living. I will pay close attention to the middle class because of its close association with literacy and formal education. I want to explode the myth that the middle class is boring and show that the use of the term as a pejorative is unfounded. The middle class has historically been the source of innovation and revolution in society; in fact, it emerged as a result of literacy.

The appearance of social class is also relatively recent. Before the Neolithic revolution some 10,000 years ago, hunting-and-gathering societies were organized clans and tribes. A clan was an extended family; a tribe, a small group of extended families working together to ensure their mutual survival. There was no such thing as class structure in these early societies; it is difficult to imagine members of the same family belonging to different social classes. Social-class structures only began to develop with the introduction of agriculture, in which a division between the landed or upper class and the peasant or working class took place. The middle, or managerial, class followed shortly thereafter, with the introduction of writing.

Communication and Education

Educational practices changed radically with the introduction of written communication and continued to change each time a new mode of writing (for example, syllabic or alphabetic writing) was introduced. The invention of the printing press made mass education and self-education possible. In our own time, the electric media — such as motion pictures, radio, phonographs, audiotapes, compact disks (CDs), television, and video recorders — that deliver audiovisual (A/V) information have had their own unique impacts, both direct and indirect, on education.

Preliminary data indicate that computers and the Internet will have a much more profound effect than any of the A/V media. Technology affects education not only by changing the ways information can be delivered, but also by changing what needs to be taught. As new information-processing techniques are developed, students must learn new skills. Thus the curriculum of schools, as well as industry's response to new training challenges, must change to reflect new technologies. Understanding the relationship between communications and education will be essential for studying the impact that microcomputers and the Internet are having and will continue to have on contemporary education in both the school system and in industry.

One of the chief features separating humankind from the rest of the animal world is our ability to communicate with each other through verbal language. Because of this ability, the knowledge and experiences that one human being acquires can be transmitted directly to others or stored as information. This process, independent of the medium of communication, is the basis of human education. Media of communication are not passive conduits of information. Rather, they are vortices of power, lively facilitators of social interactions and ideas. Communication media transform all aspects of human behavior, including an individual's cognitive processes and affective attitudes, as well as society's socioeconomic institutions of commerce, culture, and education. An understanding of media and their effects is essential for an understanding of all human interactions and institutions, particularly those like education, which at its core depends on communication.

Communication permitted humans to share information and knowledge for their mutual survival and to plan activities based on this knowledge. Education arose naturally, as a means whereby parents or elders shared with younger members of their community information and knowledge that would increase their chances for survival. This form of education gave rise to distinct cultural communities among groups of individuals who were in day-to-day communication with each other and hence shared a common heritage and a similar set of experiences.

Communication between communities allowed for the growth and evolution of cultures and the amalgamation of smaller subcultures into larger cultural groups. Cultural evolution and development, education, and communication are inexorably intermeshed. One cannot understand one without studying the others. All communication is a form of education and all education is a form of communication. And both are manifestations of a society's culture.

Not only is communication the medium through which educational activities take place, but communication and the development of communication skills also serve as the focus or content of many educational activities. In other words, communication is both the medium and the content of educational activities. One of the primary purposes of education is to transmit the skills of effective communication. But language includes both a communications and an informatics component. Hence, another focus of education is the development of the information-processing skills associated with the use of language. As the complexity of human language grew and new modes of expression and organization evolved, the education system grew and evolved in turn. This chapter traces that growth from the humble beginnings of education within the oral tradition to contemporary schools, in which all six modes of verbal language — speech, writing, mathematics, science, computing, and the Internet — are studied and used.

The Oral Tradition

Education in preliterate societies basically takes two different forms. One is the vocational training of young people through their participation in the work activities of their parents, and the other is the practice of storytelling, whereby the values and wisdom of a culture are transmitted by elders to the whole society. Both forms of education are mediated by the spoken word, either through oral instructions in the former case or through legends in the latter.

The basic form of preliterate education was mimesis, or imitation, just as an infant learns to speak by imitating his or her parents. The oral instruction of vocational training was supplemented by demonstrations of how to do things correctly. The young people who were learning practical new skills did so by imitating the work patterns of their elders, whom they served as assistants or apprentices. Secret societies or fraternities formed to ensure the propagation of vital skills such as those of weavers, potters, toolmakers, warriors, hunters, fishermen, builders, and canoe makers. Imitation also played an important role in the education provided by storytellers and priests. Tricks of the trade and the legends themselves were passed on through oral instruction and memorization. The exact words of each story, down to the accents, were memorized and transmitted through the ages in much the same way that nursery rhymes are preserved to this day. Plot, rhyme, and meter were an integral part of the stories of the oral tradition; they served as mnemonic devices aiding memorization. The tales were always in the form of poetry and never prose. Prose was not a viable medium for transmission because its memorization would have been very difficult. The right-brain skills of pattern recognition and music were therefore an essential part of the education system and cultural development of oral society.

In addition to the wisdom and cultural values the storytellers imparted, they also provided listeners with certain tidbits of practical information. Woven into the plots of his tales, the storyteller would explain how to hunt for prey, or how to build a canoe, or how to conduct oneself in battle. Eric Havelock (1963) describes the bard as "at once a storyteller and also a tribal encyclopedia" who taught his lessons through the narratives of his tales.

Class Structures in Preliterate Societies

Hunting-and-gathering societies are classless. Although they have leaders, decision making is largely achieved by tribal councils, where each member of the tribe has input into the tribe's deliberations. It was only with the advent of agriculture and the emergence of landowners that a two-class society arose: landowners functioned as the masters of peasants or serfs, who became the underclass.

There are economic reasons for the advent of the two-class system. In a hunting-and-gathering society, it is difficult to preserve foodstuffs. Hence, the acquisition of wealth is impossible. Basically, food is preserved by sharing. When a family kills a large animal and there is more meat than they can consume, they share it with their neighbors or other members of their clan. Through this system of sharing, which creates bonding between families, the overall survival of the cooperating tribe's people is enhanced. There is no survival advantage to being selfish in a hunting-and-gathering society.

With the advent of agriculture and the domestication of animals, the economics and politics of sharing changed. It was now possible to store food both through stockpiling grain and by maintaining a herd of domesticated animals. There was a reason to acquire wealth and hoard or store food. From the point of view of the individual family, there was a reason for being selfish; selfishness provided a hedge against starvation during bad times. There was also a reason to acquire land and seize ownership of it. The more land one could acquire, the more food one could produce and store, hence the greater one's wealth.

Preliterate agricultural society came to be divided into two classes — a ruling class of military, civil, and religious leaders and a governed class of serfs or peasants who performed the work that was required to grow the food and maintain the society. The structures of the first preliterate Neolithic cultures were quite different from those of a hunting-and-gathering society. Literacy and the associated formation of a middle class, or third class, did not emerge in agricultural societies until trading, commerce, and an urban form of civilization came into being 5000 years later in Sumer.

From what we know of Sumerian culture, it was an absolutist society; power was shared between the aristocrats and the priests while the serfs were at the mercy of their rulers. One can only surmise that the aristocratic class obtained power through superior military talent and used priests to legitimize their power. The priests, through their knowledge of nature, were able to share power with the military elite.

The Sumerian culture prospered under this two-class system. It developed a surplus of food which was used to support not only the aristocratic and priestly classes but also an artisan class and then a trading class. As a result of the activities of the commercial classes, a new system of information processing, and hence a tool for social organization, emerged in Sumer — writing. Those who developed a facility with literacy found that they were in a position to exercise influence in their society because of the uses to which writing could be put, not only in trade and commerce but also in the organization of the agricultural activities of the society. In Mesopotamia, irrigation canals were critical to the success of the crops. The construction and maintenance of the canals, therefore, required special coordination as well as a complicated system of accounting and land records to equitably distribute the life-giving water supply as well as the fruits of the labor of the farmers that used the water. As we have seen, it was the token system, employed to keep accounts of tributes paid in the form of agricultural commodities and units of labor, that evolved into the first form of writing.

Literacy and the Advent of Formal Education

There were no significant changes in the form of education based on apprenticeship and storytelling until the advent of writing in Sumer circa 3100 BCE. Shortly thereafter, the first formal education institutions, which we call schools, appeared. "The Sumerian school was the direct outgrowth of the invention and development of the cuneiform system of writing, Sumer's most significant contribution to civilization" (Kramer 1959). Schools had to be organized to teach reading, writing, and arithmetic because unlike previous skill sets, these three activities cannot be learned from observation and imitation. Speech is the only form of language that is learned naturally by imitation. Formal instruction must be organized for writing and mathematics. The secret codes of the letters and the numerals, and their proper use, have to be taught.

Infants begin to babble and imitate their parents' sounds automatically at a certain stage in their development, but there is no instinct to scribble. Speech is acoustic and surrounds the young child. There is no escaping the influence of speech. Writing can only be taught if a child's visual senses are directed toward writing, and what is seen is then explained. Being able to write requires a particular point of view that must be shared and explicated.

The desire and ability to use speech as a form of communication is an instinctual trait built into all human beings independent of their culture. Information processing, the other aspect of language, is a learned trait acquired slowly and transmitted culturally from one generation to another through formal education. Without cultural institutions, information-processing skills are soon lost, as was the case in Europe during the Dark Ages shortly following the fall of Rome (with the exception of the monasteries). The capacity for speech, however, has never been lost, although different spoken languages have become extinct.

Judging from the exercise tablets prepared by students learning to write, along with descriptions of their training by their teachers found at the most ancient levels of archaeological sites, it is evident that schools were organized almost immediately after the appearance of writing. They were organized originally for vocational reasons, to train scribes for administrative duties. Reading and writing in education were at first used exclusively to teach reading and writing. As schools evolved, they were used to teach other subjects. Despite the practical motivation for the founding of these scribal schools, which appeared in every major urban center of Mesopotamia, scientific, scholarly, and literary activities began to develop in these institutions. At these schools, lists of natural phenomena such as trees, insects, rivers, and minerals; lists of geopolitical features such as cities and rulers; mathematical tables; lexicons and dictionaries relating different languages; theological tracts; and poetry were created and used as teaching tools (Kramer 1959). The "databases" inscribed on the clay tablets represented the first textbooks or software tools and were initially used to train students to learn the medium of writing; later, they became objects of study themselves.

The teachers in the scribal schools "were keen observers of nature and the immediate world about them. The long lists of plants, animals, metals, and stones which the professors compiled for pedagogic purposes imply a careful study of at least the more obvious characteristics of natural substances and living organisms" (Kramer 1959, 136). The information on the tablets was then used to teach other topics, including mathematics, science, foreign languages, poetry, theology, accounting, and administration.

We know a great deal about the earliest school system of the Sumerians from archaeological finds made in Iraq. In actual classrooms that were unearthed, clay tablets used to teach the children were found. The organization of Sumerian schools set the pattern for schools right down to the present day. The shape of the rooms (rectangular), their size (accommodating thirty to forty students), and their structure (with rows of benches facing the teacher) bear an uncanny resemblance to our modern classrooms, which fundamentally teach the same subjects that were taught in Mesopotamia.

Mesopotamian schools, like today's, were graded and hierarchical. There were primary schools in which basic literacy and numeracy skills were taught. There were also institutions of higher learning devoted to professional training. These institutes taught technical subjects such as astronomy, medicine, architecture, and engineering, or specialized in the professions related to government service including theology (or temple service), law, commerce, teaching, and military science.

All societies that developed a formal education system possessed a writing system and all literate societies had schools. The ancient Incas are a possible exception because they had formal schools but did not have a true writing system. They did have a highly developed system of notation called *quipus*: a complex system of knotted colored strings that recorded both quantitative and qualitative information. The Babylonian, Egyptian, Hebrew, Vedic, Chinese, Mayan, and Aztec cultures are examples of the earliest cultures to have developed both a writing system and schools for training their young people.

The Egyptians were the second culture, after the Sumerians, to develop a writing system, and they were also the second culture to develop a formal school system. The Egyptians invented their writing system and organized formal schools sometime in the third millennium BCE. "The curriculum of elementary education was centered on writing" and writing was the "staple in all formal secondary education" (Power 1970).

In India, the Buddhists developed the institution of the monastery devoted to learning, which served as a model for monasteries in the Christian world, as well as for Western universities. In China, the education system served the government's need to train civil servants, who worked in the bureaucracy, a form of government that is itself a by-product of writing. The examination system was a key element in Chinese education.

An analysis of Hebrew education is particularly interesting because the Hebrew culture is one of the oldest continuous literate traditions in the Western world, and its ancient history, including its oral tradition, is documented in the Bible and the Talmud (the commentaries on Scripture). The Hebrews were also one of the first cultures to make use of the phonetic alphabet. Their education system influenced Western culture in many ways because the three principal religions of the West — Judaism, Christianity, and Islam — share a common origin and tradition beginning with the patriarch Abraham.

When they conquered and displaced the more sophisticated Canaanites, the Hebrews were a preliterate society with no formal education system. From the Canaanites, they adopted both the phonetic alphabet and an education system. They transformed the latter to accommodate their monotheistic religion. Originally, Hebrew education was family-based. Parents were required to teach their children "the testimonies, and the statutes, and the judgments, which the Lord, our God, have commanded" (Deut. 6:20). This passage was interpreted as a command to teach each child how to read so that he could read the words of the Lord and know His Commandments. The achievement of universal literacy by the Hebrews, a historic first, was motivated by religion but facilitated by the fact that the phonetic alphabet is the simplest possible writing system to learn.

In addition to home study, formal schools were organized to train scribes for government service and the study and administration of the Torah (law). The school system continued to grow and evolve, particularly as the Hebrews encountered other cultures, usually as victims of military conquest. By the sixth century BCE, Hebrew education had evolved into "a universal and compulsory system of education," which operated until the destruction of the state by the Romans in AD 70 (W. Smith 1955).

Judging from its content, the Book of Proverbs, dating from the time of King Solomon, was likely used as curricular material for instructing the young. "Incline your ear, and hear the words of the wise, and apply your mind to my knowledge; for it will be pleasant if you keep them with you, if all of them are ready on your lips" (Prov. 22:17–19). This passage indicates that in Solomon's time, a mixture of oral and written learning was employed. The practice dates to ancient Egypt, where wise sayings were also an integral part of the formal school system. Oral sayings were used to impart wisdom about life to students, as well as for exercises that they could copy to practice their writing skills. Hindu education applied a similar mix of oral and written learning, its students copying the Vedic texts and committing them to memory.

The Greek phonetic alphabet was the first to represent both consonants and vowels, making the learning of reading even simpler, and hence, as in Israel, a large reading public developed in ancient Greece and the Hellenistic states that succeeded it. The earliest writers in Greek culture were the pre-Socratic philosophers. The first of these, Thales and his followers, formed a school of thought, but it is not known if an actual learning institution was founded. Pythagoras formed a society to pursue philosophical studies and create an institution of higher learning. Xenophanes also founded a school. These early institutions became models for the schools founded by Plato (the Academy) and Aristotle (the Lyceum).

The Academy and the Lyceum set the pattern of scholarship for the next two millennia. Both emphasized the systematization of knowledge and the development of a methodology of learning based on rationality and deductive logic. This pattern was influenced by the use of the phonetic alphabet and the spirit of analysis, classification, coding, and abstraction that it encouraged (McLuhan 1962; Logan 1986a). "Plato encouraged his students to use logic, science, and rationality to find fresh solutions to problems instead of relying on the traditional remedies of the past. Together with a training in mathematics and logic, Plato encouraged his students to formulate the problems of human existence in scientific terms. The impact of the alphabet was to introduce both a new style of education and a new approach to problem solving" (Logan 1986a, 128).

Plato saw poets such as Homer as the enemies of his brave new world of rationality because they represented a powerful force for preserving the traditions of the past. They encouraged youth to imitate the patterns of the heroes of mythology, and hence, in Plato's view, prevented new patterns of behavior and thinking from emerging.

With Alexander the Great there was a change in the Greeks' attitude toward education, likely due to the government's imperialism and militarism. The Greeks were the first society to impose their language and culture upon those they conquered. Education became an actual instrument of conquest. Alexandria, the world's first planned city, became the site of the Mouseion (from which the word "museum" comes), a gathering place for scholars housing a great collection of geological and biological specimens and the world's largest library. The local manufacture of papyrus enhanced the literary activities of the Mouseion. Manuscripts were collected from places throughout the world and translated into Greek.

Defining the Middle Class

So far, the middle class has been referred to as the educated or literate class, that segment of society able to derive economic benefit due to the information-processing skills of its members, the class who often served as intermediaries between landlords and serfs. The term "middle class" as used here does not conform to the common usage of the term by most scholars. In fact, a precise definition has eluded social scientists. Most definitions involve strictly social, political, or economic criteria and, as a result, do not capture the essence of the middle class; they do not shed light on the reasons for the historical emergence of this group, which lie in its members' ability to exploit writing and other information technologies to advance their own and others' economic activities.

"Middle class" is defined here as that sector of society which has readily been able to make use of literacy as a tool to advance its social and economic position in society. I will show through a reexamination of the history of Western education and information-processing techniques that, in fact, the middle class is the literate class and that the growth of the middle class and literacy are correlated. In addition, I will also examine the relationship of the middle class to the ruling class and the working class to determine how its position and role in society have changed over time. Finally, I will explain how traditional middle-class values — such as concern for education and stress on hard work and thrift — grew out of an intimate association with literacy.

As noted earlier, the middle class emerged along with literacy 5000 years ago in Mesopotamia. Before the advent of the printing press, the middle class, or those who could read, were a very small minority of the population. The printing press created the conditions for mass literacy, and thus for the emergence of the middle class as a mass phenomenon and the major socioeconomic and political force of modern times.

It is increasingly clear that computers will have an impact on contemporary society as great as literacy had on previous generations. This impact could lead to the emergence of a new socioeconomic class, the computer class, which could replace the middle class as the vanguard class of the Internet age. In order to test this hypothesis, it is useful to examine the relationship between the middle class and literacy.

One of the problems that has plagued students of social class has been their inability to arrive at a precise technical definition of the "middle class," despite its unambiguous meaning for the layperson. "Nobody has ever found a definition of the English middle class which is short, satisfactory, and watertight. To attempt to evolve one is to be lured into an interminable study of the social sciences" (Lewis and Maude 1949, 13). Commenting on the definition of the middle class as the "not-so-rich and not-so-poor individuals between the proletariat-labor group and the wealthy capitalist and social aristocracy" (Harkness 1931, 45), F.C. Palm (1936, 3) remarked that "such a 'sandwich' definition indicates how difficult it is to characterize the middle classes. Anomalous, mutable, with tenuous fringes, the middle classes never have been and are not now a fixed entity, to be encompassed by a simple, rigid definition . . . Thus, the meaning of the middle classes is likely to remain with good cause in a state, so to speak, of suspended definition . . . a precise definition is virtually impossible."

The term "middle class" was coined in the early years of the

Industrial Revolution. "The first known mention of the term middle class is given by the *Oxford English Dictionary* as appearing in 1812" (King and Raynor 1981, 45). *Webster's* definition of the term, which reflects common usage and hence no particular theoretical bias, reads as follows: "middle class — the social class between the aristocracy or very wealthy and the lower working class." This definition reflects the etymology of the term as the class residing between the rich and the poor. The definition, however, provides no insight into the nature of the middle class, and therefore has been dismissed as inadequate by those social scientists who have tried to capture the essence of the middle class in a simple definition.

The middle class is often referred to as the "bourgeoisie," which leaves us with the problem of defining what that is. Another equally vague definition is the identification of the middle class as white-collar workers and the working class as blue-collar workers (King and Raynor 1981, 1–20; Roberts et al. 1977, 170). Still another definition associates the working class with productive labor (as in manufacturing) and the middle class with nonproductive labor (supervisory work) (Poulantzas 1978, 270). Closely related to these definitions is one which regards the middle class as non-manual workers and the working or lower class as manual workers. "The middle class is often negatively defined as the residual category which remains when the manual working class has been subtracted from the population" (Gerrard et al. 1978, 1). Within the context of this definition, there are "three major approaches (Bain and Price 1972, 325–39) to defining manual and non-manual work: the brain-brawn, the functional and the eclectic" (King and Raynor 1981, 1–20). According to the brain-brawn criteria, the middle class earn their living through their brains and the working class through their brawn. This somewhat pejorative definition is highly inaccurate because of the impossibility of separating, in many instances, the mental and physical components of a task. The functional approach defines middle-class activities in terms of four major job functions: administration; design, analysis and planning; supervisory/managerial; and commercial (King and Raynor 1981, 1–20). In the eclectic approach, the physical separation of the office and the factory is used to distinguish the middle class from the working class.

These three approaches to the manual/non-manual criteria for distinguishing the middle class are not inconsistent with the definition of the middle class as the literate class, since literacy involves the use of brains rather than brawn, since each of the four functions defined as middle-class activities require literacy, and since literacy is used more often in the office than the factory. The question is to what extent the criteria are useful. As they are tied to an industrial form of the economy, their validity for analyses of the Internet age or the historical preindustrial era are not as valuable as the criterion of literacy.

Most social science definitions of the middle class occur within the context of a theory of social class operating within an economic system. The seminal thinkers in developing economic theories of social class were Karl Marx and Max Weber. Marx does not divide society into three classes — upper, middle, and lower. He confines his analysis to the capitalists, who own the means of production, and the proletariat who are exploited by them. The middle class appears as the bourgeoisie, defined as the capitalists and their agents. According to the Marxist view, the possession of a skill such as literacy does not determine class structure; the only thing that matters is the actual physical and political control of the means of production, that is, the factories. The weakness in the Marxist analysis of class is that its heavy emphasis on materialism and hardware does not allow for the consideration of information patterns or the social interactions of the knowledge era. The control of the means of production in the age of information translates into possession of the skills of literacy or computer literacy or a combination of the two.

Weber (1946) identifies class in terms of economic interests and, in particular, the labor market. "According to our terminology, the factor that creates 'class' is unambiguously economic interest, and indeed, only those interests involved in the existence of the 'market.'" However, he recognizes the role that skills such as literacy play in the way a class operates in the "market."

Of all the economic-driven definitions of the middle class, none is crasser than that of R.H. Gretton (1919, 8): "The Middle Class is that portion of the community to which money is the primary condition and the primary instrument of life." Other simplistic definitions classify the middle class in terms of certain brackets of earning power (Hulton Press Survey 1948, 19–20). "Except as a rough measure of what an income-earner has to spend . . . these brackets are inadequate to delimit the social classes in the nation" (Lewis and Maude 1949, 20). There are many instances when individuals who are clearly middle class earn less than well-paid laborers. Investigations with well-paid car assembly workers "revealed that even affluent skilled workers, whose relatively high income depended substantially on overtime and shift work, neither emulated middle class styles of life, nor mixed socially with non-manual neighbors" (King and Raynor 1981, 20–22). The middle class cannot, then, be defined strictly in terms of income or spending or other economic measures.

Another definition that incorporates the notion of education and technical skills reinforces the hypothesis being developed here that the middle class is in fact the literate class. Giddens (1981, 107) argues that advanced capitalistic societies are characterized by a threefold categorization of classes: upper, middle, and lower — based on three distinct sorts of market capacity, respectively: the ownership of property in the means of production, the possession of educational or technical qualifications, and the possession of manual labor power (King and Raynor 1981, 39–40).

Each of the definitions examined here has had some degree of validity, and thus some usefulness. Some come closer than others to my characterization of the middle class as the literate class, but all of them can be understood in terms of the notion that historically the middle class has been able to share power with the ruling class because of the information-processing skills they acquired through their literacy and educational background. In fact, a historical review will show that the origins of the middle class can be traced to the origins of literacy itself.

Literacy and the other skills to which literacy provided access enabled the middle class to dominate economic life, and hence to either obtain the best jobs or to start their own businesses or enterprises. Thus the middle class has always enjoyed a better than average standard of living. Many of the members of the moneyed or upper class were actually the children (or more distant descendants) of middle-class entrepreneurs who became extremely wealthy. History is full of examples of aristocrats with middle-class roots, including the Medici, the Rothschilds, and the Rockefellers. In short, literacy has always translated into economic power, an observation that was noted by Claude Levi-Strauss:

> And when we consider the first use to which writing was put, it would seem quite clear that it was first and foremost connected with power: it was used for inventories, catalogues, censuses and instructions; in all instances, whether the aim was to keep a check on material possessions or human beings, it was the evidence of the power exercised by some men over other men and over worldly possessions.
>
> (CARBONNIER 1969)

Acquiring literacy and the other forms of specialized knowledge based upon it has been the economic strategy of the middle class throughout history. "The middle class American shrewdly committed himself to the proposition that educated knowledge was the beginning of power, and power was the source of spiritual and material riches" (Bledstein 1976, 30).

Of all the definitions of the middle class, the one that comes closest to the ideas being developed here is that of Janet Coleman, who describes the emergence of the middle class in her book *Medieval Readers and Writers* (1981, 63): "There is an argument to be made in favour of defining a middle class in terms of literacy — which determines social rank — as well as with some contact with at least a market town, rather than defining them simply as those urban dwellers directly devoted to and in control of urban commerce and industry."

The Link between Literacy and the Middle Class

If the hypothesis is correct that literacy was the tool that enabled the middle class to arise from the working class or peasantry, to prosper economically, and to evolve a unique lifestyle with an emphasis on education, thrift, and morality, we should be able to find empirical evidence for a correlation between the existence of a middle class and literacy, as well as a link between literacy and the evolution of middle-class values. In fact, historical evidence reveals that the middle class emerged with literacy at the dawn of Western civilization and that there exists a one-to-one correspondence between increases in middle-class population and the level of literacy. The advent of the printing press, for example, marked a dramatic increase in both literacy and the influence of the middle class, two events which are not unconnected, as this chapter will show.

The middle class can be said to have first emerged with literate civilization as the group of self-made individuals with a rank lying between the nobility and the proletariat. They are also those members of society concerned with commerce, crafts, administration, and the priesthood. They served as a bridge between the upper class and the working classes, allowing the aristocracy to control the proletariat without direct contact. They organized and operated the irrigation systems that made large-scale agriculture possible. They collected tributes from the farmers so that they could support the irrigation workers as well as look after their own needs. They entered into trade so that the surpluses generated by the agricultural system could be stored for lean times or traded for other commodities of value. The ranks of the middle class were also filled by the civil servants who operated the administrative offices of the governments of the city-states and the empires into which the city-states evolved.

The existence of a commercial middle class in the rich Mesopotamian valley is amply shown by the law code of the Babylonian king Hammurabi (2067–2025 BCE), which has numerous provisions dealing with merchants and the carrying on of commerce. Typical of such legislation is the following: "If the merchant has given to the agent corn, wool, or any sort of goods to traffic with, the agent shall write down the price and hand it over to the merchant; the agent shall take a sealed memorandum of the prices he shall give to the merchant" (Palm 1936, 8). What is interesting about this is the reference to writing. An integral aspect of the activities of the middle class, or bourgeoisie, from their very earliest history is an association with written records.

Direct evidence for the relationship of the middle class and literacy is provided by ancient records dating to 2000 BCE, in which some 500 individuals listed themselves as scribes, and provided the occupations of their fathers, as well, presumably for further identification. Their occupations as governors, city officials, ambassadors, temple administrators, military officers, sea captains, high tax officials, priests, managers, supervisors, foremen, archivists, and accountants (Kramer 1959, 3) clearly show the relationship between, or overlap of, the middle class and the literate class.

Ancient Egypt, the second civilization to develop a writing system, also had an active bourgeoisie. Egyptian artisans, merchants, and priests, most of whom were literate, accumulated wealth and pursued a middle-class lifestyle. Two other literate cultures arose in the territory between Egypt and Mesopotamia, each with an active middle class. One of these states was Phoenicia, "a nation of traders, [whose] citizens demonstrated astonishing initiative and persistent progress in domestic manufacturing, ship construction, foreign colonization, and general commerce" (Palm 1936, 10). The other was Israel, which was also a trading nation, particularly under King Solomon. Its most important contribution to Western civilization was not commercial but rather lay in its ethical writings and development of monotheism. The teachings of the Hebrew Scriptures have served as the paradigm for and the moral basis of the Western middle-class lifestyle and value system. For the larger part of its history, the Hebrew nation has adhered to a middle-class pattern of existence despite long periods in which it has endured poverty and other hardships. The Protestant work ethic of the North European middle class was strongly influenced by the teachings of the Old Testament.

Ancient Greece, the fount of Western civilization, represents a culture in which literacy and the middle-class way of life thrived. "A merchant class grew up, active, keen, and enlightened. It formed guilds . . . which stoutly defended their interests. It demanded written laws, and brought democracy into the constitutions . . . It even placed its stamp on the new intellectual life of the new Greece" (Glotz 1926). "Athens, during the Periclean democracy which followed, became a bourgeois state. With birth no longer a qualification for political preferment, the business classes played a foremost role in the selection of government officials. Many of the prominent leaders were of bourgeois origin . . . In cultural as well as in the economical life the Greek bourgeoisie played their part. Believers in education and individualism, they glorified Greek culture in all its forms, producing as a result many prominent members of the Greek intelligentsia from the middle classes" (Palm 1936, 12–13).

The role of the middle class and the lifestyles of its members within the context of Periclean Athens introduced a pattern that repeated itself a number of times in the ancient world, including the Hellenistic empires, Rome, Byzantium, and the Islamic empires. Wherever urban centers developed within a national or imperial state, there thrived a literate middle-class society engaged in commerce, administration, and the arts, pursuing more or less the same goals and values as today's middle class.

Medieval Education and Class Structure

During the Roman period, the motivation for education and literacy was largely to pursue practical goals such as civil administration, commerce, or law. Literature and scholarship for their own sake were not as valued as they had been with the Greeks. Consequently, when the Roman empire collapsed, together with trade within Europe, so too did the Roman administrative and legal infrastructure, along with the desire and motivation to be literate. Formal education in Europe fell into almost total decline, except for the activities of the Church, and monasteries such as those of the Benedictines, where sacred writings and some classical texts were preserved. Thus, when a nobleman or land administrator needed scribal services, he turned to the local clergy for assistance.

Although the monks were able to maintain the Western tradition of literacy, society in general reverted to the two-class system of a ruling class and a working class of serfs. The ruling class consisted of the civil authorities, the lords of the manor and other nobles (or members of the first estate), and the clergy (or members of the second estate). The peasantry, or serfs, formed the third estate of this society. The middle class in early medieval Europe disappeared. The Roman forms of organization couched in literacy and formal bureaucracies were replaced by the feudal system, which was based on personal loyalties in the form of fealty and oral oaths. These forms of social organization paralleled the tribal and oral traditions of the Germanic tribes that took political control of Europe. The fundamental unit of economic activity was the manor, which, for the most part, was self-sufficient and did not engage in commerce or trade. There was no need for a middle class, and the only members of society who were literate were monks, isolated from everyday life.

Very little new literature was authored from immediately after the Fall of Rome until the latter part of the Middle Ages. Beginning in the eleventh century, literacy entered the mainstream once again because of an increase in trading. Learning for the lay public was offered at cathedral schools, which were usually located along the principal trading routes. Starting in the fourteenth century, these schools evolved into the medieval universities, which provided training in the arts, theology, law, and medicine.

Learning in the medieval university was determined and con-strained by the need to create the texts that the students needed to study. The chief teaching methods were lectures, repetitions, and dis-putations. The ordinary lecture was usually nothing more than a dictation. The students copied the lecturer's dictation, which they then studied later. In a sense, the university lecture functioned as a means to reproduce texts deemed worthy of study. In some instances, the teachers were allowed to comment on or interpret their texts, but in many cases they were permitted only to perform straight dictation of the text. Repetitions, in which the text was read out again, were given so that students could check their copied texts for inaccuracies, although in some cases the text was also discussed. It was only at dis-putations that ideas were actually discussed and debated. The oral transmission of written texts was the only practical way of creating textbooks that the students of the day could afford. (During classical times, slave labor was used to create books for those privileged enough for higher education, so the reproduction of books was not as great a concern as it was in medieval Europe.)

Although the focus of study at medieval universities was on clas-sical texts, a great deal of the learning occurred in the oral mode. The content of the education system was written texts but the medium was the spoken word. The actual curriculum of the medieval university consisted of the seven liberal arts, grouped in the trivium of grammar (literature), rhetoric, and logic, and the quadrivium of arithmetic, geometry, astronomy, and music.

Originally, education was open only to young men who were to enter the clergy. Later it was opened to include clerks who would become high officials under kings, including lawyers, judges, diplomats, scholars, or teachers. The numbers that were formally educated were extremely limited. The education experienced by the vast majority of young men was apprenticeship training in a trade, usually the same one as that of their fathers.

The two-class social structure of the early Middle Ages began to change not only as a result of trade, but also because of technical breakthroughs that had a dramatic impact on agriculture and hence on the economy. The new technologies included the heavy plow, innovative techniques of irrigation and drainage, the harnessing of water and wind power, the stirrup, the cart, and harnesses for workhorses.

F.C. Palm (1936, 21, 25) attributes the reemergence of the middle class in the late Middle Ages to five factors:

1. A dramatic increase in agricultural production, which enabled a number of serfs to pay for their land from the proceeds of selling their surplus and thereby enter the ranks of the rural middle class.
2. The traders and craftsmen who served the needs of these new farmers organized their activities in market and fair towns and became burghers.
3. The Crusades, which promoted the interests of the middle class by opening new trade routes with the East.
4. The depletion of the ranks of the nobility due to wars, the Crusades, plagues, epidemics, and famines, which led to the distribution of their land to independent peasants.
5. The monarchs of the powerful kingdoms that arose during this period, who promoted the interests of and formed an alliance with the middle class to reduce the powers of the feudal lords and to promote the commercial and industrial interests of their kingdoms. The middle class were the vanguard of the new economic order of light industry and international trade.

These five factors led to the emergence in the thirteenth and fourteenth centuries of "a well established, prosperous, independent middle class" (Palm 1936, 21, 25). "To complete the middle classes, there arose from the ranks of the simple artisans, organized mainly in

the town craft guilds, the class of capitalist merchant-manufacturers"
(Lewis and Maude 1949, 29–33).

These factors changed the nature not only of the middle class but
of all three classes. There emerged in the upper classes two bases of
wealth, power, and influence, namely, the land, as before, and now,
with the coming of the Industrial Revolution, ownership of the means
of production. The source of the new aristocracy of capital and industrialization was twofold: the old money of the landed aristocracy, which
was invested in new industrial schemes; and merchant manufacturers,
whose middle-class business operations grew into large-scale industrial enterprises creating wealth and influence almost overnight. A
third source of the new industrial aristocracy came courtesy of the
middle class: The inventors, scientists, and engineers and their technological innovations created great wealth through the amplification
of mass production. The ranks of the middle class increased with the
addition of factory managers who served as liaisons between factory
workers and owners. With industrialization, the working class, or proletariat, consisted of two distinct groups, the factory workers and the
peasants.

Writing played an important role in the activities of the new middle
class. It was used by merchants to keep records and organize commercial activities, and by municipal authorities to organize civic
affairs. Writing was also used to express, through literature, the sec-
ular and moral concerns of the middle class. It is during this period
that there was a major shift in the reading public from the first and
second estates (the nobility and the clergy) to the merchant class.
William Langland, author of *Piers Plowman*, was not supported by "a
court patron but with the patronage of a devout 'middle class'"
(Coleman 1981, 22).

There is a correlation between "the growth in lay literacy and social
mobility as it was expressed in fourteenth century literature, a literature that did not merely passively reflect its time and context but was
written as an encouragement to critique and change" (Coleman 1981,
17). Literacy not only became the tool that helped the members of the
middle class create a new economic niche for themselves, it also
became the medium through which they rallied their causes and won
political concessions from the first and second estates. "The literature

of complaint, then, while seeming to express the grievances of the third estate, appears largely to be a literature by and for that most fluctuating estate, the wide-ranging 'middle class,' newly literate and newly vocal" (Coleman 1981, 64).

Renaissance Education, the Printing Press, and the Commercial Revolution

During the Renaissance, with its emphasis on humanism and individualism, many schools were founded to educate the young and make them literate. One of the factors that contributed to the growth of education and literacy was the greater availability and lower cost of learning materials in the form of books. This was made possible by two technological inventions — paper and the printing press. The arrival of paper in Europe from China had a major impact in reducing the costs of books. It also provided the motivation for the invention of the printing press because a supply of inexpensive paper to print on made the printing press a cost-effective technology.

The greater availability of books made it easier to operate a school; consequently more schools were established. Moreover, as more books found their way into society, there was greater opportunity for individuals to access reading material and hence additional motivation to become literate or to ensure that one's children became literate.

The printing press changed education by promoting the use of vernacular tongues rather than Greek and Latin, which had been the exclusive language of scholarship and learning. Indeed, until the printing press created a vernacular literature, children were taught to read Latin and not their own spoken language. Printers were eager to publish books in vernacular tongues because they needed to expand their markets in order to realize a return on the significant investment they made in purchasing their presses, type fonts, and other equipment. The absolute number of books and the percentage of books printed in vernacular tongues, as opposed to Latin and Greek, increased markedly. A vernacular literature also increased the number of individuals who could learn how to read and write, since they did not have to learn Latin first.

While it was in the late Middle Ages that the middle class first established itself as a permanent fixture of Western society, it was only during the Renaissance and the Industrial Revolution that followed that this class grew into a popular or mass movement, with the help of the printing press.

One of the features of the commercial revolution during the Italian Renaissance was the increased use in business affairs of literacy and the organizational techniques that grew out of alphabetic literacy, such as the double entry system of bookkeeping, the bill of exchange, and other banking instruments. A measure of the influence of this period is the current use of business terms derived from the Italian words *disconto*, *netto*, *deposito*, *foglio*, and *bilancio* (Palm 1936, 32–33).

There was a practical side to education, as well. The bourgeoisie considered education "a means of fostering the moneymaking powers of their sons, for as bankers, traders, manufacturers, and landowners, they could readily see the practical value of education; consequently, children were hastily schooled in the rudiments of business and put directly to work at the occupations of their fathers" (Palm 1936, 38).

The commercial revolution fomented by the emerging middle class also had an enormous impact on cultural patterns, including the revival of learning and the championing of the individual. Once firmly rooted economically, the middle class sought outlets for the expression of their wealth. Not only did they become patrons of the arts, like the nobility, they also participated directly in the production of works of art and literature. "Italian middle class people tried to attain social distinction by personal achievement in art and literature as well as good manners. Most of the Renaissance artists and scholars were of the business classes and proletariat" (Palm 1936, 39).

With the reemergence of the middle class in the thirteenth and fourteenth centuries, there were now two literate sectors in society, the merchants and the clergy. The members of the original first estate remained largely illiterate, but with the advent of new forms of social, economic, and political organization, a change occurred in the makeup of the ruling class. This development resulted partly from the upward mobility of the literate middle class who entered the ruling classes by virtue of their commercial successes, like the Medici family. Those upper-class families whose ancestors arose from the middle class often retained their tradition of and interest in literacy.

This phenomenon may give rise to some confusion in terms of defining the middle class as the literate class because of the existence in it of literate members of the upper class. There is nothing exclusive about these categories, however. If we define a member of the ruling class as one who is able to exercise control in society by virtue of wealth or power and a member of the middle class as one who is able to exercise control in society by virtue of facility with literacy and all the skills associated with it, the conflict disappears. These two categories are not mutually exclusive. It is possible for a member of the upper class to have all the characteristics of a member of the middle class, and to adhere to that value system. Since this definition does not refer to earning power or level of wealth, an upper-class person can also be middle class, just as a struggling artist or writer can be extremely poor and middle class at the same time. Some of the confusion in class structure analyses of society occurs because classes have been defined in terms of their financial situation rather than their function within society.

Since I do not define a class in terms of earning power, I must also provide a definition of the working class. Members of the working class are members of neither the middle nor upper class, and hence are unable, due to lack of wealth, power, or education, to exercise any level of control in society, even over their own existence, except by virtue of selling their labor. Thus a moderately well-to-do member of the working class cannot really be considered a member of the middle class. My division of classes, then, is in terms of the power base of the individual in society. For the upper class, this is through wealth or power, and, for the middle class, through literacy and education. Unfortunately for the members of the working class, their power base is limited and confined to collective action through the trade union movement or through political revolution.

Beginning with the humanist movement at the beginning of the Italian Renaissance and continuing through the commercial revolution, the Enlightenment, the rise of democracy, the American Revolution, and the French Revolution, the members of the middle class fought a steady battle with the aristocracy to win a greater share of the political power and wealth of their society. They did this by mobilizing politically through the use of the written word and the printing press, proving Voltaire's adage that the "pen is mightier than the sword." In the commercial world, they were able to improve their well-being materially by implementing the latest techniques of business organization based on literacy. In the industrial world, they prospered because their superior level of education allowed them to take advantage of the latest developments in science and technology.

As a force within society, the middle class began to play an increasingly important role in the affairs of European society in the late Middle Ages. As the technological base of economic activities increased, so too did the influence and importance of the middle class. Also, the ranks of the upper class changed dramatically, for two reasons: the continuing social migration of the prosperous middle class into the ranks of the upper class; and a migration in the opposite direction as members of the old aristocracy joined in the literacy revolution and adopted some of the values of the middle class through acculturation.

Interactions between the middle class and the upper class have remained much the same to this day. The working class, however, has been able, beginning in the nineteenth century, to change its position in society through the trade union movement. This, along with the increasing affluence of Western industrial civilization, has permitted the members of the working class to earn a decent standard of living in the past century, at least in Western Europe and North America.

The Rise of Nationalism

The availability of books, made possible by paper, the printing press, portability, and a vernacular literature, made possible another educational phenomenon, the self-learned man, an individual who educated himself by reading a great variety of books. One such was Tartaglia, who translated Euclid's *Elements* into Italian. Those who learned informally through their readings — practical men involved in the commerce of their society — began to rival the universities in terms of learning. A society of men interested in developments and learning began to develop in the late fifteenth century around the print shops of the major cities of Europe. As the publishers of new ideas, the printers were in a better position to be current with the latest developments in science, technology, commerce, and scholarship than the professors at the universities who were bogged down in the traditions of the

Middle Ages. Printing presses were first set up in the commercial, not the university, towns of Europe with the exception of Wittenberg. Knowing how to read soon became an essential feature of commercial life. By the sixteenth century, the acquisition of writing had become "absolutely necessary in virtually every aspect of middle-class life" (Bowen 1972, 402).

One consequence of the creation of a vernacular literature made possible by the printing press was the rise of nationalism. Nationalism, in turn, gave rise to the desire for national education systems. The printing press made this goal a reality by allowing uniform national curricula based on mass-produced textbooks to come into existence. "Henry VIII could require all schools to use a single textbook in grammar and no other" (L. Cole 1950). The use of the same textbook at the national level also led to a uniformity of language and the notion of "correct" grammatical uses of vernacular tongues in both their written and spoken forms.

Protestantism, Education, and the Middle Class

The printing press had an indirect impact on education through the Protestant Reformation of the early sixteenth century, a movement that was closely tied to this technology. The new style of commerce, which may be characterized as capitalism, came into conflict with the teachings of the Roman Catholic Church, which was opposed to usury and excessive profits. During the Middle Ages, the church had sup- ported the guild system of a just price, which regulated and protected the trade of the middle classes. Now this class was finding itself restricted by the Church. The result was that this conflict fuelled, to some extent, the Protestant Reformation (Weber 1948). Naturally, other factors contributed to this revolt, but these were also tied up with the social and political aspirations of the members of the literate middle class. Their desire for political freedom and the expression of their indi- vidualism contributed to the social ferment that led to the Reformation.

Literacy also played an important role in the evolution of the Protestant Reformation. Protestants were encouraged to read the Bible on their own. It was in the Protestant territories that printers began to publish vernacular forms of the Bible. In fact, even before the Reformation began, the first use made of the Gutenberg press was to print the Gutenberg Bible. The printers also played a key role in spreading the reforming ideas of Luther and Calvin through the many broadsheets and pamphlets they published. Luther's famous 95 Theses, which he had nailed to the church door in Wittenberg "were said to be known throughout Germany in a fortnight and through Europe in a month" (Aston 1968), thanks to the services of the printing press.

Empirical evidence for the thesis that the emergence of the middle class, mass literacy, the printing press, capitalism, and Protestantism are interrelated and mutually reinforcing is found in the historical correlation of these activities in centers such as Holland and Geneva. "With the victory of the Calvinists in Holland the Golden Age of Dutch printing had dawned" (Eisenstein 1979, 409). Holland was not only a great center for Calvinism and printing, it was also a haven for trade and commerce where the middle class prospered and democracy grew strong.

Universal Education, the Industrial Revolution, and the Rise of the Middle Class

The evolution of education systems into a universal and compulsory system was due to the Industrial Revolution and the factory system of mass production. The factory not only permitted the mass production of goods, it also created wide-ranging social changes. For example, it triggered a mass migration of families from farms to towns and cities by people seeking work in the factories. At first, at the beginning of the eighteenth century, all the members of a family — children and adults — worked in the factory. The working conditions were deplorable until, after a public outcry, child labor laws were passed preventing children from working in factories. This created another social problem of equal magnitude: There was no longer a role or useful activity for working-class children in urban society, unlike on a farm, where they could perform chores, help their parents, and be properly supervised. Elementary schools offering universal education to the young were organized in England in 1870 to address this social need.

Alvin Toffler has suggested that mass education evolved as it did because many of the children of the publicly supported school system were destined for factory work once they became adults. Schools were organized to train them for that activity. Toffler (1980, 45) writes: "Built on the factory model, mass education taught basic reading, writing, and arithmetic, a bit of history and other subjects. This was the overt curriculum. But beneath it lay an invisible or covert curriculum that was far more basic. It consisted — and still does in most industrial nations — of three courses; one in punctuality, one in obedience, and one in rote repetitive work." These lessons were intended to make sure that workers showed up on time, took orders from their bosses without questioning, and stayed on the job "performing brutally repetitious operations" all day long.

Within the new industrial order, work was no longer individualized as it had been during the Middle Ages, when production was based on craftsmanship. The education system that developed during the Industrial Revolution reflected the mass-production assembly-line style of production. The factory served as a model for education, which was delivered to a mass audience in assembly-line fashion. This was not true for universities and private schools, which had been founded earlier and were attended by the privileged members of society, but it was certainly true for the public school system, which was organized to serve working-class populations. The modern industrial state took over education to ensure that its economy would benefit from a uniform, productive working force.

The uniformity that the printing press and industrialization encouraged also influenced how children's education was planned and their performance evaluated. Unless a child was able to learn at exactly the same rate as his peers and advance through the curriculum lockstep, he fell behind and was demoted or demoralized, often both. (As we will see, one of the refreshing aspects of the microcomputer and Internet revolutions is that they re-individualize education and retrieve many of the patterns of education of the oral tradition and the medieval era. They also re-individualize work and provide scope for personal input and achievement.)

A major step in the growth of the middle class and its influence was the Industrial Revolution. The invention of the steam engine in 1769 by James Watt allowed the full mechanization of manufacturing and greatly improved transportation through the steamboat and the steam locomotive. The application of science and technology to agriculture, medicine, and sanitation also contributed dramatically to an increase in population and an improved standard of living. More people were capable of supporting the middle-class lifestyle. "It was the Industrial Revolution which gave the middle class a new self-consciousness and for the first time the sharing of a common identity which seems to have lasted to the mid-nineteenth century" (King and Raynor 1981, 48).

The Effects of Electric Media on Education

Beginning with the discovery of electricity in the mid-nineteenth century, a host of inventions have influenced education, including the light bulb, the telegraph, the telephone, the phonograph player, moving pictures, the microphone and loudspeaker, radio, television, slide projectors, overhead projectors, audiotape and videotape recorders, hand-held calculators, fiber optics, compact disks, and optical disks. The effect of these devices on education is quite different from that of computers. There is also a difference in the delivery of computer-based instruction and training depending on whether the medium is a CD-ROM or the Internet.

To properly assess the effects of the A/V media, a distinction must be made between these media and the interactive media of written language and computers. Users of A/V media are passive consumers of the information, sounds, and images that these media deliver. The users of both written language and computers, whether they are receiving or transmitting information, must interact with that information through a process of coding (if they are writing or inputting data) or decoding (if they are reading or accessing data). These media therefore stimulate cognitive development in a way that A/V media cannot.

The educational value of A/V media is restricted to their being a source of information, whereas written language and the computer are a source of information as well as a medium for organizing and processing information. Interacting with the written word on a computer contributes to the cognitive development of the user in a way that watching television or some other A/V medium cannot. Even reading, because of the decoding it requires, involves an organization of the material presented. The reader is constantly deciphering, understanding, interpreting, editing, rereading, or studying the material that is presented.

Nevertheless, the use of A/V media has a number of important educational implications. Their use is not without some cognitive impact. The cognitive skills that are stimulated by A/V media are similar to those activated by the reception of oral communication. Perhaps the most significant impact of A/V media on education is not the way in which they stimulate cognitive development but the manner in which they compete with, interact with, or complement the more interactive media or languages of writing, mathematics, science, and computing.

The general impact A/V media have had on society has already been discussed in Chapter 2 and their effects have been contrasted with those of the written and printed word. The observations made there also apply to education and can be summarized as follows: The written and printed word encourage patterns of information processing and organization that are linear, sequential, analytic, specialized, and logical. Electric and electronic media, on the other hand, encourage information-processing patterns and organization that are holistic or global, integrated, synthetic, generalist, and metaphorical.

Changes in the education system began to occur with the invention of the telegraph in 1844. The dimensions of the world suddenly shrank to those of McLuhan's global village. The study of other cultures and nations took on new meanings as news from distant events arrived by telegraph almost as they happened and were reported the next morning in the newspaper. An invention as ostensibly simple as the light bulb also had its effects. It made possible individual study late into the night, as well as night school for those who had to work during the day. The telephone, like the telegraph, increased interpersonal communication over long distances and brought the world closer together. Radio, movies, slide projectors, phonograph records, audiotapes, and television provided listening and viewing audiences with a rich panoply of sights and sounds gathered from across the world, reinforcing the notion of a global village. These media also provided important new channels for the delivery of information that did not depend on text. One implication for education was that many phenomena that were difficult to describe verbally could be experienced directly thanks to A/V media.

Television provides a fascinating example of the complex relationship a medium can have with education. At first, television was touted as a medium that would have a major positive impact on education. Now that we have experienced more than forty years of commercial television and every viewer has access to one or more educational channels, we are in a better position to evaluate television's influence on education. It has certainly had a major impact, but not always what was expected and not always positive.

Some of the promise of television has been realized. It is an excellent medium for the dissemination of information and for giving the viewer a sense of "being there." Educational television has provided, on balance, informative and entertaining fare, but there are limits to how effective it has been. For example, *Sesame Street* has helped correct some of the negative racial stereotypes that abound in North American society, but it has not achieved all of its literacy and numeracy goals for ghetto children.

My quarrel with television, if I have one, is not with the failure of the dream of a positive contribution; rather, it is with the extremely negative influence television has had on education, particularly the education of youngsters. By providing information and entertainment in such an easy and effortless manner, television has discouraged children from reading more. Television occupies such a large chunk of the leisure time of children, it robs them of the opportunity to spend more time reading, takes away their desire to read, and destroys their attention span. Too much effort is required to obtain, through reading, the same amount of information and excitement that can be obtained effortlessly from watching television. Television provides children with carefully digested and packaged nuggets of information in extremely short time intervals of approximately ninety seconds in length. Because television destroys children's attention span, the painstaking process of learning the three Rs has been made more difficult. Luckily, however, the computer and, more recently, the Internet have reversed some of children's disinterest in learning. They stand poised to undo some of the harm that television has incurred.

The Microcomputer Is the Medium and Learning Is the
Message: Learning, Work, and the Sixth Language

The discussion of the evolution of communications, information-processing technology, and language, and the ways these have influenced the development of social institutions, has provided the background for an understanding of the enormous changes computing and the Internet will have on contemporary social institutions. The next step is to examine in detail the evolution of computing from the first mainframe computers through to personal computers (or microcomputers) and the Internet. I will then review the impact of microcomputers on education and work. This chapter will also address the following questions formulated in Chapter 1:

- What are the relationships among language, communications, information, technology, and knowledge?
- How will computers and the Internet change our notions of what we mean by communication, information processing, language, learning, education, and work?

The Computer and the Internet, Extensions of the Human Psyche

The character of data processing has been completely transformed because of the speed with which simple operations can be performed using computers. Each of the individual steps of information processing done by a computer can also be done by the human mind. What makes the computer so powerful is the speed (orders of magnitude faster than human thought) with which simple calculations and/or operations can be processed. This makes it possible for the computer to perform certain tasks that would otherwise be impossible because of time limitations. The computer perfectly illustrates that a quantitative change can become a qualitative change if it is large enough.

I have described the computer's capabilities as if "the computer performs tasks." This description tends to anthropomorphize the computer and may give the reader the impression that the computer possesses a form of intelligence. The use of the word "intelligence" is an unfortunate shortcoming of our limited vocabulary, which was not designed to deal with machines capable of automated processes. To be more accurate, one should talk of the computer performing tasks *as directed by human intelligence*. As it is tedious to add the qualifier, "as directed by human intelligence," each time I mention the "performance" of the computer, the reader is asked to keep this qualification in mind.

This distinction is not a linguistic quibble but an important pedagogical and philosophical point. The computer is not a tool that thinks for us; it is one that extends human intelligence. Moreover, it is not the first tool to do so. Computational devices such as the abacus and the adding machine, a primitive forerunner of the computer, are examples of technologies that enhance human intelligence. Information-storage devices such as books, encyclopedias, and libraries are examples of other tools that extend human intelligence. The computer incorporates the computing capability of calculators and the information-storage capability of print or written records.

By increasing the amount of information that the human mind can comfortably access and use, the computer creates new patterns of information usage and facilitates the process of discovery. Because of the computer's power in creating new knowledge and solving problems, a notion of artificial intelligence has emerged that can be misleading. The danger is, we may begin to allow computers to do our thinking for us and make decisions based on preprogrammed instructions. Many of us, no doubt, have encountered situations in which employees of a large organization are forced into what seem to be stupid decisions because their computers provide them with no other alternative. To avoid such situations, it is essential to regard the computer as an extension of human intelligence directed by human volition. The designers of computer programs should make more allowances for human interaction whenever the computer forces its users to violate common sense.

Not only is the processing of information enhanced by computers, but so too is the storage and retrieval of information. The computer is able to store extremely large quantities of data. This is also true of a book or a library filled with books. The essential difference, however, is that because of its processing capabilities the computer can access information rapidly. The computerized search for and retrieval of information represents a quantum leap over traditional paper methods. The ability to search for and link information allows new forms of information processing and organization to emerge such as the electronic spreadsheet, the relational database, and word processing. The storage of information by computers has the added convenience that information can be retained in the computer's memory and then accessed, as needed, in either hard copy (a paper form) or on a video screen. The quantitative changes in information storage and retrieval generated by computers create qualitative changes, and hence warrant the consideration of computing as a language different from the other forms of notated language — writing, mathematics, and science.

The Internet has had a profound effect on the storage and retrieval of information. The Internet pools all of the information that is stored on the servers linked to the Internet to create the largest collection of data and information ever assembled in human history. Local intranets allow the pooling of information within an organization so that information whose distribution must be restricted can be shared internally.

Because information is so easily accessed by users around the world, writers and the creators of information are motivated to make their material universally available by publishing their information on the Internet. Papers, reports, and even whole books (through Project Gutenberg) are appearing online. The Internet is a library without walls. Traditional libraries are augmenting their physical collections by providing their users with access to the Internet.

Computers have also transformed the organization of information. While the forms of activities and functions encompassed in desktop publishing, word processing, database management, and spreadsheet analysis existed in purely paper forms, the existence of computers has transformed these four activities. Before computers, the activities encompassed by desktop publishing and word processing were confined to typewriters, traditional typesetting, and scissors and paste or other mechanical layout procedures; database management relied on mechanical indexing and cataloging techniques; and spreadsheet analysis consisted solely of standard bookkeeping techniques, enhanced by the use of adding machines and other electromechanical computational devices. Word processing, desktop publishing, database management, and spreadsheet analysis have become the principal forms of information organization for the work world in the computer age. They dominate office procedures and are carried out primarily with the help of microcomputer systems.

Word processing, desktop publishing, databases, spreadsheets, and general systems theory are specific techniques that the computerized organization of information encourages. Each of these techniques in turn encourages a style of organizing information that differs from manual systems and is perhaps best characterized as integrated. The integration occurs at many levels. First, there is the integration of qualitative and quantitative data, or put simply, the integration of numbers and words. The computer, as its name implies, began its existence as a high-level calculator, a number cruncher. Because the computer is actually a manipulator of abstract symbols, whether they are numerals or letters of the alphabet, it also became a manipulator of text very early in its existence. In fact, one of the first applications of computers during World War II was the deciphering of intercepted coded messages. Spreadsheets and databases are excellent examples of the way in which computers integrate numerical and textual data.

Not only are the processing, storage, retrieval, and organization of information transformed by computers, so too is the communication of that information. The computer has three basic forms of outputs by which it can disseminate information. These include the traditional print format through the use of a variety of printers (dot matrix, daisy wheel, laser, or bubble jet), a video format through the use of cathode ray tubes (CRTs) or light emitting diodes (LEDs), and electronic digital signals (used primarily for computer-to-computer communication). Modems connected by telephone lines allow computers worldwide to swap information instantaneously.

The Natural Language for Data Integration and Hybrid Systems

The use of computers to process graphical and musical elements of human expression is also growing. Specialized software packages allow computer users to create still graphic images either for print or for projection slides (35mm or overhead); to scan existing images and edit them to create new images; to create engineering and architectural drawings (CAD); to create animation; to edit video and motion picture film; and to synthesize, compose, and notate music.

Desktop-publishing software, which allows the user to create professional-looking page layouts, has transformed the nature of publishing and printing. Integrating text and graphics, desktop-publishing software has served as a model for multimedia software, which integrates graphical, video, and audio material with interactive mechanisms. Multimedia programs, which present information in a variety of formats, offer the possibility of meaningful and active interactions with the information rather than making the user a passive consumer. Another application is a multimedia educational package in which a software package combines textual material, including interactive questions, with computer-simulated material or video and audio material presented by a videodisk or some other video medium (Hannifin and Hughes 1985, 236). The possibilities are endless.

A new class of media that has rapidly populated the World Wide Web and given it its special characteristics is hypertext (and hypermedia). Hypertext works in the following way: Textual information is connected within a relational database so that there are multiple ways of accessing and linking information. A hypertext system is a database in which information has been organized into smaller units of information called nodes; these nodes can be easily joined to other information nodes within the database. Hypermedia is an extension of the hypertext concept in which the nodes of information are in multi-media formats rather than text. Hypertext and hypermedia, because of their distinctive organizational principles and methodology of user interaction, constitute a new and distinctive medium with the potential to radically change both our education system and the workplace: They permit easy access to information and allow users to choose their own path to and the level of depth of that information, depending on their interest.

The computer allows the integration of a number of information-processing tools because the output from one software package can be fed into another as input and then passed on to still another package for further processing. Computers provide this level of integration because of their ability to network different users and systems through the use of local area networks (LANs), wide area networks (WANs), and the Internet. Not only does networking enhance communication, it also facilitates information processing and organization by making data that reside in many different computers available to a single user. In principle, all computers could be connected through modems and the worldwide telephone network, creating a "global computer," an analog to McLuhan's notion of the global village. The Internet is rapidly making this possibility a reality.

A Paradigm Shift from Information to Knowledge

Like computing, the Internet has radically transformed the organization of information, due to its extensive use of hypertext and search engines. These tools, which are also available in intranets and client-server systems, allow multiple levels of detail to co-exist within the same document. Users can decide what level of detail they wish to drill down to. They can also navigate to related themes in other documents if the author provides cross-links to related Internet-accessible documents. The information topology of the Internet is extremely complex because of all these cross-linkages to other documents and other Web sites, yet the user or reader can move easily through this multi-dimensional space simply by pointing and clicking a mouse.

Whereas computing encouraged integration, the Internet promotes both integration and alignment. Because all of the elements of a Web page are topologically connected and can be accessed by one or two clicks of the mouse (assuming an intelligent design by the Web master) these elements can be designed to work together, which brings them into alignment. If the information elements or business processes of an organization are not aligned, their misalignment becomes transparent on the Web. One of the ways an organization can begin to align its business processes is by creating a Web page.

Information that is aligned begins to take on the structure of knowledge, just as data that are integrated and contextualized become information. The terms data, information, and knowledge are sometimes confused for each other (data for information or information for knowledge), so I provide here definitions of these terms, along with a definition for wisdom, so that there will be no confusion:

Data are the pure and simple facts, the basic atoms of information;
Information is data that is structured, adding meaning and context;
Knowledge is the ability to use information strategically to achieve one's objectives; and
Wisdom is the capacity to choose worthwhile objectives consistent with one's values.

These definitions help us understand how the alignment of information makes the acquisition or the sharing of knowledge possible. If knowledge is about achieving an objective by exploiting information, that information must be aligned in such a way that one's objective is more easily reached or achieved. Hypertext is, therefore, a powerful tool for the organization and alignment of information to create knowledge structures. Hypertext allows the acquisition of information to become a genuine learning experience in which new knowledge is acquired. Well-designed microcomputer-based learning environments were able to achieve this objective, but the Internet and the use of browser technologies greatly facilitate and enhance the process, making the Internet an ideal medium for knowledge management, networking, and co-creation.

A Short History of Computing: Three Paradigm Shifts, from Mainframes to Micros to the Internet

In order to understand the nature of the fifth language of computing and the sixth language of the Internet it is useful to review the historical development of the technology that gave rise to these two forms of linguistic expression. The evolution of computing is usually described as a continuous process. Dan Tapscott and Art Caston (1993), however, saw a discontinuity in the way that computing developed. They describe a paradigm shift in the use of information technology from the original exclusive use of mainframe computers to the current mixed use of networked mainframe, minicomputers, and/or microcomputers typically configured as distributed client-server systems in which a host computer is serving information to computer workstations distributed throughout the workplace. Tapscott and Caston labeled the initial period of computing dominated by mainframes as Era I of the information age and the more recent period dominated by microcomputers as Era II. They published their schema in 1993, long before the Internet became such a dominant force. I will extend their ideas by suggesting that the Internet and the World Wide Web may be regarded as a third paradigm shift and represent Era III of computing, as well as a paradigm shift from the information age to the knowledge era — which may also be described as the transition from the computer age to the Internet age.

Era I computing began just after World War II with the development of the mainframe computer, first with electric relays, then with vacuum tubes, and finally with transistors. Initially, only technically trained computer experts performed calculations for those requiring computing services. Eventually, end users were allowed to use the computer by submitting jobs on punched cards that were batched together with other jobs and read into the computer with a card reader. The computer would process these jobs together and send the results to a centralized printing device. After the jobs were printed out, they were distributed to the users. The punched card and centralized printer system was eventually replaced with terminals that allowed the user direct communication with the computer. The next development in computing was the minicomputer, which greatly reduced both the scale and the cost of computing. A greater range of applications became affordable. Minicomputers could be dedicated to specialized tasks, which led to some decentralization of the computing function in large organizations.

The next breakthrough was the introduction of microcomputers, or personal computers, which created a revolution. They democratized computing totally because they lowered costs dramatically, as they have continued to do since their introduction in the late 1970s. They also provided a computing environment that could be dedicated to the needs of the individual user, hence the appellation "personal computer." The microcomputer gave individuals freedom from costly and hierarchical mainframe and minicomputer solutions that did not always serve the end user's needs.

The breakpoint between Era I and Era II information technology was created by two developments: first, the emergence of stand-alone microcomputers, and second, their integration with mainframes, minicomputers, or other micros to form distributed networks or client-server systems in which the host computer downloads software and information for processing on local microcomputers. The first step in the development of client-server systems was the creation of local area networks (LANs) of micros through the use of communications cards inserted into the microcomputers, together with specialized communications software. The second step was the creation of a similar linking between micros and a mainframe or mini host computer. The purpose of LANs was to allow information to pass between users and thereby recapture some of the advantages of mainframes. The linking of a host computer with micros was motivated in part by the desire to reintegrate the community of computer users after the disintegration caused by the use of stand-alone micros.

The creation of client-server systems achieved these goals and provided microcomputer users with a richer computing environment in which resources such as software and databases could be shared by many users. The client-server environment is superior to the former host-based systems because individual users in the network are no longer tied to a centralized computing authority. They are free to pursue their own development, to meet their individual needs, and at the same time to take advantage of shared resources.

The Internet system, which will be described in greater detail in Chapter 9, is an example of a global client-server system in which users from around the world link into a virtual host consisting of all Internet nodes to share information, knowledge, and software files and to dialogue with each other either synchronously or asynchronously. The breakpoint between Era II and Era III was the emergence of Mosaic in the eighties. The release in 1994 of Netscape, which was based in part on ideas contained in Mosaic, marked the entry of the Internet and the World Wide Web into the everyday world of work and education.

Eleven Critical Technology Shifts

Tapscott and Caston (1993) describe the transition from Era I of information technology to Era II of information technology in terms of the eight critical technology shifts listed below. I have added three more critical shifts (see pages 175–76) to explain the transition to Era III, the knowledge era, or the Internet age.

Shift 1: From Traditional Semiconductors to
Microprocessor-Based Systems
This shift allowed for the miniaturization of computers so that they could fit on the worker's or student's desktop. The microcomputer permitted a dramatic reduction in price that made its use in business extremely practical and its use in schools and for personal development affordable, hence contributing to the democratization of computing. It also contributed to the decentralization of computing power and thus the general leveling of industrial-age hierarchical structures.
Shift 2: From Host-Based to Networked-Based Systems
This shift also contributed to the decentralization of computing power and the leveling of hierarchical structures. It provided a hardware environment for the integration of communications between computer users in the workplace and in the schools.
Shift 3: From Vendor Proprietary Software to
Open Software Standards
This shift enabled each organization to develop its own affordable computing environment without being held hostage to arbitrary pricing or the technical expertise of a third party.

Shift 4: From Single to Multimedia: Data, Text, Voice, and Image
This development enriched the information environment that the computer user could access and integrated visual, aural, oral, and textual information.

Shift 5: From Account Control to Computer
Vendor-Customer Partnerships Based on Free Will
As with open systems, this shift allowed organizations greater freedom in developing their own systems.

Shift 6: Software Development: From Craft to Factory
This shift greatly reduced the cost of software and permitted the development of standards and generic skills. It provided a basic set of information-processing tools consisting of word processing, database management, spreadsheets, presentation, and desktop publishing that could be universally accessed and used interchangeably between organizations. It has now provided learning tools for use in the classroom that allow children to discover in a systematic and relatively simple manner basic generic information-processing skills.

Shift 7: From Alphanumeric to Graphical, Multiform User Interface
This shift has also contributed to the democratization of computing by giving many more people access to computing. The graphical user interface makes software easier to use and faster to learn. It lowers the age at which children can begin to use computer applications. It integrates analytic data-handling techniques characteristic of left-brain processes with spatially oriented strategies of information processing characteristic of right-brain processes. This allows children and adults suffering from dyslexia greater access to computers and a viable strategy for overcoming their cognitive deficits.

Shift 8: From Stand-Alone to Integrated Software Applications
This shift, together with network-based hardware, has permitted the integration of communications and information sharing among computer users.

The shift from Era I to Era II computing has profoundly affected the way computers are used in schools and the workplace. The difference in education is, perhaps, more dramatic because Era I computing had almost no impact on education. There were a few isolated applications of computer-assisted learning that merely automated learning and teaching strategies from the paper-and-pencil era. The only really significant use of computers was as the object of study in computer science courses delivered in high schools and postsecondary institutions. Era II computing, on the other hand, has created a revolution in education.

The transition from Era I to Era II information technology has been dramatic in the workplace, as well. It has resulted in completely new patterns of organizing work. Contemporary business is currently in the process of carrying out this reorganization, which frequently goes under the name of business-process reengineering. The reorganization entails new patterns of work for the individual worker, but perhaps more importantly, promises the greater integration of business processes and communications both within and between organizations.

The eight shifts listed above changed work patterns from those of the industrial age to those of the information age. But the way computer use has been organized in the workplace, ironically, owes more to the patterns and organizational principles of the industrial age than to the information age; in the case of software production, the pattern has resembled the preindustrial era of crafted technology characteristic of the Middle Ages. In order to understand this paradox, we will return to the communications theories of Marshall McLuhan in the next section.

The Shift to Era III: The Internet Age and the Knowledge Era

The three shifts in technology that made possible the widespread use of the Internet are:

Shift 9: From Networking through LANs and WANs
to the Use of TC/ICP
This shift allowed the networking of stand-alone computers and computer networks through the Internet, by making use of the worldwide network of telephone lines (and in some cases cable).

Shift 10: From Desktop and Server Navigation to the Use of Browsers
This shift was prompted by the release of Netscape, and led to the lift-off of the Internet and the creation of intranets.

Shift 11: From Modems to Routers
This shift made it economically feasible for whole organizations to access the Web through their local client-server system, thus pro-

moting business-to-business applications of the World Wide Web and internal corporate-wide webs or intranets.

These three shifts, which have made popularization of the Internet possible, have resulted in the emergence of knowledge management techniques and the beginning of a new way of doing business I have named the knowledge era, in which knowledge is regarded as an abundant quantity that can be shared to enrich the community at large.

A McLuhan Perspective on Era I, II, and III Computing

Chapter 2 examined how, beginning with the telegraph, the electric flow of information created new patterns of work (McLuhan 1962; 1964). By the time McLuhan first formulated his ideas in the early sixties, the technologies of the telegraph, telephone, radio, television, and photocopier had begun to break up the specialized, centralized, hierarchical structures of industrial-age business into more decentralized, more integrated, and flatter organizational structures. McLuhan's analysis of the effects of electric information led him to predict that work patterns would also be characterized by decentralization, non-hierarchical, generalist, and integrated structures.

How is it that McLuhan was able to observe the organic, decentralized, and integrative patterns of Era II of the information age a full twenty years before the introduction of microcomputers, in the heart of Era I and thirty years before the Internet, when the use of mainframe computer technology was characterized by the opposite patterns? McLuhan understood that when a medium first appears, it exclusively uses the content of another medium for its content until its users have learned to exploit the new medium to develop new forms of expression. To make the most of McLuhan's insight, we must take into account the nature of the mainframe computer. Like the factory, the mainframe computer represented a considerable capital investment and therefore its use had to be organized to increase the efficiency of the equipment. As with factory workers, shifts were organized to minimize equipment or machine downtime. Jobs run on the computer were organized in batch modes to maximize the machine's throughput. The user had to organize information processing to accommodate the needs of the computer and often the high-paid staff that operated and programmed it.

Mainframe computers were first put to use to gather information and create reports identical to those that had been created before the advent of computing. Instead of creating new business procedures, computers were used to automate the old tried-and-true methods for conducting business. The content of the new medium of the mainframe computer was the old-fashioned business techniques. Mainframes provided managers with the information they needed to command and control those below them in the hierarchy that characterized the management structures of industrial-age and Era I information-age firms. Actually, this use of mainframes was the last gasp of this style of management: The information environment in which business operates today has simply become too complex for command-and-control management to survive. The management information systems (MIS) that mainframes provided merely prolonged the life of the hierarchical management style for another thirty years, but its eventual demise was inevitable.

As in the industrial model, the organization of MIS personnel in the mainframe computer environment was centralized and controlled hierarchically by MIS specialists who advanced through the ranks from programmer to analyst to senior analyst to project director to manager of MIS. The ranks of MIS personnel were very much like those of the military. There was a degree of uniformity in terms of the experience of the MIS personnel and the skills they were taught. Because the training of MIS staff was so specialized and required the logging in of long hours tediously programming the computer line by line, most MIS personnel did not have much experience with other aspects of their firm's activities. Because of the investment in time required to be a computer programmer or systems expert, virtually none of the non-MIS personnel of the company became involved in the operations of the firm's computers.

This total split of MIS functions from the business activities of the firm created two cultures with little or no understanding of each other's functions or needs. The division was absolute until the advent of microcomputers and their integration into the work flow of virtually all organizations, from the largest to the smallest. It also helps explain the difficulties that many microcomputer end users had with their MIS departments, and vice versa. MIS personnel and end users come to computing from completely different perspectives. It is only through a process of dialogue and the integration of work groups that these two diverse groups can learn to work together.

The development of software was one aspect of MIS operations during Era I that did not conform to the model of industrial organization. Each manufacturer of a mainframe computer had its own proprietary operating system; once a firm committed to a supplier, it was locked into a unique system and could not purchase software developed by any other suppliers. In fact, for most of the information-processing jobs that a company wanted its computer to perform, software had to be created specifically for that application. With some few exceptions, software had to be crafted by a team of programmers and analysts for each application. The code that they created could not be used for other information-processing activities.

Era II computing changed all this dramatically. There are only three standards for operating systems: One was developed by Microsoft (MS-DOS) for the IBM personal computer, one by Apple for the Macintosh, and the third, UNIX, is an alternative to MS-DOS. The Macintosh system, which featured a graphical user interface and a mouse for clicking on icons, was much easier for the unsophisticated end user to work with. Microsoft, the creators of MS-DOS, duplicated many of the features of the Macintosh graphical user interface with one of their own called Windows. These two current standards for operating systems are now compatible and many applications run on both platforms.

An important feature of Era II software that distinguishes it from hand-created Era I software is that it is mass-manufactured and can be purchased shrink-wrapped directly off the shelf, with no or little need for individualization or installation by a professional. It is ironic that modular software, mass-produced using industrial-age techniques, became the engine for Era II computer usage. End users network with co-workers, suppliers, and customers, and students working in the classroom or at home have the freedom to customize information-processing activities in a decentralized, nonhierarchical, and fully integrated environment that fully embodies the spirit of the information age. Era II computing, which is microcomputer-based, nonhierarchical, networkable, and open, is having a profound effect on learning, on the workplace, and on the relationship between schools and work.

Era III computing has once again changed the dynamics between end users and MIS specialists. MIS was able to wrest control of the microcomputer environment in their organizations by installing client-server systems. They were able to impose enterprise-wide standards for software and hardware. Then along came the Internet; now the end-user community has a new channel of access that they can use to do an end run around MIS. In many organizations to this day the greatest resistance to the expanded use of the Internet or intranets comes from MIS specialists, who cite problems of security, some real and some imaginary or exaggerated. What makes MIS uneasy, namely, the unbridled and uncontrollable linkages of their computer users with resources and servers worldwide, is exactly what makes the Internet such a potent agent of change for work and learning and the relationship between them.

Era III Internet-based computing is also changing the way software is distributed. There is no longer a need to buy a shrink-wrapped software package to install onto one's system; software can now be downloaded and rented from the Internet on an as-needed basis. The advantages to consumers are that their software can now always be up to date and their hard drives need not be cluttered with a bunch of software that is not being used.

The Impact of Microcomputers on Learning and Work

There has been a steady invasion of microcomputers into our schools and workplaces for the past twenty years, resulting in the transformation of both domains. This new technology challenges us to evaluate the way we have organized our education system and workplace environments. We must understand the ways in which the new information technologies will continue to change education and work, requiring our schools and businesses to perform tasks they never before had to take into account. The impact of computer systems and the social interactions they engender will therefore become a mandatory subject of study for all those concerned with industrial and/or educational planning. While this section will focus on the impact of computing on learning and work I will make reference to the Internet as it impacts on the use of microcomputers. A more detailed discussion of the direct impact of the Internet on learning and work can be found in Chapter 9.

As discussed in Chapter 5, the education system is particularly sensitive to the influence of communications media and, consequently, has been shaped by them over the centuries. The origins of schools and the formal classroom style of teaching can be traced to the need in Sumer some 5000 years ago to train young people to use the medium of writing. Many aspects of school and classroom practice have changed surprisingly little since that time. If the invention of writing was the impetus for starting schools, the Gutenberg printing revolution represents another benchmark in the evolution of education. Low-cost printed material made possible the delivery of educational services to a mass audience. It inspired a system of schooling whose primary task was to teach children to function in the new print environment. Its goals and values, which came to be colored by a print mentality, still color today's schools.

We are now in the midst of a third major communications revolution, one created by electronic information devices. This revolution promises to have as profound an impact on society and education as the printing press had 500 years ago.

Computing devices entered the school system in the early sixties as an administrative tool in the form of mainframe computers. This technology was initially used to teach computer programming courses, primarily in secondary and postsecondary schools. Mainframes were later used as delivery systems for computer-assisted instruction (CAI), in which students mastered the content of lessons introduced by their teachers through drill and practice, or were introduced to new content through tutoring. CAI was based on a behaviorist model in which the user was a passive recipient of information. CAI offered the advantage of individualizing the student's learning program and automating certain of the teacher's functions such as tracking and evaluating a student's progress (Kurland and Kurland 1987, 319–20).

The advent of microcomputers, which entered the schools at the grass-roots level, decentralized and dramatically changed the nature of computer use in schools. Because of their affordability, microcomputers found their ways into virtually every school in North America, with high schools averaging forty to fifty machines per school and elementary schools about twenty machines per school (Becker 1991*a*, 6–9).

At first, microcomputers were used as delivery systems for CAI, but soon new applications began to appear: these included word processing and LOGO, a programming language for primary-school children, in which students could more actively control their learning experience. As computers began to proliferate, computer literacy and programming became educational goals in their own right. LOGO and other programs, such as Rocky's Boots and Gertrude's Puzzle, created microworlds that elementary-school pupils could explore on their own to create their own learning experiences. The tool use of computers for functions such as word processing, spreadsheets, and databases allowed the greater integration of computers into the general curriculum. As already discussed, new applications such as hypertext and multimedia, in which images, sounds, and texts are integrated, hold promise for more changes in the use of computers in education.

A number of authors (Papert; Kelman et al.; Pitschka; Bitter and Camuse; Taylor) suggest that the microcomputer will be a source of revolutionary structural change in the modern education system and in the contemporary workplace. What is the basis of this thesis? Other media introduced into the business world and the education system have had significant impacts, but they have not made truly revolutionary or structural changes. Certainly, the telegraph, the telephone, and electric lighting made significant changes in how business was conducted; but not enough to affect its hierarchical structures. The impact of these inventions on education was even less.

The mass media of radio, recordings, television, and movies had a greater impact on education than on work, but they were not the radical change agents they had been touted to be. Educational television is one of the more valuable forms of television programming, but it has not had a lasting impact on education or been the source of any cognitive breakthroughs. Mainframe computers had very little, if any, effect on education. Their effect on business has been significant from a quantitative point of view but not from a qualitative one. They have allowed firms to expand the scope of their operations and have automated a number of traditional business processes, but they have not changed the basic corporate hierarchical structure that has character-ized companies since the beginning of capitalism and industrialism. What is different about the microcomputer and its power to effect structural change that distinguishes it from other media?

I will respond to this question by postulating nine significant impacts that make microcomputers, as a medium of communication, a pro-found and liberating influence on both work and learning:

1. The microcomputer is the first medium to successfully vie with television for the attention of both adults and young people since the advent of commercial television.
2. The microcomputer is interactive, and hence has the potential to promote exploration and discovery.
3. The microcomputer promotes educational activity, and hence can liberate untapped potential in students and workers.
4. The microcomputer is an ideal medium for delivering and promoting individualized and self-directed learning and/or individualized work productivity.
5. The microcomputer has the potential to promote a positive attitude toward work and learning and encourage a positive self-concept.
6. The microcomputer has the potential to profoundly change teaching patterns within the classroom, as well as the social interactions of pupils and teachers in schools and of staff and management in the workplace.
7. The microcomputer is the first educational technology to be introduced into schools at the grass-roots level by teachers, parents, and students, and into the workplace by workers and middle managers rather than by senior administrators.
8. The microcomputer is a medium through which the curriculum can be integrated in the school and the flow of work can be integrated in the business world.
9. The microcomputer will act as an agent of reform, challenging the notions that hierarchical control-and-command structures are the most efficient way to conduct business and that a formal school structure is the best setting for educating children.

The nine postulates of microcomputers I have identified suggest that microcomputers will play an important role in the future development and reform of education. If these ideas are correct, then studying the effects of microcomputers will be essential for understanding how to plan training and education.

The following elaboration of the nine features of microcomputers as they relate to education should be treated as hypotheses that require further study and confirmation. These hypotheses were first formulated almost fifteen years ago on the basis of direct observation of computer usage in classrooms (Sullivan et al. 1986). A recent visit to one of the schools that was part of this original study has revealed that these postulates have stood the test of time. Although the Internet is a new factor not present fifteen years ago its role has been to reinforce the impact of microcomputing as identified by the nine postulates above.

Currently, the Internet principally serves as a resource for information that students can grab and integrate into one of their computer-based projects, such as creating a database or word processing a report or a research project. Computer usage in schools has not changed all that much in the last fifteen years. The amount of time devoted to computer work is, on average, still less than an hour a day. Even at River Oaks Primary School in Oakville, Ontario, in which a special effort has been made to integrate computers into the school curriculum, daily usage averages only two hours. The greatest impact of the Internet, as will be seen in Chapter 9, is on education outside the classroom milieu.

Microcomputers and the Ninefold Enhancement of Education in the Schools

We are only beginning to understand the potential range of the applications of computers in education. The only way to study this new medium and its effects on education is through the collection and analysis of observational data from a variety of classroom sites. This process will help us understand the issues surrounding the planning, use, and implementation of microcomputers in the school system.

The nine postulates formulated above are tested against the wealth of observational data on the classroom use of microcomputers collected in a comparative ethnographic study in which I participated (Sullivan et al. 1986), plus some more recent observations made in the fall of 1999. The conclusions reached in this study of the use of computer technology in elementary schools were based on classroom observational data, information gathered in interviews with teachers and pupils, a survey with the pupils, and historical data (Innis 1950, 1972; McLuhan 1962, 1964; Logan 1986*a*; McLuhan and Logan 1977) on the use of traditional media such as writing and print.

1. Attention Span

The microcomputer is the first medium to successfully vie with television for the attention of young people. I do not wish to overstate the case and claim that all children are attracted to this new medium or that once they are attracted to it, they never tire of it. The students' attitudes toward computers are not uniform and those who are generally enthusiastic are sometimes bored, while those who are generally bored are sometimes enthusiastic. But there were instances where we observed increased attention span and concentration as a result of the technology. Thoughtful instruction or guidance is a necessary ingredient to ensure the successful use of computers in the classroom.

The microcomputer's capacity to engage children and capture their attention through interactive video images is a property shared with video games. This property, not shared by textbooks, can be exploited to design engaging educational software, which offers competition to the fast-paced, rapidly changing images of television. Microcomputers, however, are not an automatic draw; a well-designed book can and must compete successfully with computers. While microcomputers are a versatile educational medium, there are still many valuable educational experiences that can only be obtained with books.

When microcomputers are linked to the Internet, interest and attention span increase due to the richness of resources that are available. No hard drive can carry the variety of experiences that a student can find on the Internet. Many Web sites contain exactly the kinds of elements that school kids enjoy, namely, graphics, music, videos, and animation.

2. An Interactive Medium

The microcomputer is interactive, and hence has the potential to promote exploration and discovery. Television, in sharp contrast, is a totally passive medium. Children watching its flickering mosaic images quickly become mesmerized. Commercial television is mental junk food that leaves the minds of its viewers unnourished and inactive. The microcomputer, on the other hand, if suitably programmed, can be used to stimulate an active response. When used skillfully and creatively by the classroom teacher, it can function as a medium of exploration and discovery. Moreover, the microcomputer provides the user with a sense of control both over learning and over the data or information contained within or generated with the computer.

The microcomputer is not the first interactive medium in education; the written word is certainly another example. Although the book is only a delivery vehicle, it engages the mind interactively because of the reader's need to decipher its message. Writing and reading entail the active coding and decoding of information from visual signs into language and vice versa. Alphabetic writing also requires the active analysis of spoken words into their basic phonemes so that each phoneme can be coded by a letter of the alphabet. Writing has traditionally functioned as a medium for exploration and discovery for both schoolchildren and adults. Indeed, the creative output of science and the humanities would not have been possible without this evocative medium. "Ideas develop from interaction and dialogue . . . especially with one's own writing" (F. Smith 1982, 204).

The computer also stimulates the development of new ideas because it, too, is an interactive medium, on two accounts: as a medium of communication for the written word, and as a data-processing device. The computer provides the user with a dimension of interactivity in addition to that of writing, namely, the capacity to manipulate data. It is the most powerful research tool and stimulus to new ideas developed since the invention of writing, numerical notations, and the printing press, and, like the use of these media, its use will contribute to the further cognitive development of its users.

The microcomputer is an interactive medium that pupils are able to operate in an exploration-and-discovery mode. But the microcomputer by itself is not necessarily interactive; it must be programmed in a particular way to realize this potential. Even with an interactive form of software like LOGO, however, its use does not necessarily lead to exploration and discovery on the part of the pupil. Students still require the guidance of a teacher to integrate their use of the micro-computer with the rest of the educational program and to show them how to use the software in a way that will promote self-growth.

There are those who would claim, however, that LOGO is not truly interactive. It is an "example of a closed system in which the content is pre-defined, responses are anticipated, and action is controlled by the designer alone." Its weakness is that, unlike the Internet, its interac-tivity does not entail "the mutual, autonomous, and simultaneous activity of both participants (designer and user) working toward a common goal." (Ryder 1996)

The Internet increases the interactivity of microcomputers because of hypertext and the ease with which interactive Web sites can be cre-ated. The Internet is the ultimate medium in terms of interactivity and there are three unique dimensions to this interactivity:

i. There is a greater variety of resources on the Internet, as compared to the microcomputer's hard drive.
ii. The navigation of the Web to find resources and items of interest provides another dimension of interactivity. The Web is an endless source of materials and tools that can occupy an individual for hours on end. The exploration of this world by surfing, directed only by curiosity, provides an important learning experience.
iii. The Internet allows for true interactivity because it enables two-way communication. (This point will be elaborated in the Internet section.)

3. An Educational Medium
The microcomputer promotes educational activity, and hence can liberate untapped potential in students. In most cases, we observed at our six classroom sites modest educational gains with word processing, drill and practice, and programming. Particularly impressive were the results achieved in the area of special education, where the computer supported all aspects of the teacher's program, and students working

independently on the computer increased both their computer and academic skills (Sullivan et al. 1986, chap. 8).

Because it is interactive, the microcomputer allows users to develop new cognitive skills, as well as to reinforce their literacy skills. Television, on the other hand, does not promote learning because it is a basically non-interactive medium that merely transmits information to passive viewers. Television informs, but it does not educate. Television viewers do not develop new cognitive skills as a result of using it. This helps explain why television was such a disappointment as an educational medium. Information does not equal education; the ability to process information is an essential part of education, and television does not promote this activity.

The fact that television allows children to become better informed has actually had certain negative consequences. From a very early age, youngsters in the television age are exposed to almost all aspects of life through the medium of television, and as a consequence are "gray at the age of three," to quote McLuhan (1964). This may explain why the present generation of children seems to know so much, yet understand so little. They are already jaded about life, so their teachers have little new information to offer them and, as a consequence, find it difficult to hold their attention. Children in the television age also become intellectually lazy because no effort is required to absorb TV-transmitted information, as compared to learning from written material.

Print promotes educational activity because, in addition to informing its readers through its content, its use, unlike that of television, requires that the individual possess certain cognitive skills to decode its content. To use the alphabet (Logan 1986a), a writer (or a reader) must first learn to analyze each spoken word into its basic phonemes and then code (for writing) or decode (for reading) those phonemes into (or from) meaningless visual signs, the letters of the alphabet. In addition to promoting the skills of analysis and coding, alphabetic literacy teaches abstraction and classification. Computer literacy involves similar skills of analysis, coding, abstraction, and classification, and hence reinforces the skills of literacy and the left-brain modes of organization associated with them. Moreover, computers promote right-brain forms of patterning and organization because of their use of more global categories such as files, fields, and databases.

This is one of the reasons that the microcomputer has the potential to become such a powerful teaching tool.

Television, on the other hand, has none of these features; it can only inform and cannot really educate. An education can be defined as what is left over after you have forgotten all that you learned. This definition is facetious, but it contains an important insight into the effects of interactive media such as the written word or the computer. Learning facts is not an education; learning how to process information or data is.

A possible reason that higher learning or science did not develop in preliterate societies is that there was no interactive medium available to store and process information. Writing provided such a medium and print reinforced or enhanced it, creating the sudden burst in education, scholarship, research, and science, first after the invention of writing in Sumer and Egypt, then after the development of the phonetic alphabet in the Levant and Greece and, finally, after the invention of the Gutenberg printing press in Renaissance Europe (Logan 1986*a*). We are experiencing a similar explosion of activity with computers.

The microcomputer combines the educational advantages of the written word with the graphic capabilities of video. This graphic effect is even stronger with the Internet. Computers and the Net are multisensory media capable of providing the same information in alternative modes (textual, graphic, or animated). Computers and/or the Net can deliver more data to students in easily accessible forms, and, if programmed cybernetically, only as required.

A recent study indicates that laptop computers are even more effective than desktop computers in terms of engaging schoolchildren in their schoolwork. "The results of the data analysis indicate that the Laptop Project was successful in encouraging students to use computers for schoolwork. Before the project began, less than one-quarter (15%) of the sixth graders reported that they used a computer frequently at school. After the first year of the Laptop Project, three-fourths (75%) reported using computers a lot at school" (Stevenson 1999).

By providing a rich source of information and learning activities, the Internet is both an electronic classroom and an electronic library, one of the largest libraries (if not the largest) ever assembled, with instant access to its resources. The Internet itself can be used to find resources. The Maricopa Center for Learning & Instruction (MCLI), part of the Maricopa Community Colleges in Arizona, operates a Web site at http://www.mcli.dist.maricopa.edu/tl/index.html that lists hundreds of resources. It provides 39 topics from anthropology to zoology. One of these topics, education, has links to 62 educational Web sites. One of these listed Web sites, the "Australian Correspondence Schools (ACS) Online Study," offers the following features: "over 280 distance Education courses (hobby & career), how to study on line/using the Net, new international accreditation system, free 88 page handbook posted anywhere in the world." (Its Web address is http://www.acs.edu.au/distance/.) It is one of many sites that provides such information. "With the Internet and the World Wide Web, time previously spent getting information can now be used for the much more important business of assessing the information and examining its usefulness" (Thorpe 1999).

4. Individual and Self-Directed Learning

The computer is an ideal medium for delivering and promoting individualized and self-directed learning. At all of the classroom sites we observed, children used their computers to a certain extent in an individualized mode. A factor that contributed to the success of the individualized instruction at one classroom site was the considerable talent the teacher had developed for juggling the needs of five or six students by answering their questions and encouraging their work as she moved from one workstation to another. We found less success if the teacher was not as skilled in this way. Care must be taken to make sure pupils are properly supported when they are working at the computer in an individualized mode.

The microcomputer supports individualized instruction, but it is not an automatic teaching machine. "To move beyond 'gift-wrapping' in the context of self-directed learning leads to the following requirements for computational environments. Such systems must: be simultaneously user-directed and supportive; be sufficiently open-ended and complex that users will encounter breakdowns; provide means for significant modification, extension, and evolution by users; support a range of expertise; and must promote collaboration" (Fischer and Scharff 1998).

One of the advantages of microcomputers for individualized and self-directed instruction is their ability to provide instant feedback without embarrassing the user if a mistake has been made. Conversely, children derive a great deal of pleasure from sharing with their classmates the positive feedback they receive from the computer.

The use of microcomputers in education reminds us of the importance of individualized and self-directed learning, not only with computers but with other media, as well. Individualized learning is not unique to computers. The book is also conducive to individualized learning. Before the advent of printing, books were a precious handcrafted commodity chained to tables and studied by individual students rather than by a class of students at once. Before printing, each student studied the manuscript most appropriate for his level of knowledge. The printing press and the mass production of textbooks changed the pattern of book usage in school. The self-taught person who does not attend school but learns by reading books continues to pursue an individualized style of learning. Schools, however, where an entire class studies the same printed textbook and is expected to learn lessons at the same time, no longer provide individualized instruction. Textbooks in modern schools are used as a broadcast medium, which students must follow in a lockstep program of learning. It is up to teachers to individualize the instruction of their pupils. It takes more time and effort on their part, but it is worth it when one considers that each child has his or her own special needs and cannot be treated as an indistinguishable unit on an assembly line.

Even though computers invite an individualized approach to learning, there is still the danger that they, too, can be used in the broadcast mode. At present, this danger is not grave because there are still relatively few computers in the schools, but that will not always be the case. Computers should not be used the way textbooks were, to coordinate the studies of all pupils in the same classroom. Indeed, computers can be used as dynamic tools to individualize the use of text-based information.

The Internet provides the opportunity to individualize learning because of the vast richness of its resources. Students follow their own individual paths on the Internet. They can bookmark their favorite Web sites so that they can return to those places that pique their curiosity and inspire their best learning experiences. The personalized desktop "model of computing is one that lets a child access personalized information from any computer any time. (The) student quickly sift(s) through Internet sites, television shows, video conferences, and e-mails to gather the information needed for his report" (Krochmal 1998). The fact that the Internet provides access to such a rich array of resources means that individual students can find topics and information that appeal to their specific interests and needs. The teacher becomes less dependent on a textbook that forces all the students in a class to work with the same material.

5. The Affective Domain

The microcomputer has the potential to promote a positive attitude toward learning and encourage a positive self-concept. Microcomputers and the Internet have both enjoyed wide acceptance and enthusiastic responses from schoolchildren worldwide, across all socioeconomic classes, grade levels, and ranges of aptitude (intelligent, normal, remedial, learning-disabled, physically challenged, and so on). There is, however, a small but significant percentage of children in every group who are either hostile or indifferent to these media. But most pupils like computers because the interactivity captures their interest and imagination.

The enthusiasm for microcomputers often translates into a positive attitude toward schoolwork and learning in general. This is not to suggest that every child who uses a computer and/or surfs the Net automatically begins to enjoy school. Computers are not a panacea, but they do provide a significant number of children who may be frustrated by the predominantly print-based education program of our education system with an alternative mode of expression and learning.

The use of the Internet in postsecondary education also posted very positive results and motivation: "It was found that students enjoyed the process of learning exercise physiology via the Internet and, given the opportunity, would take additional Web-based courses. With our student populations demanding higher access to Internet-based courses, colleges are shifting their focus on learning rather than teaching" (Pankey 1998).

6. Social and Learning Interactions

The microcomputer has the potential to profoundly change teaching patterns within the classroom, as well as the social interactions of pupils and teachers. One of the earliest fears surrounding the use of computers was the concern that schoolchildren would become antisocial automatons, so transfixed by their interactions with computers that they would lose interest in interacting with one another. The intense social interaction and cooperation that surround computer use in classrooms (Sullivan et al. 1986) show that these fears were ungrounded, illustrating once again that the effects of media are sometimes counterintuitive. The microcomputer actually promotes cooperation and social interaction.

Whenever schoolchildren use computers, either in small numbers (one or two per class) or in a lab with many machines, their social interactions are very intense. The students constantly converse with one another, answer one another's questions, and discuss what they are doing. They often verbalize and describe their exploits on the computer, even when no one is there to listen to them.

Books do not invite the same level of intense social interaction. There is something intrinsically private about reading. Silence is requested in a library but not in a computer laboratory; mandatory silence would kill the social interactions necessary for the successful use of computers. People use books in public places such as trains or airports to achieve privacy; one hesitates to interrupt someone who is reading or writing (either manually or with a typewriter), but one feels less compunction about talking to someone working at a computer. Somehow, it is not as disruptive to distract a computer operator as it is a typist. If you cause the typist to make a mistake, it is a real intrusion because of the special effort required to correct errors, whereas with word processing little harm can be done because of the ease of correction.

On the whole, our observations (Sullivan et al. 1986) confirm that the social interactions of students increase when they use computers, whether in a classroom or laboratory setting. The teachers at the various classroom sites confirmed this. One claimed that young people are more social at computers, which she thought was beneficial if properly controlled. Another found the increased social interaction disruptive. "It is more difficult keeping students on task and getting them to organize their time" (Sullivan et al. 1986, chap. 7). Another teacher agreed. "The noise that the children make using the computers was distracting to the other children. Sometimes, a whole lot of children went up suddenly to look at the computer, and the teacher would have to yell at them from the back of the room to sit down" (Sullivan et al. 1986, chap. 6).

Data from our interviews and surveys with the schoolchildren at the classroom sites also confirm the hypothesis that their social interactions around the use of the computer are intense. The children indicated overwhelmingly that they preferred working with others rather than alone because they could help one another. However, the loners preferred the absence of interference, and most of the children reported that there were times when other students interfered with their work on the computer without being asked, which they found to be a nuisance. They also indicated that some students copied their work, but they did not seem to mind this. They indicated that they enjoyed talking about their computer activities with other children, although some found that it distracted them from their work. The children said they spent a good deal of time helping one another and felt that many of their classmates knew a lot about computers.

Thorpe, in a recent study (1999), identified a shift from "learning that takes place primarily through each person's working alone to learning in collaboration with others. Computers, for a variety of reasons, always have welcomed and seemed to require several minds working together. In classrooms where projects and problem-solving dominate the learning process, students get to work together to accomplish goals. Beyond being good preparation for the kind of work environment students are likely to encounter when they leave school, this opportunity is especially important to girls."

The most constructive social interaction around the use of microcomputers in the classroom is peer teaching. Many teachers take advantage of this phenomenon. If they wish to teach a new technique to their class, they often show it to the three or four computer whizzes in their class; within two to three weeks, the entire class will know the new technique. The knowledge has diffused through the whole class as a result of peer interactions. One school board encourages its teachers to take advantage of peer instruction and even provides guidelines for identifying "student facilitators."

Peer teaching completely restructures social and pedagogical patterns in the classroom. Instead of all learning interactions radiating, often in an impersonal manner, from teacher to pupils, a much richer network of interactions emerges. The teacher no longer possesses a monopoly of knowledge, because the microcomputer democratizes expertise. Frequently, one or two experts who know more than the teacher about certain aspects of computers come to the fore. These students alter the social structure of the classroom. The phenomenon of student experts is not a transient one that will disappear once teachers learn to use computers. Because the technology will continue to evolve and improve rapidly, it is likely that the present generation gap between teachers and their computer whizzes will continue for many years.

Peer teaching, the presence of student experts, and the intense socialization surrounding the use of computers all contribute to a completely different teaching style. Although the role of teachers has changed, their importance has not been diminished. The success of computer activities in classrooms depends heavily on the teacher.

Because of its capability for two-way communication, the Internet can change the social interplay of a traditional classroom setting. Students can make links outside the classroom. They can develop meaningful learning experiences with individuals or classrooms in another neighborhood, city, or country. They can find resources to challenge the authority of the teacher. The concept of the classroom without walls can expand right across the globe.

7. A Grass-Roots Movement

The microcomputer is the first educational technology introduced into the school system at the grass-roots level by teachers, parents, and pupils rather than by administrators. Microcomputers, and later the Internet, which allows learning in the school to be effortlessly extended into the home, were not introduced into the classroom as the result of decisions made by educational planners or administrators, as was the case with educational television. Teachers who owned their own personal computers found them to be useful tools. In many cases, microcomputers were first used for administrative purposes by teachers, then by students for their schoolwork. Once computers were in the school, and the Internet began to command the attention of computer users, students and teachers demanded to have their computers linked to the Internet. The response of school authorities was much more rapid than it had been to the use of microcomputers in the classroom, probably as a result of the previous learning experience.

The grass-roots response of pupils and teachers is the key to the success of microcomputers in schools. Suddenly, an alternative learning environment came into existence that suited the learning styles of a much greater variety of schoolchildren. Microcomputers create new opportunities for those who are at a disadvantage operating in a purely print environment, and hence further democratize educational opportunities by providing an alternative medium to print.

One of the factors that paved the way for the use of microcomputers in the school system was how the organization of primary-level classrooms changed after the introduction of television. The shift from desks bolted to the floor at regular intervals in neat rows to ones that could be moved around was the start of a revolution in education. Teachers began to react subliminally to the competition of television by introducing activity centers into their classrooms to more effectively engage their pupils and break up the monotony of sitting at a desk all day long. The use of audiovisual aids encouraged this development even more. By the time microcomputers were introduced to the classroom, the stage had been set for their use.

One of the important and interesting effects of the use of microcomputers is the autonomy it provides a teacher. The traditional classroom, where most learning aids are print-based and used in a non-individualized manner, has been completely controlled by centralized authorities such as school boards or ministries of education through the choice of textbooks (using instruments such as Ontario's Circular 13) and setting curriculum guidelines. The only options open to teachers have been those regarding teaching style and delivery. With microcomputers, the teacher has more options and greater control. The same is true for students because of the greater opportunity this technology affords to individualized learning. So, the microcomputer democratizes and decentralizes authority by giving users greater control over their activities, whether they are learning or teaching.

One danger that the grass-roots movement faces is its own success. Once it is perceived that microcomputers are here to stay (and we are not far from that point), there will be a natural response from bureaucratic structures, such as school boards, to control the phenomenon, as was the case with textbooks. This impulse is dictated by the logic of bureaucratic organizations, and their need to rationalize and explain the large expenditure that microcomputer-based education requires. The only way to avoid unnecessary bureaucratic interference is to create meaningful communication between administrators and their clients, the teachers, parents, and pupils at the grass-roots level of education. Breaking the lines of communication, even for the shortest time, will be disastrous. The imposition of standards, equipment, or software on teachers without the teachers' support will be counterproductive.

One of the reasons for the grass-roots acceptance of and enthusiasm for the microcomputer has been its human scale. Remember, before the introduction of microcomputers, mainframe computers had only a marginal effect on education. By contrast, students are able to conceptually grapple with micros. They can "get their arms around the computer," so to speak. They are able to see all of the components of the machine at once. The operation of the disk drive is familiar to them because of the parallel of the floppy disk with the CD disk and the tape cassette. The ability to control and be aware of all the inputs is a great advantage to students first learning how to use a computer. Indeed, it provides them with a sense of pride and independence.

8. Integrating the Curriculum

The microcomputer is a medium through which the school curriculum can be integrated. One of McLuhan's basic insights into the nature of electronic media was that they tend to encourage the integration of information rather than its fragmentation, as is the case with print. The current school curriculum, a product of the print era, is organized into separate subjects that are, more often than not, taught independently. The spirit of specialism can be found throughout the education system from the primary grades to postgraduate studies. The arrival of the computer has done very little to reverse this trend. For McLuhan, however, the integration of the curriculum is inevitable. "In education the conventional division of the curriculum into subjects is already as outdated as the medieval trivium and quadrivium after the Renaissance. Any subject taken in depth at once relates to other subjects" (McLuhan 1964, 347). Note that this thought was expressed thirty-one years ago, long before the advent of microcomputers and the use of computers in schools.

Word processing is one computer application that integrates English language and communication skills with other subjects such as the natural sciences, history, geography, and other social studies. Other applications such as spreadsheets and databases have shown preliminary promise for the integration of mathematics, science, and social studies. While the level of integration is still quite modest, the potential for the future is unlimited and will be an important source of reform in the education system.

9. Alternative Forms of Education

The microcomputer will act as an agent of reform, challenging the notion that a formal school is the best setting for educating children. This fact was recognized by D. Mersich as early as 1982: "Advances in computer-aided learning (CAL), together with the discretionary attendance provisions of the law, will soon make it possible for private enterprise to go into competition with the public education system, whip it in quality, and make a profit at the same time" (Mersich 1982, 37).

The competition that private entrepreneurs might give to the school system will not force public education out of business. It might siphon off some of the best teachers, however. We can only hope the competition will force the publicly supported education system to reform some of its practices to better meet the needs of its clientele. This is an extremely healthy prospect for contemporary education and should have an effect similar to the one the printing press had on the reform of medieval universities and the preparatory schools that fed them. The printing press updated and revitalized the education system of its day. The microcomputer will have a similar effect, with proper implementation in the school system.

The claim that the microcomputer has the potential to revitalize education cannot be empirically validated, because the presence of microcomputers in the school system is such a new phenomenon. There were a number of promising features of computer usage in the six primary-school sites we observed, perhaps foreshadowing the type of reform and renewal of the school system that computers could help generate. While the successes that were observed were modest, they are the type of experiences that educators can build on to exploit the educational potentials of microcomputers. The fact that the special-education teacher at one classroom site was able to use the computer as a tool to engage her pupils' attention and then use their interest to deliver an individualized program of education that stimulated their literacy skills is significant, given the rudimentary level of our under-standing of how to use computers effectively in schools.

The moderate success of the computer labs is another hopeful sign. Even the very modest educational gains in the classroom use of com-puters portends well for the future. What is important is not just the level of success we observed in the course of one year of observation, or the progress that has been made in the few years since the intro-duction of the first primitive microcomputers into the school system, but rather the trend line and the rate of growth of the phenomenon. There is evidence that microcomputers possess the potential to renew our education system, but renewal will not be automatic. The question is how the implementation of microcomputers within the education system can be organized to realize that potential. This constitutes one of the major challenges facing today's teachers.

Another trend we observed that could contribute to the renewal of the school system was the strong interaction between school and home computer usage, which the Internet amplifies. Children with computers at home enjoyed a definite advantage. While this advan-tage represents an equity issue between working- and middle-class children in the short-term, the drastic reduction in the cost of com-puters expected in the future should cause this disparity to disappear. What is important is that computer usage represents one of the first activities in a long time that integrates schoolwork and home recre-ational activities. Computers could become an important tool to combat the alienation children feel between their schoolwork and what they experience outside of school. Given the increasingly impor-tant role computers will play in the world of work, school computer programs will inject the element of relevance that educators have been desperately seeking to motivate their pupils.

The Internet reinforces and amplifies all of the reforming features of microcomputing. The Internet, by providing the possibility of operating a school totally online, becomes an agent for reform by virtue of its threat to literally replace the school as an institution that must co-locate the teachers and the students. A number of online institutions are now successfully operating, and many more are planned. Some operate as complete stand-alone online operations, while others provide online services to complement their off-line or traditional offerings. This theme will be explored in greater detail in Chapter 9.

Microcomputers and the Ninefold Enhancement of Learning in the Workplace

Today's workers and employers are under enormous pressure just to remain employed or in business. During the industrial age, workers or employers needed to learn only one set of skills that would in most cases last them a lifetime. This is no longer the case. More and more, workers and businesses are finding themselves displaced by technology. Their salvation lies in ongoing learning so that their skills remain relevant to the current environment of rapidly changing technology and skill requirements, especially due to computers.

All technologies, as noted in Chapter 2, are a source of both service and disservice. Job displacement by technology is a disservice. The increased productivity that microcomputers permit is a service. So, too, is the fact that microcomputers stimulate learning on the job and make lifelong learning more possible. Just as the microcomputer has stimulated reform of the school system, it can perform a similar task in the world of work, and for basically the same reasons. The ninefold enhancement of learning by the microcomputer, which I originally formulated for children in the classroom setting, also provides a good description of increased productivity and learning in the workplace. The conclusions that follow are based on reports in the literature and some direct observation of computer usage in the workplace and at a computer-training center in Toronto.

1. Attention Span

The microcomputer is the first medium to successfully vie with television for the attention of adults. Workers are by and large enthusiastic about microcomputers. There are a few exceptions, generally among individuals who have had difficulty learning how to use their computers because of poor training or no training. For workers who have mastered its use, there is satisfaction with computing for a variety of reasons:

i. Users feel that they are more productive.
ii. They find that their work is easier and less tedious.
iii. They enjoy the fact that they are constantly learning new skills or improving their existing skills.
iv. They enjoy following the ongoing and continuous development of the technology.
v. They feel less trapped in their positions because they have generic skills that can be transferred to other jobs, in their firm or elsewhere.
vi. They enjoy the intellectual challenge of using the technology.

As with schoolchildren, adults enjoy the graphical features of microcomputers. The graphical user interface with pull-down menus has made the use of computers simpler and more enjoyable. Indeed, there is an almost game-like aspect to some functions. The loss of attention span created by the medium of television applies to today's adult population as well. Graphical user interface helps users overcome weak attention spans and allows them to deal with information in small, digestible bytes. Their aversion to print is similar to that of children, and therefore computers, particularly graphically configured computers, make it easier for them to work with text-based information. This is another reason that Era II computing is so different from Era I computing. In Era I, computer-generated information was accessed by the end user through printouts and had to be read just like print. Era II computing involves much more direct, graphical contact with the data.

Another parallel of work-based learning with that of schoolchildren is the importance of proper instruction and guidance. Proper training, which includes a general understanding of the hardware system and its operation, as well as specific knowledge of software application, is the factor that most contributes to user satisfaction.

The Internet also successfully competes with television given the large number of information and knowledge workers who will return to using a computer in the evening so that they can surf the Internet. The introduction and the anticipated expansion of WebTV, whereby users can surf the Internet from their television set, speaks volumes as to the draw and attraction of the World Wide Web.

2. An Interactive Medium

The microcomputer is interactive, and hence has the potential to promote exploration and discovery. One of the chief benefits of microcomputers and client-server systems is that they allow end users to interact directly with data. This provides users with more potential for exploration and discovery. It also provides them with a sense of control over the data and information they are working with, so that they do not feel overwhelmed by the increasingly greater amount of data. Because end users are able to interact with their data, they have a sense of ownership of it and consequently a better understanding of it.

The interactivity that microcomputers make possible fully accrues when they are used as a tool to generate new information, as when word processing a report, using a spreadsheet, or working with a relational database. New ideas develop from the interaction and dialogue that the use of computers allows, enriching the work of users and helping them to develop as individuals and as workers.

The two-way communication with other users is perhaps the most valuable contribution of the Internet to the world of work. This interactivity can improve relations within an organization and result in a better sharing of knowledge and information internally. It can also improve relations with customers and suppliers. One can learn how to better meet customer needs, and teach suppliers how to better meet your organization's needs.

3. An Educational Medium

The microcomputer promotes educational activity, and hence is capable of liberating untapped potential in workers. Because it is interactive, the microcomputer allows users to develop new cognitive skills, as well as reinforce their literacy skills. The skills developed in learning how to use the computer are generic and apply to all forms of information processing, which is the root activity of most work today. Computer use provides another benefit, in that it allows workers to integrate left-brain analytic problem-solving techniques with right-brain forms of patterning and organization, just as the computer integrates textual and graphical information. The use of the microcomputer is probably the best form of education that a manager can provide employees to prepare them to operate in today's business environment. And the beauty of this form of education is that the worker is learning these skills in the midst of generating productive work. The only time-investment outside the office is one or two days every six months to allow the user to upgrade computer skills and stay abreast of this rapidly changing technology.

The Internet is a rich source of work-related learning in two ways:

   i. It provides the resources of the World Wide Web to help users find work-related information;
   ii. It can deliver formal online training courses that employees can take at their convenience without the problems of scheduling that classroom training entails.

4. Individual and Self-Directed Learning

The computer is an ideal medium for delivering and promoting individualized learning and/or individualized work productivity. Its ability to provide instant feedback without embarrassing the user makes it a very powerful educational tool in the hands of all employees, assuming they receive enough initial instruction to get started. The microcomputer is also an excellent medium for individualized productivity because it provides workers with an information environment in which they can work in peace and at their own pace. The microcomputer has also given rise to a huge increase in the number of people working at home, in what Toffler (1980, 26, 210–23) labels the "electronic cottage."

The Internet enhances the individualization of learning by allowing users to bookmark the Web sites that are most effective for them. It is also possible for users, on certain select Web sites, to create their own individual file folders, so as to have continuity in their learning experience. Other Web sites that do not have individual file folders keep track of each visitor and allow them to continue their learning experience from the point where they left off on their last visit. The Internet allows the delivery of online training to employees that they can study at their own leisure when they have the time and inclination to learn something new. The delivery of training in the classroom instructor–led mode forces students to learn at a particular time not of their own choosing and to learn at a pace that works for the group as a whole. It is impossible to conduct classroom instruction at a pace that satisfies everyone. For some the pace is too fast and they fall behind, while for others it is painfully slow and they get bored and eventually disinterested.

5. The Affective Domain
The microcomputer has the potential to promote a positive attitude toward work and encourage a positive self-concept. Adults feel a sense of pride when they are able to create a professional-looking product. Another factor motivating workers to use computers is their belief in its importance for the advancement of their careers. The computer relieves much of the tedium of work because it completes repetitive tasks so easily. It also provides stimulation and a constant source of challenge, and hence makes work more interesting.

6. Social and Learning Interactions
The microcomputer has profoundly changed the pattern of social interactions among staff and management in the workplace. It is generally recognized that the use of this technology has flattened out hierarchical structures and led to a team-oriented rather than a command-and-control style of management. The intense social interaction and cooperation that surround computer use in the workplace parallel the experience in the classroom. The microcomputer promotes cooperation and social interaction because the users feel united by a common bond to overcome their perception of the machine as "stupid." The cooperation that develops between users helping one another translates into good teamwork, which carries over to other activities.

The Internet and e-mail allow more peer learning to take place within an organization, and a network of coaches and mentors can be easily identified and accessed over the Net. The Internet allows the network of co-learners and coaches to extend beyond the confines of the organization.

7. A Grass-Roots Movement

The microcomputer is probably the first major piece of technology that was introduced into the workplace at the grass-roots level by workers and middle managers. And this was much against the wishes of the MIS (management information systems) departments, who ran their organizations' information operations through the use of mainframe computer systems. Many MIS personnel regarded microcomputers as a nuisance, an attitude they have extended to the Internet because of their inability to control it.

For the end users and their managers, the microcomputer and then the Internet were godsends because they allowed each department to control its own computing and information access, and they could be used to get work done more efficiently. This grass-roots response was the key to the initial success that microcomputers enjoyed in large organizations.

One of the reasons for the grass-roots acceptance of, and enthusiasm for, the microcomputer was its human scale. Before the introduction of microcomputers, mainframe computers were inaccessible to the ordinary worker (defined as someone not in MIS); even after the introduction of terminals, the end users' use of the mainframe was severely limited.

The introduction of the Internet into the workplace also occurred as the result of grass-roots support for the medium. Workers who surfed the Net at home found that the Net was rich in resources that helped them in their work. They began to demand this capability in the workplace, and encountered two lines of resistance. One was from MIS, who worried about security issues and perhaps, in some cases, their own role in the organization. The other line of resistance, which usually came from somewhere near the top of the organization, was that this medium, despite being a valuable source of useful information, is also an electronic playground in which workers could easily waste time and perhaps even visit politically incorrect, and hence inappropriate, Web sites. These concerns were largely overcome at most companies, but there are still many organizations that place certain restrictions on the use of the Internet. In some cases access is given only to managers; in others Internet use is policed to make sure it is appropriate.

Another vein of resistance to the use of the Internet in the workplace came out of the concern for the security of proprietary information, which began to leak out of organizations because of the spirit of collegiality and community that the Internet engenders. This security issue has been addressed with fire walls, but many companies are still wrestling with the problems created by the free sharing of information.

8. Integrating Business Processes

The microcomputer, configured in a client-server architecture, has the potential to provide a medium through which the flow of work can be integrated. McLuhan long ago pointed out that computers would integrate all information processes in an organization rather than fragment them, as had been the case with print. Without ever using the term, he conceived of business process reengineering more than thirty years ago. "With electricity as the energizer and synchronizer, all aspects of production, consumption, and organization become incidental to communications. The very idea of communication as interplay is inherent in the electrical, which combines both energy and information in its intensive manifold" (McLuhan 1964, 307).

9. Alternative Forms of Education

The microcomputer will act as an agent of reform, challenging the notion that a hierarchical control-and-command structure of management is the most efficient way of conducting business. The Internet amplifies the effect of the microcomputer as an agent of reform by providing direct channels of communication between all members of the organization. This is not to suggest that management will be replaced by computers and intranet-linked communications. The firm will self-organize to some extent, but leadership will still be required to set goals and to create a vision for the organization. Managers will be needed to plan the overall direction of an organization, define its objectives, and develop its strategies for achieving those objectives. But management will no longer need to bother with the day-to-day tactics of running an organization. Client-server systems with appropriate communication links, information-processing tools, and adequate information will allow tactical decisions to be made by employees. The managers' jobs will be to set up the tools and to provide the training. The client-server system will become the "virtual manager," a tool that will allow its users to self-organize.

The printing press updated and revolutionized the world of commerce in its day. The microcomputer will have a similar effect. A number of promising features of computer usage in the world of work foreshadow the kind of reform and renewal of commerce that computers could bring. These features involve the transformation of today's firms into "learning organizations," as has been suggested by Peter Senge (1993), and the transformation of workers into "lifelong learners."

7

Learning a Living in the Wired World

Schools can no longer perform the whole job of providing students with all the tools and knowledge they need for their careers. Technology is changing too fast for that. Today, the best the schools can do is to prepare students for the task of keeping themselves continuously updated.

Given these facts, every employer must plan some form of in-service education; otherwise, their employees will fall hopelessly behind. In addition to staying up to date with technology, employers should also be actively concerned with their employees' educational development, given that most workers are now or soon will be "knowledge workers" who have to deal with information all day long. The operation of a business or any other mission-oriented organization, therefore, requires an educational strategy or plan as urgently as it needs a marketing or financial plan.

The job of a company's human resources department entails the constant upgrading of employees' skills, as well as their general intellectual development. And employees who want to advance must make a plan for their own personal development through a program of life-long learning. An educational program is essential for survival in the business world for both the organization and the individual.

This chapter will help readers develop a plan for their own development or for their organization. It attempts to answer four of the questions posed in Chapter 1:

- How is computing changing work patterns and the organization of social institutions?
- How can computing be harnessed to inculcate students with the desire for lifelong learning?
- How can work be organized to naturally promote learning?
- How can education in the workplace be better organized to improve productivity, so that learning becomes a lifelong activity and workers are properly trained to do their jobs?

In answering these questions I will draw heavily on the ideas of Marshall McLuhan, who understood many years before the introduction of microcomputers and the World Wide Web the effects electricity would have on learning and work. Many of his predictions that were scoffed at and regarded as hype in his day have come to pass and are now part of our general understanding of the effects of computing and the Internet.

From Global Village to the Wired World

> Real, total war has become information war. It is being fought by subtle electric informational media.
>
> (MCLUHAN 1967, 138)

Despite the fact that computers have begun to alter our notions of language, communications, culture, education, commerce, and government, most people are largely unaware of the profound impact of technology, and carry out their activities largely unaffected by the changes surrounding them. This is not altogether surprising; those who lived through the Gutenberg revolution were equally unaware of the major shifts brought about by the printing press. The pattern of unawareness repeats itself each time a new technology is introduced. As McLuhan wrote (1962, 187), "Every technology contrived and outered [sic] by man has the power to numb human awareness during the period of its first interiorization." We are currently passing through such a period. The rate of change, however, is so great that we can no longer afford to ignore the process of change. The Gutenberg revolution stretched over centuries; the time scale of the computer revolution is only a matter of years. Nevertheless, in this very short period of time, our institutions are falling out of sync with contemporary economic and social realities.

That we live in a knowledge era is a twentieth-century cliché destined to become a twenty-first-century reality and archetype. The planet *has* shrunk to the dimensions of a global village. All of the institutions of our post-industrial, postcapitalistic society, including the family, the economy, corporations, small businesses, primary and secondary schools, universities, local and national governments, the civil service, political parties, and the media, are undergoing rapid and profound structural changes. As a result of these changes, we suffer from a number of information-age maladies, including future shock, information overload, political gridlock, resurgent nationalism, and ethnic xenophobia. These are the symptoms of the "information war" shell shock and the post-traumatic stress with which we struggle daily.

We are desperately trying to establish a balance between the change represented by the hundreds of technological opportunities that the future holds and the stability and comfort of our traditional institutions. Our collective response to the challenges of the information revolution has taken the interesting form of both a move forward into a new era, a new millennium, by embracing the use of computers, the Internet, and other forms of new information technology, and, at the same time, an attempt to return to some of the values of our past by reengineering our businesses, restructuring our government and its social assistance programs, reforming our education system, managing our knowledge, and renewing our spirituality.

The key idea in all the schemes of renewal, reform, reengineering, and restructuring is that the relentless flow of information cannot and must not be stopped or even slowed down, but must be controlled and harnessed by the use of information-technology hardware, advanced software systems, expert systems, cybernetics, general systems theory, and artificial intelligence. Our planet will be encircled by one continuous grid or network of information connecting homes, business, banks, schools, government offices, and information providers through computers, LANs, WANs, e-mail, the Internet, telephones, fax machines, cable, television, video, radio, film, smart cards, ATMs, and electronic banking services. The global village has become the wired world.

The standard approaches to the "information crisis" — that is, those approaches that focus exclusively on the technology and the flow of information — can only offer partial solutions to the challenges of living in a wired world. The problem we face is neither technical nor quantitative, but qualitative. The challenge is not that the amount of data and information has exploded exponentially, but rather that we must deal with new patterns of communication and information processing and the impacts they are having on institutions that were designed for different methods of data handling. A quantitative change creates a qualitative change. I believe that the so-called information crisis is not due to the rapid increase in the amount of data that is currently being processed, nor is it due to the speedup of transactions or any of the technical challenges required to deal with this increased and accelerated flow of information. It is due to our lack of the "soft" skills required to integrate the new techniques of data handling and information processing with the organizational structures of the social, political, economic, and cultural institutions of our society.

Our ability to handle vast amounts of information quickly and economically is prodigious and growing rapidly. It is the transformation of our society and its institutions to accommodate the new wired reality that is lagging behind. Institutions designed to handle a much slower and smaller flow of data, and based purely on paper forms, can no longer cope with the information explosion; hence the feeling of information overload. It is incumbent upon us, therefore, to redesign and reengineer our institutions to cope with the increased information demands of the Internet age. Moreover, radical changes in the way individuals are trained to work with information must be made. The older forms of education and training simply do not work. They must be redesigned.

The solution to the problem we face is not technical but social, and, of the two, social problems are always more difficult to solve. The problem lies in the conflict between the techniques, processes, and attitudes that are in place to deal with the older forms of literary and paper-based information and the reality of the newer electronic forms of information that are swamping today's institutions. The current mismatch between the newer forms of information processing and the institutions designed for older forms is not historically unique. In every age and in every society that has undergone significant technological development and change, a mismatch between the new techniques and the old institutions has been a problem. Our era is no different, except that the transition between the old technologies and the new ones has been more rapid and hence the mismatch has been greater.

Why Our Industrial-Age Institutions Are Not Working

Our computer skills have evolved faster than our organizational skills. Institutions organized to address the challenges of the industrial age cannot cope with the vastly increased and accelerated flow of information. The force driving the transition from the industrial age to the information age is computing and other forms of information-processing technology. They are producing what Toffler (1980) called "the third wave of human change." The pace of change is quickening, and with the introduction of the Internet we are passing from the information age to the knowledge era, which, by appropriating Toffler's terminology, we might label a fourth "wave of human change." If our institutions are to remain relevant and serve the needs of society, they must make better use of these communications and information-processing technologies.

Most modern institutions such as the nation-state, the civil service, the corporation, the labor union, the free-market system, the banks, and the education system, however, developed during the Industrial Revolution, or the "second wave" of human change, when mass production was inaugurated. Many of our institutions such as the stand-alone school, the church, the city, can be traced to an earlier date. They began with the advent of writing during the agricultural revolution, or the "first wave." They have undergone the same bureaucratization as those institutions that originated in the industrial age. In fact, all of our bureaucratic organizations are products of the type of organization that swept in with industrialization.

If the goals and objectives of today's institutions were shaped by the needs of an economy based on mass production, their breakdown, with the dominance of informatics as the principal driving force of our economy, should come as no surprise. The industrial model, which stressed uniformity, fragmentation, and specialization, has been replaced by a cybernetic model that stresses diversity, integration, and the generalist approach of systems theory. McLuhan attributed the transformation to the transition from a print-based communication system to one dominated by electricity and electronics. McLuhan's analysis, developed in the early days of computing before microcomputers were conceived, foreshadowed many of the themes that have been developed in the nineties by the business analysts discussed later in this chapter. McLuhan's ideas, read in light of today's developments, seem to have anticipated Toffler's observation (1980, 1990) of the crucial new role of knowledge in the production of wealth, the need for Hammer and Champy's technique (1993) of business process reengineering, Tapscott and Caston's notion (1993) of the extended enterprise, Senge's idea (1993) of the learning organization, and Drucker's ideas (1993) of postcapitalistic society and the demise of the dominance of the nation-state.

I realize that as a friend and former colleague of McLuhan's, I might be subject to a bit of bias. Moreover, it is always easy to read predictions into people's work after the events have come to pass. Having duly warned readers, I will support my position by quoting liberally from McLuhan, so that readers can examine his exact words and form their own opinions. The quotes I am using all come from the introduction to *Understanding Media*, and from the last chapter, entitled "Automation — Learning a Living" (McLuhan 1964).

The fact that McLuhan's ideas needed thirty years to germinate, and required rediscovery by other authors can be attributed to four factors:

1. McLuhan's prose style was cryptic and difficult for many to follow, or to put it more charitably, he wrote like a poet, and business people do not generally look to poetry as a source of inspiration and direction.

2. McLuhan had no business experience and was not considered to have any particular insight into the nature of business. As a scholar with a literary bent, his ideas were largely ignored by the business community, with the exception of creative professionals in the advertising field.

3. McLuhan was not taken seriously by business people, most academics, and even many of the writers I refer to, who advocate interdisciplinary approaches. Specialism dies hard even for information-age interdisciplinarians. They were unable to embrace notions such as McLuhan's idea (1964, 359) that "the social and educational patterns latent in automation are those of self-employment and artistic autonomy." The elevation of McLuhan to the position of patron saint by the editors of *Wired* magazine suggests that perhaps a new generation, the generation of McLuhan's grandchildren, is ready to accept his mantle.

4. Finally, McLuhan's ideas were truly ahead of their time, and not enough collective experience with information technology and, in fact, none with microcomputers or the Internet, had been logged in at the time of the publication of *Understanding Media* in 1964. Now that millions have experienced what McLuhan wrote about fifteen years before the introduction of microcomputers and thirty years before the introduction of the World Wide Web, his ideas, properly contextualized, have gained popular acceptance, often without proper attribution.

Knowledge: The New Source of Wealth

In *The Third Wave* (1980) and *Powershift* (1990), Toffler documents how our economy has undergone a radical transformation due to information technology. Manufacturing and distribution activities once dominated the economy. It is now the information and service sectors which comprise the majority of activity. Furthermore, the information and service sectors are merging. In describing his company, the founder of one of Europe's largest computer manufacturers remarked, "We are a service company just like a barbershop" (Toffler 1990, 74).

All sectors of the economy are affected by computing. "Farmers now use computers to calculate grain feeds, steelworkers monitor consoles and video screens . . . A United Parcel Service driver handles boxes and packages, drives a van, but now also operates a computer"

(Toffler 1990, 74–75). Auto mechanics at Ford dealerships are using a computer-based expert system. All of these observations led Toffler to the conclusion that knowledge will play a "crucial new role . . . in the production of wealth. Instead of metal or paper money, electronic information becomes the true medium of exchange" (Toffler 1990, 238).

The economist Peter Drucker (1993, 8) came to a similar conclusion: "The basic economic resource — 'the means of production,' to use the economist's term — is no longer capital, nor natural resources (the economist's 'land'), nor 'labor.' It is and will be knowledge." McLuhan published this idea twenty-six years before Toffler and twenty-nine years before Drucker, when he wrote: "The very same process of automation that causes a withdrawal of the present work force from industry causes learning itself to become the principal kind of production and consumption . . . The peculiar and abstract manipulation of information [is] a means of creating wealth" (McLuhan 1964, 351, 354). He also captured the idea of the connection between wealth and information in the following quote, which also calls for the type of restructuring of organizations known as business process reengineering (BPR): "Wealth and work become information factors, and totally new structures are needed to run a business or relate it to social needs and markets" (McLuhan 1964, 357).

Business Process Reengineering

The first use made of computers was to automate the fragmented business processes inherited from the previous era of mechanization. This approach does not take full advantage of the technology. In business process reengineering, the processes by which an organization conducts its business are reorganized and reengineered to take full advantage of the information handling that computers make possible.

The use of computers to automate the old processes illustrates McLuhan's adage that the first content of a new medium is always an older medium. "The content of this new environment [the electronic age] is the old mechanized environment of the industrial age" (McLuhan 1964, vii). Business process reengineering reverses this phenomenon and finds a new content that is more naturally suited to the patterns of the new technology. According to the management analysts Michael Hammer and James Champy (1993, 90), "The real power of technology is not that it can make the old processes work better, but that it enables organizations to break old rules and create new ways of working — that is, to reengineer."

McLuhan predicted in 1964 that all industries would have to go through a reengineering exercise because the effects of electric speedup would be to integrate the processes that industrial mechanization had fragmented and create the need for new types of organization and talent. He predicted that firms would have "to rethink through function by function," their place in the economy. In a later publication, teaming up with Barrington Nevitt, McLuhan (1972, 220–1) formulated the dilemma of trying to speed up mechanical processes in the following way:

> The United States moves into a period of 'inefficiency' and break-down resulting from the application of electric speeds to mechanical processes. The computer-system specialist, in practice, is entirely a product of old literate and mechanical training. He thinks of electric technology as a quantitative increase in the performance potential of the old mechanized system. In practice, what occurs is that the old system is simply shaken to pieces by the 'vibes' to which it is subjected.

Hammer and Champy (1993, 27–28, 49) came to the same conclusions as McLuhan through their study of management and economics:

> Reengineering is about reversing the Industrial Revolution. Reengineering rejects the assumptions inherent in Adam Smith's industrial paradigm — the division of labor, economies of scale, hierarchical control, and all the other appurtenances of an early-stage developing economy. Reengineering is the search for new models of organizing work . . . Task-oriented jobs in today's world of customers, competition, and change are obsolete. Instead, companies must organize work around process.

McLuhan (1964, 347), too, had identified the importance of process, but much earlier: "Electricity . . . gives primacy to process, whether in making or learning." Hammer and Champy (1993, 25) arrive at a similar conclusion: "It is not products but the processes that create products that bring companies long term success."

Businesses are reengineering their operations not only to obtain the most efficient use of computers, but also because they are pitted in a struggle for survival and, in most cases, must restructure or perish. Hammer and Champy (1993, 17) have identified three factors that are driving this process, which they call the three Cs — Customers, Competition, and Change.

Customers have taken charge; it is a buyer's market. Customers now have access to so much information and so much choice that they are forcing business to respond to their needs. This phenomenon was also predicted by McLuhan (1964, 349–50): "The consumer becomes producer in the automation circuit . . . Marketing and consumption tend to become one with learning, enlightenment, and the intake of information." Toffler developed a similar idea in 1980 in *The Third Wave*. During the first wave, the consumer and the producer were identical: People produced for their own consumption; then during the second wave, a wedge was driven between the producer and the consumer. During the third wave, however, the "prosumer" reemerges. There is "a progressive blurring of the line that separates producer from consumer" (Toffler 1980, 284). They are "reunited in the cycle of wealth creation, with the customer contributing not just money but market and design information vital for the production process" (Toffler 1990, 239).

The second factor driving restructuring is competition. Consumers or prosumers armed with information technology can do many things for themselves like design their own business forms or create their own newsletters. So businesses must compete with their own customers. Moreover, the number of competitors has grown at the same speed with which the world has shrunk to the dimensions of a global village. The number of people and organizations that can compete is much greater than it was when business was conducted on a local level. Start-up companies are another source of competition. They carry no organizational baggage and "do not play by the rules" (Hammer and Champy 1993, 22). McLuhan (1964, 350) warned of the ease with which new enterprises could be started: "The separation of power and process obtains in automated industry, or in cybernation.

The electric energy can be applied indifferently and quickly to many kinds of tasks."

The third factor driving reengineering is constant change, which Hammer and Champy suggest is a change in the nature of change itself, a point that was also made much earlier, in 1970, by Toffler in *Future Shock*. The very first author to sound the alarm of the accelerated pace of change was McLuhan, who, as noted in Chapter 2, introduced the notion of electric speedup.

Postcapitalist Society

In addition to increasing the level of competition that individual firms face, the globalization of trade has also undercut the importance of the nation-state, according to Peter Drucker (1993, 10–11): "The sovereign nation-state has steadily been losing its position as the sole organ of power. Internally, developed countries are fast becoming pluralistic societies of organizations. Externally, some government functions are becoming transnational, others regional . . . and others are being tribalized."

This latest development in the geopolitical sphere was predicted by McLuhan (1964, 353) based solely on his understanding of communications. "Electric speed requires organic structuring of the global economy quite as much as early mechanization by print and by road led to the acceptance of national unity." McLuhan pointed out that nationalism "wiped out many of the local regions and loyalties" because of the speedup of information due to the printing press. In a similar manner, he suggested, the speedup of information flow due to electricity would undercut national organization in favor of global and continental associations such as the United Nations, European Union, and NAFTA.

There has also been a return to and revitalization of local and regional loyalties. The decentralizing effects of electricity predicted by McLuhan and the flip back to tribal or oral structures are surfacing, so that many people now embrace the credo: "Think globally, act locally." The national institutions are being caught in this squeeze play. This is not to suggest that the nation-state is about to disappear, but only that it will no longer dominate the geopolitical and economic systems as it once did.

McLuhan also saw that the electric speedup of information would neutralize the great ideological conflicts that were the basis of the cold war. "The electric changes associated with automation have nothing to do with ideologies or social programs" (McLuhan 1964, 352). The end of communism and the restructuring of capitalism have had nothing to do with the years of military and propaganda posturing of the Eastern and Western blocs, led respectively by the former USSR and the United States. The transformation took place as a result of economic and social forces, driven largely by information technology.

There was a reason the Communists banned private ownership of the personal computer: They recognized that the electric flow of information was the one thing that their centralized hierarchical command-and-control system could not defend against. And indeed, in the end it became impossible for them to do so. Their system was inundated by information and collapsed under its weight. The *coup de grâce*, ironically, was actually Gorbachev's introduction of *glasnost* (openness) and *perestroika* (restructuring), which finally brought down the whole system.

The face of capitalism has undergone a similar but less dramatic transformation, as old-style forms of command-and-control hierarchical corporate structures give way, due to the Western form of *glasnost* and *perestroika*, namely, open nonhierarchical computer-based communications and flow of information, and business process reengineering. McLuhan's predictions have come to pass, as Drucker (1993, 4, 6) proclaims in his latest book, *The Post-Capitalist Society*: "That the new society will be both a non-socialist and a post-capitalist society is practically certain. And it is certain also that its primary resource will be knowledge . . . Instead of capitalist and proletarians, the classes of the post-capitalist society are knowledge workers and service workers."

The Extended Enterprise

In their book *Paradigm Shift*, Tapscott and Caston discuss the transformation of business operations due to the interconnectivity that networked computing environments make possible. They describe three spheres of networked operations within a business organization that are replacing the departmentalized fragmented corporate structures that characterized industrial-age firms. They are: (1) the high-performance work group, (2) the integrated organization, and (3) the extended enterprise, which is the integrated organization together with its network of associates, including its suppliers, customers, distribution channels, and strategic allies or partners.

The high-performance work group is an interdisciplinary team working together within the organization through a network of computers that "provides personal and work-group tools, information, and capabilities to directly support all categories of people in the information sector of the economy . . . Enterprise architectures provide the backbone for the new open, networked enterprise" (Tapscott and Caston 1993, 15, 17).

The integrated organization consists of work groups that are able to communicate and exchange information with each other so that the organization operates in an organic and purposeful manner.

The extended enterprise consists of the integrated organization together with the network of associates with which it is doing business, whether they are customers, suppliers, allies, or partners. The extended enterprise represents a group of organizations linked by one continuous stream of information flowing between them. This integration maximizes the efficiency of the business transacted between the associates of the extended enterprise.

The Tapscott and Caston model is based on the integration of automation and communication and the need for people working together to coordinate their activities. McLuhan's insight into the integrative nature of electricity foreshadows many of Tapscott and Caston's ideas: "Total interdependence is the starting fact . . . With electricity as energizer and synchronizer, all aspects of production, consumption, and organization become incidental to communications" (McLuhan 1964, 354, 359). Without understanding any of the details, McLuhan developed the notion of the extended enterprise based on his understanding of the effects of electric information. "Naturally, when electric technology comes into play, the utmost variety and extent of operations in industry and society quickly assume a unified posture . . . Many people have begun to look on the whole of society as a single unified machine for creating wealth" (McLuhan 1964, 348).

The Learning Organization

There is one point on which all of the models of today's economy agree: that knowledge and information are the keys to the production of wealth. Combine this idea with Tapscott and Caston's notion of high-performance work groups and the integrated organization, and one has derived the notion of the "learning organization," which forms the central theme of management analyst Peter Senge's provocative book, *The Fifth Discipline*. Senge, quoting *Fortune* magazine, wrote, "Forget your tired old ideas about leadership. The most successful corporation of the 1990s will be something called a learning organization" (Senge 1993, 4).

A learning organization is one that makes a commitment to team learning, continual lifelong education, and a general systems approach to its operations. These are themes that McLuhan began to talk about in the sixties. He observed that the electric speedup of information meant that a single set of skills would not last a worker through his or her lifetime. The only solution to this dilemma is lifelong learning and the acquisition of generic skills rather than specialized skills. Just as electricity separates the source of its power from the processes to which it directs its energy, and is thereby flexible and easily directed to different tasks, so too must today's worker possess flexibility. The acquisition of generic skills is the only assurance or security that an individual has in an economy that moves like quicksilver. Electricity be my metaphor! (with apologies and thanks to Dylan Thomas).

McLuhan did not use terms like "general systems theory" and "team learning," but he embraced these notions using terms like "cybernation" and "feedback." "Feedback is the end of the lineality that came into the Western world with the alphabet and the continuous forms of Euclidean space" (McLuhan 1964, 354). He also stressed interrelation and the need to reverse the fragmentary nature of industrial-age education. "Education designed to cope with the products of servile toil and mechanical production are no longer adequate. Our education has long ago acquired the fragmentary and piece-meal character of mechanism. It is now under increasing pressure to acquire the depth and interrelation that are indispensable in the all-at-once world of electric organization" (McLuhan 1964, 357).

Senge stresses the importance of research within a learning organization. All solutions are "always subject to improvement, never final . . . When people in an organization come collectively to recognize that nobody has the answers, it liberates the organization in a remarkable way" (Senge 1993, 282). He saw the role of the manager in a learning organization "as researcher and designer" (Senge 1993, 288). McLuhan also recognized the importance of the research process, and the participation of the staff of an organization in that process, through his interpretation of the Hawthorne effect. Industrial psychologists observed at the Hawthorne plant of General Electric that no matter how workers' conditions were changed their productivity increased. McLuhan attributed this to the fact that their participation in the experiment motivated them and made them work harder.

In Search of Learning Organizations

McLuhan, Toffler, Hammer and Champy, Tapscott and Caston, and Senge agree that knowledge now plays a critical role in the creation of wealth. Their observation is both trivial and profound. It is trivial in the sense that it is a cliché that no one would deny, yet profound because there has been no significant response by the education community, and only a minor one by the business community, to this new reality transforming our lives. Despite the dynamic changes in the nature of our economy, the training and preparation of personnel are based on the industrial model. The world that our present forms of organization and our education system address is rapidly disappearing, yet the way our school system relates to the world of work has not changed significantly since its founding at the beginning of the Industrial Revolution. The classroom has traditionally been isolated from the basic realities of work and the economy. The stereotype of teachers pedantically dispensing book learning unrelated to the needs, concerns, or interests of their pupils is, regrettably, far too accurate.

Nevertheless, the school system demonstrates some measure of success in that it supplies technically trained individuals. Unfortunately, these successes are limited. Today's educational goals serve yesterday's needs. They are built into the system because education was organized to supply the work force for a hierarchical society. Its function was to stream the general population into an elite of highly specialized experts and technocrats, the managing class, and a general population with enough literacy and basic skills to consume industrial products and provide a disciplined labor force. The hierarchical structures of industrial organization are rapidly disappearing, however, and therefore the high-end products of the school system — the middle managers — are no longer needed.

This is slowly being recognized in the private sector and is resulting in a reorganization of firms along the lines outlined earlier and a reengineering of their business processes. There is a flattening of the hierarchical management structures and a movement away from command-and-control management. The public sector has been much less responsive to this form of reorganization than the private sector, but the idea has been gaining general acceptance. Least responsive to these trends has been our education system, perhaps the most reactive and hierarchically structured institution in our society.

We can no longer afford to entertain an educated technocratic elite who take the responsibility of operating and administering economic, political, and social institutions for the less-educated lower echelons of society. The fragmentation of knowledge among different social classes cannot succeed in the computer age as it did during the industrial era, when tasks were also fragmented and only managers needed to be fully informed.

Today's economy demands greater integration of job function with knowledge and information. "The 'leap' to a higher level of diversity, speed, and complexity requires a corresponding leap to higher, more sophisticated forms of integration. In turn, this demands radically higher levels of knowledge processing" (Toffler 1990, 81). There are two implications to this observation for the training of post-industrial workers. First, the present practice of dividing the school curriculum into specialized packages of information called subject disciplines will no longer serve today's need for a systemic approach to the use of knowledge. According to McLuhan (1964, 346), "Automation is information and it not only ends jobs in the world of work, it ends subjects in the world of learning." Second, all members of society, whether they are production workers, service sector workers, or consumers, will require both a knowledge base and a set of information-processing skills to function at even the most rudimentary level. Clearly, our school system must be capable of preparing individuals for the new demands of post-industrial society.

Toffler's analysis of the economy and society as developed in *Powershift* (1990, 81) can be applied to education and provides an explanation for the present failure of our school system: "The disintegrative or analytic approach, when transferred to economics, led us to think of production as a series of disconnected steps. Raising capital, acquiring raw materials, recruiting workers, deploying technology, advertising, selling, and distributing the product were all seen as either sequential or as isolated from one another." Toffler's description can be paraphrased to diagnose with equal acuity the problems with today's education system: "The disintegrative or analytic approach, when transferred to schools, has led us to think of education as a series of disconnected steps. Reading, writing, mathematics, science, social studies, computer literacy, commerce, engineering, medicine are all seen as either sequential or as isolated from one another." The origins of reading, writing, math, and science are all connected and hence these disciplines should be studied in an integrated manner. An integrated curriculum not only better prepares people for the reality of today's economic and commercial climate, it also makes learning easier.

The lesson of the integration of learning and doing does not apply solely to our schools. It applies with equal validity in the workplace, in which job function and training must also be intermeshed. Industry has done little to reform its educational practices. It was forced to introduce training programs for staff, and in some cases companies now operate in-house training departments. But these training departments have been formed more often to save on the cost of training than out of a real commitment to employee training and development. Most in-house training departments operate at a level below that of outside organizations whose sole business is education. In the field of computer training, for example, an in-house training group will confine its expertise to the software and hardware platform that the organization is using. The in-house trainers may read about other computer products, but they do not immerse themselves in the operation of those products, and therefore do not have the same breadth of understanding of the current computing environment as do trainers in an educational company working with a large number of software applications and platforms.

Industry still operates on the antiquated premise that the basic education of employees has been provided by the school system and their only responsibility is to upgrade the skills of employees from time to time. In too many instances, in-depth education of personnel is viewed as a waste of money and resources. The cost of training is often looked at as an additional expense, like taxes, that must be minimized no matter what the consequences — and the consequences can be significant. Since wealth production and knowledge are synonymous, the first price to be paid is the inefficiency in wealth production due to personnel who do not have the basic skill sets needed to do their jobs. The analogy in the industrial age would be to consider the hardware or machinery necessary to operate a factory as an ancillary cost of doing business that needed to be reduced as much as possible or avoided altogether.

Industrialists realized that the advantage their factories would have over their competitors' would be the efficiency of their equipment and machines. Today's chief advantage is not just the equipment, which is still critical, but the knowledge base of one's employees at both the staff and management levels. The early industrialists understood the importance of their machinery: Its results were so tangible. The unit cost of production using machines was dramatically lower than hand production, making the need to invest in equipment obvious. The only exercise was the calculation of the time needed to recoup the capital investment. In the early days of industrialization, marketing and competitive analyses were not even required because there was little or no competition and an undersupply of consumer goods; it was a seller's market. Undercutting the price of handcrafted goods was a no-brainer.

Obviously, recouping the investment made in employee education and development is not as easy to gauge as was the investment in hardware in the industrial age. Increased productivity due to training may be marginal at first, so it is difficult to calculate the payback time. Given the low cost of training, however, relative to the cost of hardware, operating costs, and salaries, a modest incremental increase in productivity will result in a payback time of only two to six months. Let us estimate the payback time for a typical training scenario, assuming that the cost of training per day is twice the employee's daily salary and the training session lasts two days. The cost is therefore six paydays, four for the actual cost of the training and two for the lost productivity during the two days of training. A modest increase in productivity of 10 percent due to the training will result in a payback period of only sixty working days or roughly three months. No manager should ever think twice about providing each employee with a minimum of two days of training every six months.

The other benefit accrued from training is the general intellectual and cognitive development of an organization's employees. Not only will they be able to do their jobs more effectively, they will also be better able to develop new ideas to make their firms more competitive and/or more productive. A knowledgeable employee is a more effective employee and also a happier employee. When workers' skill sets are being continually updated, they feel more confident about their work. They have pride in what they are doing. Because workers feel that their companies care about their well-being and personal development, employee training and education not only make for a more knowledgeable worker but also a more motivated one. Even if employees are thoroughly trained for their jobs, excuses should be invented to train them just to increase their sense of participation and harness the Hawthorne effect (McLuhan 1964, ix).

Finally, the bottom line for training employees is the need to remain competitive. Progressive firms are benefiting from the enormous dividends that employee education pays. It will not be too long before the rest of the business world catches on to the obvious: that in an information-based economy, knowledge is the prime ingredient in the production of wealth. The number-one asset of a company, therefore, is not capital, not equipment, but knowledge and a well-trained staff — intellectual capital, if you will, and that intellectual capital must be spread uniformly throughout the organization. This idea provides a striking contrast to the practice of the industrial age, where the knowledge sat at the top of the pyramid and was carefully guarded and hoarded by the owners and managers, and a program of de-skilling employees and segmenting work was considered the best way to increase efficiency.

Toffler's description of the new production paradigm can be easily adapted and used as a prescription for remedying the ills of today's school-based and workplace educational practices. We need only substitute the word "education" for "production" in the following quote from *Powershift*: "The new model of production [education] that springs from the super-symbolic economy is dramatically different. Based on a systemic or integrative view, it sees production [education] as increasingly simultaneous and synthesized. The parts of the process are not the whole, and they cannot be isolated from one another" (Toffler 1990, 81).

The skills learned in one discipline must feed the study of another. Topics must be studied holistically, where the literary, mathematical, scientific, social, economic, and environmental aspects of the topic are treated simultaneously. "Real-time" or experiential involvement in a topic must supplement book-based learning. "Connectivity rather than disconnectedness, integration rather than disintegration, real-time simultaneity rather than sequential stages — these are the assumptions that underlie the new production paradigm" (Toffler 1990, 82), and by extension the new education paradigm.

Toffler (1990, 85) describes the impact that the new mode of production is having on business and the distribution of knowledge: "Just as we are now restructuring companies and whole economies, we are totally re-organizing the production and distribution of knowledge and the symbols used to communicate it." Unfortunately, a similar restructuring of our education system has not yet taken place, which is why our schools and industrial training continue to fail us.

When I refer to the failure of our education system, I am not referring merely to the system of publicly and privately funded schools to serve the primary, secondary, and postsecondary educational needs of the community. My remarks also include the failure of the industrial training programs in both the public and private sectors, as well as the lack of integration between the training provided by the formal education system and the needs of the workplace. And even if we succeed in reforming the system, the rate of change of technology is still too rapid to rely on schools to meet all our educational needs.

To succeed in its mission, today's business organization must give careful thought to its education strategy. It must strive to become a "learning organization, where people continually expand their capacity to create the results they truly desire, where new and expansive patterns of thinking are nurtured, where collective aspiration is set free, and where people are continually learning how to learn together" (Senge 1993, 3). Unfortunately, most of our educational institutions, even those of higher learning, are not "learning organizations" by Senge's definition. More about that in the next chapter.

Nomadic Gatherers of Knowledge and the Total Social Process

McLuhan certainly demonstrated an uncanny ability to describe the landscape of cyberspace, a term I am certain he never heard. What is remarkable about his achievement is that in 1964, when he wrote *Understanding Media*, workplace computing was in its infancy and restricted to mainframe computers in which jobs were run on a batch basis using punched-hole cards and card readers. His musings on computers filled fourteen pages of the last chapter of his book and two pages in the introduction, yet as we discovered in this chapter, he seems to have covered the gamut of issues facing computing and learning in today's workplace. He even seems to anticipate, albeit obliquely, the phenomenon of surfing the Internet. He suggested that with electricity and automation, human behavior would change: "Men are suddenly nomadic gatherers of knowledge, nomadic as never before — but also involved in the total social process as never before; since with electricity we extend our central nervous system globally, instantly interrelating every human experience" (McLuhan 1964, 358).

This quote, like many of McLuhan's pithy observations, is packed with insights. The image of nomadic knowledge gatherers certainly describes today's users of the Internet, but possibly an even deeper insight is the idea of electrically configured knowledge as a "total social process . . . interrelating every human experience." In the thirty-five years since McLuhan formulated this idea, those who promote the notion of knowledge management have made a careful distinction between explicit knowledge and tacit knowledge. This distinction was first formulated by the philosopher Michael Polanyi and introduced into the knowledge management literature in a book by I. Nonaka and H. Takeuchi, *The Knowledge Creation Company*. Tacit knowledge is "deeply rooted in an individual's action and experience as well as in the ideals, values or emotions he or she embraces" whereas explicit knowledge is rational, "formal and systematic" (Nonaka & Takeuchi 1995, 8). Tacit knowledge is personal, subjective, intuitive knowledge that grows out of practice, whereas explicit knowledge arises from study, is objective, and is the kind of knowledge that can be learned from a book. There is a vast difference between book learning and experience-based learning.

The logic that characterizes tacit knowledge is analog logic, while the logic of explicit knowledge is deductive. Although Nonaka and Takeuchi do not mention it, tacit knowledge follows the patterns of oral culture, whereas explicit knowledge follows the patterns of literate culture. This is a distinction made long ago by McLuhan, who used the categories of percept and concept rather than tacit and explicit knowledge. Within the framework of McLuhan's thinking, tacit knowledge is associated with right-brain patterns of thought while explicit knowledge is associated with left-brain patterns of thought.

In the knowledge era the explicit forms of knowledge that dominated literary culture and the tacit forms of knowledge that characterized oral culture are forming a new amalgam. The Internet will play an important role in this transformation because of the way it encourages the exchange of personal information, or tacit knowledge. It is important to keep this in mind when planning an intranet or Internet environment. A certain amount of personal information, especially if it is related to one's work, helps create a climate that encourages the exchange of tacit knowledge. The knowledge era will be an eclectic age in which all forms of knowledge — tacit and explicit; subjective and objective; oral, multisensorial, literary, numerical, scientific, and cybernetic — are valid and have a role to play in understanding our social, economic, and cultural worlds.

Knowledge has come around full circle to re-embrace the concrete, after going through a steady chain of ever-increasing abstractions as language evolved from speech to writing and math to science to computing. The information age was the high-water mark of explicit knowledge. Computers provided the medium for the most extravagant display of explicit knowledge, but they also created an environment for the dialogue and the sharing of all knowledge, explicit and tacit, through the connectivity of the Internet. It is fascinating that McLuhan, long before the Internet came into existence, understood that the new electrically configured knowledge would involve individuals in a "total social process."

Charles Savage, one of the pioneers of the concept of knowledge networking, has added a very important dimension to our understanding of knowledge structures and their relationship to social institutions and dynamics, by introducing the verb "knowledging," to remind us that knowledge is more than just content, as in a body of knowledge, but rather the end product of the active process of knowledging. "Knowledge is not something that is possessed like a commodity . . . Known facts can be possessed, but the human process of 'knowledging' is a much richer and more dynamic phenomenon . . . 'Knowledging' is more than just 'knowing,' because it suggests an active and continual process of interrelating patterns." (Savage 1996, 121) Savage, like McLuhan, understands that a "total social process" is required for the sharing and exchange of knowledge.

Karl Erik Sveiby (1997), another knowledge management pioneer, who developed the notion of knowledge capital (also known as intellectual capital), has developed an interesting understanding of the relationship between wisdom and knowledge, on the one hand, and information and data on the other. Sveiby's approach is also based on the dichotomy between tacit and explicit knowledge. For Sveiby, wisdom and knowledge are tacit, and difficult to represent and transfer. They can only be achieved through experience. Information and data, on the other hand, are explicit, easily represented, stored, transferred, processed, and reprocessed.

It takes wisdom and knowledge to write a book or an article: the wisdom to choose a subject and an audience that are aligned, and the knowledge to order the information gathered and to write intelligently with insight about the subject. In the end, however, what is created, the book itself, is nothing more than information and an assemblage of data. Readers, by virtue of their tacit knowledge and experiences, can use that information and data to create their own knowledge, and perhaps add to their store of wisdom, but only as a result of the interaction of their knowledge and wisdom with the data and information contained in the book or article. This insight is at the root of Marshall McLuhan's famous one liner: "the user is the content."

8

The Student Is the Curriculum and the Process Is the

Content: Computers, the Internet, and the New Curriculum

This chapter will attempt to answer the following questions:

- How can computers and the Internet be used to achieve present educational goals?
- How must present educational goals change to accommodate changes in the nature of work due to the widespread use of computers and the Net?
- How can the school system be restructured so that the goals of education and the vocational needs of society in the Internet age or the knowledge era can be better matched?
- How can computing be harnessed to inculcate students with the desire for lifelong learning?

Computers: Cognition, Communication, and Education

The ostensible objective of an education system is the transmission of a body of knowledge, but equally important is the transmission of the methodologies and techniques for organizing information. A body of knowledge or explicit knowledge minus the understanding of the processes and methodologies that went into creating that body of knowledge is nothing more than information. Information without knowledge, as we have already pointed out, has little or no value. The heart of an education program is not the information with which one becomes acquainted, but the tacit knowledge in the form of communication, information-processing, problem-solving, and cognitive skills that are developed or acquired through understanding and using a body of knowledge. The histories of education, cognition, information processing, communication, and language are therefore intimately connected and must be studied together. "Language and human intelligence can be thought of as two aspects of the same evolutionary development" (Hickerson 1980, 13).

In fact, information-processing skills are basically equivalent to cognitive skills, as the following definition by a cognitive scientist suggests: "Cognitive psychology attempts to understand the nature of human intelligence and how people think . . . Cognitive psychology is dominated by the information-processing approach, which analyzes cognitive processes into a sequence of ordered stages" (J.R. Anderson 1980, 3).

In order to study the role of computers in education, it will be necessary to study the three domains of communication, education, and cognition (or information processing), and examine how these three domains relate to one another and how they are affected by technology. The boundaries between the three domains have begun to blur, partly because of the integrative power of computers and the Internet. Perhaps, then, cognition, communication, and education are not the three separate categories that the analytical objectivist approach of Western science and social science, with their bias toward classification, would have us believe. Perhaps cognition, communication, and education are simply different projections or facets of the same phenomenon — human thought.

It is difficult, for example, to imagine one of these activities being carried out without the involvement of the other two. Indeed, none of them can be pursued independent of the other two. Cognitive activities require both the communication of information and the skills acquired through education. The linguists Edward Sapir (1921) and Benjamin Lee Whorf (1964) argue convincingly that human thought or cognition sprang from humankind's unique capacity for speech or language. As children begin to develop mentally, many of their cognitive processes are learned within the context of their social and information environment. Hence, cognition is a product of both communication and education.

Communication, on the other hand, requires both the development of cognitive skills and participation in an educational process. Language, too, is learned from the child's interactions with his or her parents and family. The development and deployment of a child's communication skills, however, also depends on his or her cognitive skills. Communication is, therefore, also a product of the domains of education and cognition.

Finally, education is not possible without both the communication of ideas and the deployment of cognitive skills. My argument that each domain depends on the other two comes full circle with this last observation.

The relationship between cognition, communication, and education is impossible to formulate in a reductionist manner because the interactions between these three domains are so strong and interwoven. I believe these processes arise together, each creating the conditions for the others' development.

Any two of the domains in this model can function as inputs into the mind to create or generate the third. It is impossible to have one without the other two, but none of the three domains is primary. As one considers different intellectual activities, domains that had functioned as inputs can change roles to work as the output, and vice versa. If the activity is learning, the inputs are cognition and communication, and the output is education. If the activity is sharing ideas, the inputs are cognition and education, and the output is communication. If the activity is thinking, the inputs are education and communication (or language), and the output is cognition.

The link between cognition, communication, and education is related to the fact that language has both a communications and an informatics aspect. The Russian psychologist L.S. Vygotsky (1962, 6–7) formulated a similar relationship between language and thought that applies with equal validity to the relationship between communication, cognition, and education:

> The primary function of speech is communication, social intercourse. When language was studied through analysis into elements, this function, too, was dissociated from the intellectual function of speech. The two were treated as though they were separate, if parallel, functions, without attention to their structural and developmental interrelation. Yet word meaning is a unit of both these functions of speech . . . The conception of word meaning as a unit of both generalizing thought and social interchange is of incalculable value for the study of thought and language.

Vygotsky is criticizing the separation of the communication or social-intercourse aspect of language from the intellectual or cognitive function, and pointing out how this separation limits our understanding of the relationship between thought and language (or, as I have formulated the problem, the relationships among communication, cognition, and education).

I believe the connection between language and abstract thought is even closer than suggested by Vygotsky. In Chapter 3, in the section entitled "The Evolution of the Six Modes of Language," I proposed that before verbal language all mental processes were percept based, and that with verbal language humans were able to conceptualize. The first concepts that we created were the words invented as strange attractors of our percepts. This model suggests that abstract thinking and language cannot be separated. Words are the medium of abstract thought and the use of language is the beginning of cognition. Each language that is mastered expands the cognitive universe of the learner.

Technology and the Transformation of Education

An expansion of the notion that language is simply a medium for communication to include its informatic abilities to store, retrieve, organize, and process information is essential for education and curriculum planning. Contemporary education does not limit itself to the teaching of the three Rs. It attempts to develop the student's reasoning and problem-solving capabilities; thus, the information-processing aspects of language are critical for a well-rounded education. In fact, education can be defined as the learning of the use of the six languages of speech, writing, mathematics, science, computing, and the Internet. The emphasis in this approach is not learning facts, but using these languages to study one's world and to organize and communicate information about that world. This is why computing, with its emphasis on the information-processing aspects of language, has the potential to revitalize and revolutionize education.

Our model of language as communication and informatics can be extended to describe the education system. Schools have both a communications and an informatics side. Teachers and students communicate with one another, while a significant part of the curriculum teaches various forms of information processing.

Historically, each time a new medium of communication or method of information processing has been introduced, education has been directly affected and, in many instances, radically transformed. For example, the idea of formal education housed in an institution devoted to learning — a school — is a direct result of the invention of writing and the desire to train children to be literate. The advent of writing and numerical notations signaled the end of an education system based on the oral tradition and the apprenticeship mode of vocational training. Education was a natural part of everyday life in preliterate societies and was integrated with the normal activities of survival such as home-making, toolmaking, hunting, and food gathering. The new system of education that emerged with writing, however, was based on formal schooling and the instruction of a specialist, the teacher, whose sole mandate was to provide formal instruction. The education of children was separated from the other activities of society and housed in a new institution, the school.

As discussed, although the microcomputer has had hardly more than fifteen years to influence education, its impact has been significant. This technology has enjoyed great success in helping children with learning disabilities — particularly those who are dyslexic — to overcome their handicaps. Its role in the general classroom is extremely promising and still emerging. It is already clear, however, that the capacity of the microcomputer and the Internet to motivate students, encourage peer teaching, individualize instruction, and increase user interactivity holds the potential to revitalize education at both the grass-roots level of the individual student, as well as at the curricular level throughout the whole system.

Formulating a Curriculum of Study for the Internet Age

There are two areas where change will be required in the education system: the actual content of the curriculum of study and the way in which that curriculum is presented, or the way in which the curriculum will be addressed by students. The concept of the delivery or the presentation of a curriculum evokes the attitude and style of education characteristic of the industrial age, in which schools operated more or less like factories. The typical schools of the industrial era have been likened to sausage factories, where students were stuffed with knowledge and information. Each student was stuffed with exactly the same material so as to produce a uniform product. Today we recognize the shortcomings of such an approach and try to individualize education as much as possible so that each student may realize his or her own unique potential.

Educational psychologists have discovered that children (and adults) learn better when they have an opportunity to choose what they study and when they study it. According to the developmental psychology of Jean Piaget,

> Learning is an active process whereby the child constructs understanding of events in his or her environment by a process of assimilation and accommodation. The child assimilates new experiences into existing cognitive structures for understanding the world. These structures, in turn, accommodate themselves to the new experience and thereby slowly mature into the complex reasoning abilities that characterize formal adult thought.
>
> (KURLAND AND KURLAND 1987, 322)

The child must exercise some element of control over what is studied and when. Not that students should have total freedom of choice; if that were the case, there would be no need for schools.

Libraries and curricular-resource centers and the occasional visits of a tutor would satisfy all of the student's educational needs. The sixties style of education, or the human potential model, in which students are free to realize their potential by studying only what interests them, has serious shortcomings. While the student's participation in the selection of the topics or subjects of study is essential for the success of any educational endeavor, education requires structure and the guidance and devotion of a caring adult. A balance must be struck between students pursuing their own educational interests and goals and educators providing guidance and structure.

There is every reason to believe that students can pursue the goal of self-actualization while preparing themselves to live and work in society. The style of education and the specific curricular goals advocated here strike a balance between the needs of the individual and those of society.

Curriculum by Tradition

Tradition plays a dominant role in the organization of learning in our education system. There is no universally agreed-upon theoretical basis for the present curriculum of our primary and secondary schools. To some degree, today's curriculum is nothing more than a historical accident, with little or no rationale for its organization. Moreover, it is not clear that contemporary teaching practices introduce skills at the most appropriate time in the development of pupils.

There are isolated attempts to incorporate some of the insights of educational psychology into curriculum design. The insights of cognitive science tend to dominate, but elements of behaviorism still linger. The educators who have the responsibility of determining curriculum cannot be blamed for not making greater use of the insights of educational psychology. The field is in flux, with the answers to many vital questions violently debated by diverse schools of thought. In addition, educational psychology is subject to fads and bandwagon effects, making educational planning difficult, if not outright impossible. The lack of consensus among the experts generates just enough confusion and uncertainty among educational planners, curriculum designers, and school board trustees to neutralize the contribution that educational psychology could make.

A New Approach to Curriculum Planning

Rather than attempting to plan curriculum on the basis of the insights of educational psychology with all of its uncertainty, I propose a much simpler approach based on an understanding of the nature of language, communications, and informatics. Instead of trying to fathom the mysteries of the cognitive domain, I suggest that we allow the historical development of language, communications, and informatics to guide our philosophy of education. The natural evolution of language provides a model of how and when to introduce concepts and techniques in communications and informatics. This approach is pragmatic and phenomenological rather than theoretical.

The basic assumption of this philosophy of education is that the historical course in which cognitive processes developed within the human psyche can be successfully repeated in the education of the individual. The basic idea can be expressed in terms of the concept used in the field of biological evolution that "ontogeny recapitulates philogeny."

In essence, I propose that formal education focus on the integrated development of the communications and informatics skills involved in the use of the six verbal languages of speech, writing, mathematics, science, computing, and the Internet. Conceptual tools or cognitive skills that arise from the use of the earlier forms of language will prove useful in mastering the later modes of language. Thus, the tools of analysis and classification acquired through learning writing and mathematics can be used in the study of science and computing. The primary focus of education becomes the development of the generic cognitive skills associated with the six modes of language, whereas the mastery of any particular body of knowledge becomes a secondary goal.

Examples of generic cognitive skills include analysis, abstraction, classification, matching, measuring, coding, decoding, metaphor creation, model making, and synthesis. By adopting an integrated approach to education, students will not only acquire the communication and information-processing skills associated with the six languages, but they will also develop the problem-solving skills and creativity necessary to apply these skills to new situations.

This model of education is based on the notion that all modes of language must be mastered and incorporated into an individual's repertoire of skills. Some would argue that, with the exception of those who want to become computer scientists or office workers, learning to use computers and the Internet is a frill for most students. They would argue that the use of computers and the Internet is a luxury that most schools and jurisdictions cannot afford. I believe the opposite is true: Computing and familiarity with the Net are just as essential to a complete education today as was learning how to read and write after the advent of literacy.

Including Computer Technology in Today's Curriculum

At each stage in the evolutionary chain of language the information-processing capacity of human language has increased. Each new development was motivated by the need for a higher level of informatics to combat the information overload that arose from the previous mode of language. Therefore, as each new form of language emerges, it is inevitably adopted by the information elite of society. Not only does the new form of language help alleviate the information overload of the previous mode, it also creates new applications of language and thus eventually gives rise to new forms of information overload.

Computers, which were developed by science and business to cope with the enormous amount of data generated by the success of industrial society, have given rise to a new information explosion in the post-industrial era. The increased linkages that computer networks made possible gave rise to the need for the instantaneous and universal access to information and other computer users, which inspired the development of the Internet. Once a luxury or a convenience, computers and the Net are now a necessity. They are here to stay and their use will only increase with time.

Once a new form of language emerges, we can never permanently revert to the information environment that existed before its advent. There are examples in history of cultures that fell into a period of temporary intellectual regression and reduced the use of an advanced form of language they had previously adopted. The use of writing in Europe ceased almost entirely with the fall of the Roman empire. Only in the monasteries were book learning and the art of writing preserved in Europe. Periods of cultural decline, however, are generally followed by an intellectual restoration or renaissance in which the earlier developments are recovered and used even more vigorously than before.

Each time a new form of language was invented, it quickly established itself as the dominant mode of communication and informatics in certain domains of intellectual activity. The dominance of the new mode of language does not obsolesce the earlier forms of language, however. First, the new mode of language automatically incorporates or subsumes all of the earlier modes of language, hence preserving them. Secondly, the new mode cannot successfully compete with the older forms of language in every possible application. The complexity that the new language must possess in order to provide greater informatics power makes its use awkward in certain circumstances. The older modes of language are therefore essential to human interaction. They continue to evolve, but do so under the influence of the later forms of language.

People did not stop talking to one another after the advent of writing. But the nature of the spoken word did change as a result. A comparison of the vocabulary of Homer, representing the oral tradition, with that of the post-literate period reveals that more abstract terms crept into the ancient Greek language with the advent of writing. Today, although computers pervade almost all aspects of communication and information processing, we do not use a computer to write out a shopping list or to perform a simple mathematical calculation like balancing our checkbooks. Computers and the Net, however, have changed the way we prepare written documents, and even the way we communicate informally with colleagues using e-mail.

The Six Languages: A Core Curriculum

Because each mode of language has its own set of unique domains of applicability and areas of practicality, a well-educated person needs to be adept in all six to realize their full potential. A lack of knowledge of any of the six modes will restrict an individual's sphere of activity. The degree to which any given student will want to study each of the six modes will depend on his or her needs, interests, and aptitudes.

Mastery of the rudiments of all six is certainly a prerequisite for serious study in most areas of learning.

Learning to speak is not a part of formal schooling; virtually all children learn this skill from their parents or guardians before they reach school age. Refining the skills of oral language, or learning the art of rhetoric, however, is an appropriate part of the school curriculum. Therefore, the main elements that provide the framework for formulating a well-rounded and comprehensive program or curriculum of formal education are:

1. Rhetoric — the art of public speaking.
2. Literacy — the ability to read and write.
3. Numeracy — the ability to use abstract numbers and perform simple mathematical operations.
4. Science literacy — the ability to use scientific principles to organize knowledge and interpret information.
5. Computer literacy — the ability to use computers to communicate, store, access, organize, and process information.
6. Internet navigation and communication skills — the ability to surf the Net to access information, use the Net's various communication channels, and create a rudimentary Web site.

An education does not consist merely of data handling and information-processing skills. While developing the analytic skills of its students must be a primary concern of an education system, students must also be taught to put these skills to use and to select appropriate goals and values to which they can apply their skills. A school system cannot be content just to create technocrats who can operate the machinery of industry and society.

The core curriculum I have proposed leaves out a number of activities and studies that should be included in a total educational environment; for example, health and physical education, life and coping skills, values education, social skills, and exposure to and participation in the nonverbal languages and arts such as music, dance, painting, sculpture, photography, video, handicrafts, and so on. I fully recognize that these activities are essential to a comprehensive education and hence must complement any core curriculum that focuses on the six verbal languages. I will not deal with the nonverbal languages and the other topics in this study, however, as my focus is on language.

Still, it must be noted that these areas in the student's development are extremely important and should not be considered add-ons or mere cultural enrichments; rather, they must be integrated into the core curriculum that I am proposing. Educational reform must go beyond converting our schools from factories that produced skilled workers for the industrial age to one that produces them for the Internet age. We should strive to turn out well-rounded students who are both technically skilled and socially and culturally aware.

Process over Content

The structural interrelatedness of the six modes of languages identified in Chapters 3 and 4 suggests a design for the core curriculum for children. The actual content of the curriculum, that is, the domain of knowledge or body of information that is studied, is not necessarily significant. But making sure that students learn the techniques of informatics and communication associated with the six languages is essential. Reading can be learned from schoolbooks, or just as easily from the instructions to a board game or a computer program. Writing can be learned through personal expression, or by storytelling or reporting on a project. The principles of science can be learned by studying animal behavior, plant morphology, geological formations, or the phenomena of electricity and magnetism. Computing skills can be acquired through word processing, database management, or numerical analysis. Internet skills can be developed by searching the Web for information needed for a essay or a research project, and by sending and receiving e-mail or building a Web site.

The choice of topics to be studied should be based on the interests and needs of the pupils and the community in which they live. Obvious choices for topics are the most conspicuous features of the students' environment and the most dominant elements of their culture, such as national and local history and geography. They should also include local industries, such as agriculture in a rural community, the ocean in a maritime community, forests in a lumber community, or manufacturing and commerce in an urban setting.

The timing for the introduction of various aspects of the six modes of language should be the product of careful study and analysis within the domain of cognitive science. Until cognitive science can provide more direction, certain common-sense rules of thumb should be followed. Each new aspect of the six modes of language should be introduced at an appropriate time in the education and development of a youngster. The historical development of language can guide curriculum developers. A pupil need not, however, acquire a sophisticated grasp of one mode of language before being introduced to another. In fact, the use of one mode can help in mastering another. Cross-pollinating one language with another will integrate and align the student's use of language. For example, an interest in science or computing can be used to teach reading and writing skills; the need to solve a mathematical problem can become the impetus to learn more about computing.

As a physics professor, I have found that the inability of my students to use their reading and mathematics skills in a new environment acts as a great impediment to their ability to solve physics problems. Their reading and math skills are superficial, and are not integrated with any subjects but their English and math courses, respectively. Because their teachers introduced these skills within narrow parameters, applying these skills within a new context is difficult.

Integrating and aligning the use of the six languages will, in fact, help ensure the success of the curricular approach I propose. The computer provides a natural medium for the integration and alignment of the six languages because it incorporates elements of all of them. It is also a natural medium for integration because of the ease with which it can store and manipulate information.

Using all six modes of language to study a particular topic is a natural way to achieve integration. It also corresponds to the way problems are addressed outside of the classroom in the "real world." Reading, writing, spelling, mathematics, science, computing, and the Internet should not be regarded as subjects to be taught; rather, they should be treated as tools to be mastered, so that they can be used to learn about subjects that interest the students. These tools become the windows through which students can study the world in which they live and the media through which they communicate their knowledge to others.

According to educator John Olson, this "tool" approach to the use of computers and the Net in the general curriculum also has the effect of integrating two important streams of the educational process: vocational training and general education. "Computers can contribute both to educational and social goals. The study of them can introduce students to the 'world' of computing, increase computer awareness and develop computer literacy — all of which are aimed at coping in the working world. Computers can aid the teaching of existing subjects, or they can introduce students to whole new ways of learning. Thus we have two important dimensions to keep in mind; vocational-educational and school subjects teaching aid" (Olson 1988, 2).

I prefer to think of these two dimensions in terms of the vocational training and cognitive development of students. There are some aspects of learning about computers that are primarily vocational, but that will also contribute to the student's cognitive development. These include learning how to program, design, and repair a computer. These specific toolmaking skills, as opposed to tool-using skills, will prepare those students who wish to make a career out of computers.

The tool-use skills of the computer and the Internet also provide students with general vocational preparation, as well as with an excellent base for general learning and cognitive development. Given that so many more information transactions will take place through the medium of the computer and the Net, the dichotomy between the vocational and educational uses of word processing, spreadsheeting, or databasing is moot. Like the skills of reading and writing, the skills of using computers and the Net are not more vocational than educational, or vice versa. They are both vocational and educational. Many aspects of education and many areas of employment are denied to anyone who does not learn to read and write. The same is true for computing, and will be even more so in the future. The richness of education and the possibilities for work will be limited for those who do not learn computing. Even today, many workers are being displaced because they cannot use a computer. Thus the integration of computing into curriculum, particularly the use of computers in the tool mode, will serve both an educational and a vocational function for today's students, who will live their lives entirely in the Internet age.

The real lesson to be learned is the art of uncovering or discovering new knowledge, the art of organizing that knowledge and applying it to practical situations in life, and, finally, the art of creating new knowledge or conducting original research. This proposition does not actually differ that much from present-day views on the curriculum, but it represents a change of emphasis and a reversal of the roles played by content and technique. This approach attempts to put the power in the hands of students, so that they control the technology rather than the technology controlling them (Labbett 1988, 91).

The intended result — for students to become more experienced in using information technology to pursue their own educational goals — hinges on the successful design, management, and assessment of a classroom curriculum where teachers and their pupils can jointly develop their understanding of the world (Labbett 1988, 90).

My approach to curriculum planning can be expressed in terms of two of McLuhan's aphorisms: "The medium is the message" and "The user is the content." The "content" — or the various topics to be studied — hones the skills needed to use the "media" of the six languages. Rather than learning the three Rs in order to study other subjects, other subjects are studied in order to master the three Rs, science, computing, and Internet use. As "the user is the content," the subjects selected to be studied should be those that interest the student.

Tutor, Tool, and Tutee Modes of Computing

In a cogent formulation of the role of computers in education, educator R.P. Taylor (1980) identified the tutor, tool, and tutee modes of computer usage. In the tutor mode, the computer is used as an automatic teacher, instructing the user by delivering information, requesting responses, and matching the student's response to what might be considered the correct answer. This mode is sometimes referred to as CAI, computer-assisted instruction, or CAL, computer-assisted learning. Simulations in which natural phenomena or social interactions are modeled represent another example of the tutor mode.

In the tool mode, the operator uses the computer to achieve some information-processing or communication task. Examples include word processing, spreadsheets, database management, or graphics. In the third mode, the tutee mode, the user is teaching the computer or instructing it what to do. Programming the computer is an example of the tutee mode.

The tutor, tool, and tutee modes of computer applications in education each have merit. Educators must address the question, given the limited resources available, of what the most powerful and practical uses of computers are. I believe that the tool mode is the most effective way to use computers in education because it allows the user to master the information-processing and communication skills associated with the language of computing.

Using a computer in the tutee mode contributes to the cognitive development of the user. Programming a computer is more difficult than using a computer in the tool mode and is also more specialized. It is the kind of skill a computer scientist will need to master, but it is less useful to the ordinary end user. Some exposure to programming or related activities like LOGO is advisable, however, so that a student has a better understanding of computers and how they work.

Using a computer in the tutor mode does not contribute to the cognitive development of the user in the way the tool and tutee modes do. In addition to being of limited value, it is not clear that CAI has any advantages over traditional methods of drill and practice. "Not all studies of the effectiveness of CAI have shown consistent positive results . . . The researchers found no strong evidence that PLATO [a CAI program] either helped or hindered students . . . The studies have also consistently pointed out that the cost-effectiveness of CAI programs — one of CAI's major selling points — has clearly not been demonstrated" (Hickerson 1980, 337, 343).

CAI reduces users to passive consumers of information that is being automatically presented to them by the computer. Benefits can be derived from learning the content of material presented in the tutorial mode, but the student does not derive any additional benefits from the process of using the computer this way. The tutorial mode can be likened to television use, which, while informative, does not develop the skills of its viewers. A concern has also been raised about the overexposure of youngsters to video images (Sloan 1985, 7–8). The use of the computer in the tutor mode must have demonstrable educational benefits to justify its use. It would be hard to support the use of CAI where it was the sole or primary use of the computer.

The tutor mode also includes simulations in which a software program models a natural phenomenon, a complex piece of technology, a social interaction, or a social institution. By exploring the model, the user begins to learn about the phenomenon that has been modeled or simulated. Simulations can have a negative effect if they are used to replace experiences that can be had in the real world. On the other hand, they can be quite useful if they can show students how a system they could not otherwise access, such as a nuclear reactor, operates.

For a simulation to be used as an effective educational tool, it must be integrated into the student's overall educational program. Students and their teachers should discuss how well the simulation models reality. Field or laboratory comparisons with the processes being modeled should be attempted wherever possible. The skills developed through the software program and the topic of the simulation should be studied using other educational media such as texts and discussions. In short, simulations should be chosen for use if they reinforce other classroom activities and can be integrated into the curriculum effectively.

Of the three modes of computer usage in education, I most strongly advocate the tool mode, because it promotes cognitive development, is easy to learn, and has many practical applications. The use of computers to organize information derived from the direct observation of real phenomena provides the healthy mix of using a powerful analytic tool and, at the same time, dealing directly with nature. I propose that students use computers as tools, just as they are used in the real world of work, whether in the field of art, science, administration, commerce, or engineering. The computer can be used as a tool to capture the fleeting images of the direct observations of the real world so that the data may be examined, reexamined, and interiorized.

In summary, then, all applications of computers have merit. The challenge to educators is to choose the appropriate mix of uses that best meets the educational needs of the students for which the educational program is being designed. It is recommended that the tool mode be given the greatest priority because the tool use of computers (1) promotes cognitive development; (2) reinforces information-processing and communication skills; and (3) provides an open-ended environment for imagination, exploration, and discovery. According to one study, word processing . . . is already a sophisticated tool for the production of reports, essays, poems, books, etc. . . . . It offers an open-ended facility for the imagination. It aids revision through a variety of techniques and presents the finished product in a polished form . . . The product can then be stored, say on a database, or transmitted to others on a computer network. Similarly spread sheets offer facilities for computational analysis . . . Other open-ended tools offer the facility to produce diagrams and graphs . . . The computer offers, therefore, the chance to make real products for an audience, an audience not just limited to classmates or teachers.

(KURLAND AND KURLAND 1987, 16–17)

The microcomputer opens new worlds of expression to students and helps them develop a positive attitude to writing and, consequently, to learning in general. Because of its ability to simplify writing and facilitate editing, word processing has had a positive effect on the writing skills of students of all ages, from the earliest grades of primary school to university graduate schools. Word processing appears to have the potential to arrest or even reverse the general decline in literacy and writing skills that McLuhan associated with television and its influence. The widespread use of microcomputers for word processing should result in a renewal of our literary roots and the restoration of the pre-television level of reading.

For developing mathematical skills, spreadsheet programs are invaluable. One of the chief advantages of spreadsheets is that they allow users to visualize the information or data that they wish to understand. New relationships emerge once data are presented visually. Another benefit of the spreadsheet routine is that it allows users to easily make calculations involving the data entered into the spreadsheet. This capability facilitates inferring, predicting, and hypothesizing. The spreadsheet also places the abstract data collected by a student or a worker within a concrete context. These capabilities are particularly valuable in that they provide both a qualitative and quantitative dimension to the analysis and display of data.

Another important tool that should be integrated into the curriculum is a relational database. A well-organized database program can help students see relationships among the data they have collected that they might not ordinarily have seen. The database can help the student discover commonalities, similarities, or differences between the elements of the database. They are in a better position to analyze the various relationships that might exist as well as note trends. They might even be in a position to formulate and test hypotheses. "The capability of organizing and rearranging information in a multitude of formats offers the user the opportunity to view the data in a variety of ways. Using databases to perform queries allows relevant bits of information to become visible, while leaving the database unchanged" (Strickland and Hoffer 1989, 20). In summary, the construction of either a database or a spreadsheet is an ideal activity for the student to learn the skills of classifying, seriating, inferring, predicting, hypothesizing, and controlling variables.

For those readers interested in a more detailed discussion of the use of computers for primary and secondary schools, I have posted an Appendix on the Internet for you to download and use in any way you wish. You will find there a more extended discussion of the use of computers in the tool mode, with special emphasis on their application to teaching the natural and social sciences. The URL is http://gutenberg.com/6thlanguage/appendix.

Computers: A New Source of Alternatives in Education

One of the solid achievements of the period of intense social change during the 1960s was the emergence of alternative schools. The uniformity of traditional schools, which were organized to conform with the values of the industrial age, proved to be oppressive for many children and adults. Some children who were labeled learning-disabled within the context of traditional schools thrived in alternative educational environments. Alternative educational formats, which were initially resisted by traditionalists, are now part and parcel of the services offered by most school boards to serve the total educational needs of their community.

As already noted, microcomputers and the Internet will be a source of new alternatives in education. They provide an alternative to traditional textbooks as deliverers of information that can be easily integrated. The ease with which information can flow between computers, or between software programs on the same computer, or between different files within the same program, facilitates the integration of a variety of subjects or topics. The Internet in particular puts the student in touch with the entire world and a vast array of resources.

The computer also provides children with an alternative channel for inputting and outputting textual information. The work of special-education teachers with learning-disabled children and computers has proven beyond a doubt that computers offer many children who have difficulties dealing with print the opportunity to develop a functional level of literacy. Many children who have been labeled learning-disabled are not disabled if an appropriate mix of media is used to facilitate the development of their literacy. The microcomputer seems to be an important component of that mix.

Other teachers working with populations of "normal" students systematically report that computer usage leads to a greater competency with literacy skills compared with traditional methods. A similar increase in mathematical skills has also been reported. Many cases can be cited where the use of computers has not led to any significant educational or cognitive gains, but this is most often due to the misuse of the technology by the teacher. There is little doubt that computers and the Net offer an important alternative to the traditional approaches of teaching the three Rs.

Although it does not work for everyone, the computer is a very powerful learning tool for many children and adults. There are some people for whom the traditional methods of textbooks, pencil, and paper may be more suitable. And for still others, neither the traditional approach nor the use of computers is the answer. For these individuals, the educational techniques of the oral tradition may be the most effective. And for still others, the medium that taps their potential may be one of the nonverbal media of expression and communication, such as music, dance, painting, or theater.

There is more than one way to become literate. I know of a student labeled learning-disabled by the system, and made to feel like a failure, who found his own path to literacy through music. This individual, who dropped out of grade nine, first became a rock-and-roll drummer and later a symphonic percussionist. He eventually played with two of North America's leading youth orchestras, began a career as a composer, and graduated from a prestigious music school. He not only achieved a university level of literacy, but earned an A average because of his passion for his musical art form. In addition to his achievements in musical performance and symphonic and film-score composition, he went on to master computer programming in order to compose and record his music, became an avid reader of philosophy to better understand his nonverbal art form, and began writing poetry, a form of verbal expression closely related to his interest in music. He is now pursuing a very successful career in Hollywood, composing music for movies, TV, and video games, and is one of the tops in his field. If he had remained in the education system and not dropped out when he did, he might have been totally destroyed as a musician and as a person. The important lesson to be learned from this story is that an interest in one medium of expression can lead to proficiency in a number of other media.

Not only are microcomputers in their present form an alternative medium of expression and education, they also hold the potential for becoming the source of many additional new modes of communication and education. By integrating graphics and/or music with textual materials through multimedia and hypermedia packages, microcomputers can integrate the educational experiences associated with verbal and nonverbal languages.

The World Wide Web has spawned many new tools that combine text and graphics in a dynamic way. Through simple animation, the relationship between abstract quantities can be demonstrated. Through its combination of text and graphics, the Internet can perhaps be used to explore the relationship of music to mathematics and physics, or the relationship of the fine arts to geometry and optics.

The individualized learning that microcomputers promote has been demonstrated as another important educational alternative. Clearly, the uniformity of the mass education system that served the needs of the industrial age no longer serves the needs of the knowledge era. While individualized instruction is required, an education for all sectors of our society must be provided, and education must be made a life-long activity. In the context of the increased demand on the education system due to increasing population and the desire for lifelong education, the only way individualized education can still be provided is to make wholesale use of computers and integrate them with classroom instruction, so that the important social exchanges of peer interaction and teaching can be maintained.

Defining Computer Literacy

In order to set goals for computer education, computer literacy must be defined. Literacy itself, the ability to read and write, is a rather straightforward skill, easy to define precisely: "That person is literate who, in a language he speaks, can read with understanding anything he would have understood if it had been spoken to him; and can write, so that it can be read, anything that he can say" (Gudschinsky 1976, 3). It is not easy to provide a definition of computer literacy with the same precision, nor may it be desirable to do so. There are many different aspects of using a computer, which require various degrees of skills and aptitudes, from the simple accessing of information to programming a computer to automate a complex information-processing task. Nevertheless, some notion of what is meant by computer literacy is essential; I will therefore attempt to define it in terms of easily describable behavioral outcomes.

First, computer literacy is not a discrete state like being alive or pregnant, in which case either you are or you aren't. It is, in fact, possible to be a "little" computer-literate. Computers are ubiquitous and people are more computer-literate than they think. Anyone who has used an automatic elevator has essentially operated a user-friendly menu-driven computer with a very simple keyboard.

Computer literacy is best defined in stages, so that it is not a question of whether or not one is computer-literate, but to what degree one is. One does not need to know every aspect of computing to be computer-literate, just as familiarity with all aspects of literature is not required to make one literate or total knowledge of mathematics to make one numerate. So, it is possible to be computer-literate without being able to program or repair a computer, just as one can be a driver without being able to design or repair a car. The stages of computer literacy can be ranked along a continuum. They include the ability to:

1. turn on the computer
2. access a program from the hard drive
3. load an application onto the hard drive from disks
4. respond to a menu-driven software package
5. access information from the computer
6. input information into the computer
7. process information using the computer
8. word process with a computer
9. do spreadsheet analyses using the computer
10. operate a database using the computer
11. create a software routine using an authoring language
12. program a computer to input, access, and process information
13. develop a programming language for the computer
14. develop an operating system for the computer
15. design a computer
16. judge when the use of a computer is appropriate
17. understand the issues concerning the deployment of
    computers in different environments in society

The skills that constitute this definition of computer literacy have been ordered more or less with increasing complexity, except for the last two points. My definition of literacy does not differ greatly from that of Joel Schwartz (1989, 161):

Computer literacy takes shape as a group of behavioral skills which permits individuals to utilize computers within the parameters of societal expectations. I suggest that any computer literacy program should teach students the functions, applications, and implications of computer usage. Computer literacy training should, at minimum, promote the following outcomes: 1. promote a basic understanding of how a computer works; 2. provide basic skills for interacting with a computer to access stored information; 3. familiarize students with various applications of available software programs; 4. provide basic skills for using computers to run available software; and 5. develop awareness of the computer's impact on society.

Computer literacy as I have defined it does not necessarily entail the ability to program or design a computer, just as literacy does not necessarily entail the ability to invent an alphabet or some other new writing system. Schwartz (1989, 161) provides two reasons that programming need not be included in a basic computer literacy program. "First, specific programming skills can be viewed as vocational training as opposed to literacy training. Secondly, research findings on the effects of computer programming indicate very little lateral transfer to a student's analytic or problem solving skills."

A thorough definition of computer literacy, on the other hand, is not limited to the skills of operating or programming a computer; it includes an understanding of the social implications of the new technology. Information technology is becoming more and more pervasive in modern society. It is "unlike any previous tool. The material it shapes is the most fundamental to human action: information . . . Its impact cannot be studied in isolation from the social context . . . Education must therefore look beyond the walls of its schools and examine the social context itself and see how and in whose interests information technology is already being used, and promoted" (Schostak 1988c, 2). In order to study the social context of the use of computers, students will also have to examine the nature of computers and develop a rudimentary understanding of what they can and cannot do with the technology. Some of the issues surrounding artificial intelligence must be addressed as well.

Innis and McLuhan were pioneers in examining the myriad social, political, cultural, and economic effects of writing and other forms of communication. True literacy involves an understanding of, or at least a sensitivity to, these effects. Similarly, numeracy and science literacy entail an understanding of the social, political, cultural, and economic effects of mathematics and science. Computer literacy must not be limited to an understanding of the social context of information technology alone. It must also include an understanding of the social context of the other modes of language.

Defining Internet Literacy

Just as a definition of computer literacy was required to establish educational goals, one is also needed for Internet literacy. As with computer literacy, there are many different aspects to Internet literacy. I will, therefore, define it as with computer literacy, in terms of a spectrum of easily describable behavioral outcomes. One becomes Internet literate in stages that can be ranked along a continuum. More or less in order of increasing complexity, they include the ability to:

1. access the World Wide Web and/or e-mail from a work station
2. read e-mail messages and save them to a folder, respond to e-mail messages, compose e-mail messages, and send e-mail messages by properly addressing them
3. participate in a listserv by receiving and responding to posted messages
4. access a Web site on the World Wide Web using a browser and navigate the site to drill down to the level of detail desired
5. make use of all the features of a browser like Netscape or Explorer, such as bookmarking, printing, and setting preferences
6. use a Web search engine to retrieve needed information
7. copy files from one's computer and attach them to an e-mail message
8. use ftp to upload text and/or graphics from one's computer to a Web site
9. create a Web site using raw HTML or a software package like FrontPage
10. create links to other sites and/or create an e-mail response on a Web site
11. use CGI scripting to create a response form on a Web site
12. create simple animations for the Web
13. use Java scripting to create applets
14. design a Web site, given the objectives of the Web site and a Web strategy
15. develop a Web strategy given the objectives of the Web site

This list does not purport to be complete and certainly will be out of date very quickly. I would, therefore, be pleased to hear of any omissions at logan@physics.utoronto.ca.

The Limits of Artificial Intelligence

My approach to curriculum development or reform would be termed by some a form of computer and Internet enthusiasm. I am happy to accept this characterization of my work, but wish to distinguish my form of computer and Internet enthusiasm from that of the proponents of artificial intelligence and the LOGO microworld approach. "Researchers on artificial intelligence, like Papert, see great potential for increased human intelligence through interactions with computers. Computers act as environments for exploring ideas and stimulating higher order thinking [microworlds] . . . Enthusiasm for computers is driven by research on microworlds based on theories of artificial intelligence (AI) . . . It is important to see that the roots of computer enthusiasm lie in the promise of AI" (Olson 1988, 6–7).

While it is true that a school of computer enthusiasm derives from the AI movement, my computer enthusiasm does not. In fact, I reject the main tenets of the strong AI program. I believe the notion that human intelligence can be programmed into a computer is horribly naive and, as a consequence, dangerous. My enthusiasm for computers and the Internet stems from the same source as my enthusiasm for basic literacy and numeracy. Just as writing and mathematics greatly expanded the world of learning and became an integral part of both general education and vocational training, so too computing will play a similar role in the knowledge era.

We should not forget that writing and mathematics, like computers, created their own microworlds, that is, "environments for exploring ideas and stimulating higher order thinking" (Kurland and Kurland 1987, 319–20). Writing and mathematics, however, did not create artificial intelligence; they enhanced human intelligence and allowed it to flower. The same is true of computing. It is not nor will it be a source of artificial intelligence. Rather, it is a powerful tool that will extend and enhance human intelligence.

The notion that human intelligence can be programmed into a

computer derives from our understanding of the behavior of neurons, the individual nerve cells of the brain and the nervous system. Neurons exhibit a simple binary on-off digital logic in that they only fire an electric impulse when a certain threshold of inputs is exceeded. The neurons are networked in much the same way as the components of the integrated circuits of a computer. Hence comes the temptation to draw an analogy between human thought and the logical operations of a computer. But the AI theory breaks down because not all aspects of the human mind are controlled by the logical operations of the brain's neural nets. The human mind is shaped as much by the endocrine system and endorphins as by neurons and the flow of electrons. Human thought is as much controlled by pleasure, passion, love, morality, beauty, mysticism, and curiosity as by reason and logic. It is difficult, if not impossible, to explain in terms of logic the music of Mozart, the sculpture of Michelangelo, the paintings of Rembrandt, the poetry of Shakespeare, the philosophy of Spinoza, or the moral ideas of the great religions and their prophets.

The notion of artificial intelligence is a product of human hubris and represents an overextension of science. Each time humankind makes a little progress in understanding nature, there are those who jump to the conclusion that they understand the whole picture. There is even a term to describe this excess: scientism. The ancient Greek philosophers who invented deductive logic thought they could explain all of nature with their theoretical, rational, reductionist philosophy; they failed to understand the importance of empirical observation and experimentation. The success of Newton in describing in mathematical equations the motion of mechanical systems led to the formulation of a naive mechanistic view of the universe. The enthusiasm of Alexander Pope as expressed in his lines "Nature and Nature's laws lay hid in night; God said, 'Let Newton be and all was light,'" was typical of those who thought that Newtonian mechanics was the final word. In fact, Newton held sway for only 200 years, until Einstein formulated his Theory of Relativity in 1905. The supporters of strong AI, high on the success of modern computing, are making the same kind of mistake in oversimplifying a very complex phenomenon.

Modern science has taught us that there exist natural barriers to our understanding of nature. Goedel's theorem states that a mathematical system cannot be both complete and logically consistent. Quantum physics, through the Heisenberg uncertainty principle, limits the accuracy of measuring both the momentum and position of a particle. The universe changes each time it is observed or measured. Surely if the precise knowledge of the position of an electron interferes with the knowledge of its momentum, there must be some limits on human intelligence achieving an understanding of itself. Unfortunately, humility has not always been the strongest characteristic of modern scientists.

The danger of the AI movement is that the limited kind of "artificial intelligence" a computer generates will set the standards for what is an acceptable level of human intelligence, just as Muzak is regarded by some as music. Artificial leather is not leather, but a material that simulates some of the properties of leather. A well-written book can simulate human discourse and provide readers with a form of companionship, but cannot answer their questions or interact with them as the author can. Because the book is a medium whose interactivity with the reader is somewhat limited, it is not regarded as a form of artificial intelligence or even as an artificial storyteller.

The computer is a much more sophisticated communications technology that, when properly programmed to anticipate the different possible inputs of its users, can replicate some forms of human intelligence. If the author of the software routine is particularly clever in anticipating all possible inputs and is able to script a set of appropriate responses, it is possible that the computer will be able to fool users into believing they are dealing with a disembodied intelligence. But artificial intelligence is not human intelligence; it merely *simulates* human intelligence.

Mathematician Alan Turing's definition of AI is that if you cannot distinguish the communication of the computer from a human communication by telex or e-mail, then the computer response is a form of artificial intelligence. But people on telex lines are limited in relaying their full range of intelligence because they cannot communicate information that they can convey face to face through body language, tone of voice, and facial gestures. The limitation of Turing's definition of AI has been borne out by the experiences of people who have assumed fake identities on the Internet so as to role play. They were able to get away with their false guises as long as they remained online but, once they tried to extend their persona beyond the Internet, they met with disappointment because what they were doing was ultimately phony. The Turing criterion works as long as one remains online, whether it is with a telex machine or the Internet. But communicating online provides an extremely limited version of the reality that most of us enjoy through face-to-face interactions, where we can reach out and touch each other if we are so inclined.

If all of our interactions were mediated by telex communications, our culture would not be as rich as it is. If our culture were mediated by AI, the same impoverishment of human interactions and spirit would occur. The proponents of strong AI, those who believe that the computer can duplicate human intelligence, regard the computer strictly as an information-processing device and ignore that it is also a medium of communication. A book is not a form of human intelligence, but the communication of human intelligence through the artifact of the printed page. Artificial intelligence is not an independent form of intelligence, but the communication of human intelligence through the artifact of a computer, which is a medium for the storage and processing of information.

AI dehumanizes human intelligence by confusing the process and the artifact. An AI system is an artifact. An artifact does not contain intelligence, nor is it intelligent. It merely serves as a medium for human intelligence. A telex conversation simulates face-to-face discourse, but it does not replace face-to-face meetings. Negotiations conducted strictly by telex would prove extremely difficult if a delicate matter was under consideration. It is difficult to imagine how computer-based AI could evoke those aspects of human intelligence that encompass care, concern, compassion, love, curiosity, or any of the rich panoply of human emotions that make human companionship so valuable.

Computers have been programmed with all the rules of Mozart's music, but they have never been able to compose a piece of music that comes close to evoking the feelings his music generates. The genius of Mozart was not his use of rules of composition, which can be programmed on a computer, but his talent for knowing when to break the rules and how. This intuition came out of his life experiences, his ecstasies, and his sufferings. How do we make a computer experience ecstasy and suffering or teach it how to weep or laugh? Some human actions or reactions can be quantified and replicated with mathematical algorithms, but some are beyond analytic prescription, like those of joy, remorse, tragedy, love, and spirituality.

The excesses of strong AI parallel the historic instances when a new breakthrough in science or technology was used inappropriately. Those who believe that the time and effort needed for face-to-face interactions is not worth the effort because it is so easy to communicate via the Internet are placing limits on human potential. I will address this issue further in the next and final chapter, devoted solely to the Internet.

9

The Internet as the Sixth Language:

The Alignment of Work and Learning

$\mathbf{T}$he first users of the Internet were the military and the scientists and engineers who helped create it. The next cohort of users were academics, primarily scientists and engineers once again, who utilized the Internet to facilitate their research activities, mainly through the use of e-mail and the transfer of data and software files from one computer to another. Scientific research has always been a cooperative activity in which scientists share their data and results freely. The Internet is therefore an ideal medium for conducting scientific and other scholarly research activities. In recent years, with the popularization of microcomputing, the Net has been discovered by the business world, as well as by home users and hobbyists. The scientists' ethos of sharing ideas, information, and data, however, still dominates the use of the Internet by other communities and gives it its unique character as an open medium of communication.

The Net became an everyday fact of life for an estimated 148 million users worldwide by the end of 1998, according to the March 22, 1999, edition of *The Industry Standard* (another estimate — from www.rua.ie — puts the number at 171 million). There were an estimated 263 million e-mail accounts, transacting 3.4 trillion messages in 1998 (emarketer.com/estats/020199_email.htm). The Net straddles international borders and links continents, with users in every country and every major city in the world. It is used by children and adults from all walks of life — students, teachers, workers, business people. It has applications everywhere — in homes, schools, offices, businesses, government, research organizations, libraries, and community centers. It links workers to their colleagues, clients, and suppliers. It connects friends and complete strangers. It provides low-cost and efficient communications and provides a medium for information gathering, information dissemination, research, advertising, cataloging, buying, selling, instructing, teaching, learning, congregating, community development, planning, committee work, socializing, entertaining, amusement, killing time, and saving time. It is a place where people meet to play and work. Thousands of new businesses have sprung up on the Net, conducting business that ranges from attracting customers to electronically fulfilling transactions to buy a product or service.

There has been a marriage of television and the Web, giving rise to a new information appliance called WebTV, which allows users to access the World Wide Web through their cable-TV provider. WebTV offers a simple interface, removing any frustrations that might arise from technical difficulties or the lack of computer literacy on the part of the user. There have also been mergers of Internet companies with traditional media companies, such as the blockbuster merger of AOL.com, which owns Netscape, with Time Warner, which produces magazines, movies, and television (CNN).

The Net and the Web are giving rise to new ways of thinking, communicating, and processing information. The Internet is transforming learning and commerce, and accelerating the evolution of the information age into the knowledge era. The Internet and intranets are promoting and enhancing a new way of dealing with knowledge, in terms of knowledge management and knowledge networking. Although it has been only six years since the release of Netscape at the time I write this book, I feel justified in calling the Internet the sixth language.

The Internet and the World Wide Web have reinforced and amplified the impacts of computing, just as computing has reinforced and amplified the languages of science, math, and writing. In this chapter we will study the impact of the sixth language, whose unique semantics of Web pages, e-mail, chat rooms, and listservs and its unique syntax of TC/ICP, hypertext, and search engines create a unique environment and language for communications and information processing.

The Five Messages of the Internet

In addition to its unique semantics and syntax, the Internet is also a medium with unique effects. Every medium has its message, and the five messages of the Internet are as follows:

1. The Internet promotes two-way communication
   and hence dialogue.
2. The Internet facilitates access to information.
3. The Internet promotes continuous learning.
4. The Internet aligns and integrates information
   and knowledge structures.
5. The Internet promotes community.

These five features are contained in many other media, but the Internet is unique in that it possesses all five of these properties. As we make the transition to the knowledge era, each of these five features of the Internet propel work and learning into greater alignment.

The Two-Way Flow of Information
The Internet permits and promotes two-way communication, making dialogue and knowledge-sharing possible. For the creators of Web sites, this interaction allows feedback from their visitors and customers. For the visitors to a site, the two-way communication gives them a chance to dialogue with the supplier of a service or product that they are interested in and to test the reliability of the information they are accessing. It also gives them a voice, so that they do not feel like passive consumers of information.

Ease of Access of Information and the Role of Information Design

The ease of access to information is one of the chief advantages of the Internet for delivering training, fomenting dialogue, and sharing knowledge. Hypertext allows one to provide information and lessons at different levels of depth and detail, which users can access in an order that makes the most sense for them and that best accommodates their individual learning styles. The trick, however, is to present information, ideas, proposals, or learning material in a format that makes them easily accessible, attractive, and engaging. This requires an understanding of the techniques of information design, so that information is batched in easily digestible segments that maximize the user's learning experience.

Continuous Learning

The Internet promotes continuous learning because the information it contains is so easily accessible. Users can pursue educational activities whenever they have free time and are in the mood for learning something new. They do not have to conform to someone else's schedule, as they do with classroom learning. They can pursue an almost unlimited number of topics, depending on their interests and their needs. The Net and the Web have all of the positive learning features of computing that were reviewed in Chapter 6, with the following additional features that make learning more attractive, entertaining, and effective:

- many graphical interfaces, which help users visualize abstract concepts;
- interactivity, through which users can experience instant feedback that reinforces their learning experiences;
- two-way communication, which enables users to dialogue with other students, subject experts, coaches, and mentors;
- hypertext links, which allow users to quickly research a topic of interest and pursue multiple paths to their goals and which give users the ability to work at their own pace in an environment of their own choosing;
- a choice of different learning environments, which allows users to find a format compatible with their learning style.

For all the reasons cited above, educational and information Web sites are registering millions of hits per day, and hence represent the most important breakthrough in educational media since the invention of the printing press and the inauguration of public education. The Net far surpasses educational television or film strips in effectiveness, because the users of the Net are active participants in command of their interactive learning experience.

Alignment and Integration

The Internet provides a medium or platform for the integration and alignment of an organization's business processes. Before the existence of personal computers and the Internet, business activities could be easily divided into compartmentalized processes and addressed one at a time. The ethos of specialization, which was so successful during the industrial age, is slowly giving way to a new ethos of integration, as computers and the Internet assimilate many of today's business functions. An intranet configured as a knowledge network permits the integration of the knowledge and learning activities of all the employees of an organization. Because knowledge and information resources are available to everyone, the organization can align its knowledge-creation activities, which in turn leads to synergy.

The Creation of Community

Of all the messages of the Internet, perhaps the most important is the promotion of community. Community is fostered on the Net through its other four messages. Two-way communication allows people to feel involved. Information design helps users feel that their needs are being looked after. Continuous learning makes people feel that their minds are engaged and respected, and alignment integrates the needs of an organization with all of its stakeholders, including its customers and its suppliers. An intranet-based knowledge network, by being available twenty-four hours a day, seven days a week, is always there for members of a community, supporting their information needs and providing an environment for learning, knowledge creation and sharing, and the development of new ideas, products, services, and approaches to doing business.

The Decentralization of Information Flow and the Reintegration of Work and Learning

Marshall McLuhan long ago predicted the complete decentralization of the flow of information. An international web of computer users and computer networks, linked by telephone lines and fiber optic cables, the Internet embodies that idea. It is a conduit for e-mail. It is an information highway — a network of networks. The Net allows any two participants to communicate with each other via their modems or routers, so that they can exchange any information that can be stored on their respective computer systems. Users can surf the Net to gain access to information files. They can download onto their computers everything from documents and software to graphic images, photographs, music, multimedia presentations, movies, and videos. The Internet is a global client-server system with multiple numbers of servers and millions of clients. It is, therefore, the client-server of client-servers.

The Internet is being used to buy and sell goods, hold forums or discussion groups on a wide variety of topics, provide customer support, and promote everything from political causes and commercial products to social activities and art forms. Anyone who wants to start a new discussion group or promote something new may do so. The Internet — or cyberspace — is an open market place of ideas, products, and services. The importance of the Internet as a basic information utility is growing daily. It has already achieved a status equal to that of the postal system, the telephone network, or the broadcast system, and even threatens to surpass these venerable and established institutions. The Internet is an ideal medium for continuous learning because it makes access to resources so easy.

In oral societies, learning took place while people worked together, and, as a consequence, education was not centralized. There were no schools, no formal education, only apprenticeships or on-the-job training. With the advent of formal education, ultimately controlled by school boards, education became centralized. This trend is reversing now, thanks to the Internet and the reintegration of work and education, as learning becomes a lifelong activity associated with both work and an individual's personal development.

McLuhan predicted that electric technologies would retrieve the patterns of oral societies, including the reintegration of work and learning. "Paid learning is already becoming both the dominant employment and the source of new wealth in our society" (McLuhan 1964, 351). There is no longer any doubt that the fragmentation of work and learning is coming to an end. Toffler, Senge, Tapscott and Caston, Hammer and Champy, and Drucker all embraced this idea. Reintegration is a matter of "electronic manifest destiny." Clearly, the Internet will effect this reintegration.

The Internet: The Silent Oral Tradition

The Internet replicates the patterns of oral society. Many authors evoke McLuhan's notion of the global village in describing the Internet user community, but their analysis usually goes no further than this observation, by Internet expert Mary Cronin (1994, 64):

> "Global village" has been applied to many different situations over the past few decades, some far afield from Marshall McLuhan's original concept of how computerized communication changes society. But it seems entirely appropriate that this phrase should become the description of choice for the Internet. The millions of people linked to the network not only have the common experience of using the same electronic tools and information resources regardless of location, they are also connected to each other in a new way, free to exchange ideas, solicit advice, consult, argue, without regard to national boundaries.

This excerpt from Cronin's *Doing Business on the Internet* represents the only mention of McLuhan in her book. It does not do justice to the parallels that can be drawn between Internet usage and the patterns of communication in an oral society, which are played out every day on the Internet. McLuhan observed that electricity replaces the patterns of organization of the mechanical industrial era with those of oral culture. The microcomputer has reinforced and strengthened the patterns of electricity and, hence, oral society, and the Internet is having a similar effect.

There are many parallels between the Internet and oral culture.

Oral culture was an extension of the psyche of tribal humankind within its community, just as the Internet is an extension of its users — an extension, however, with a global reach. The protocols and rituals associated with the use of the Internet are not the formal patterns characteristic of literate communications, but are more like those of an oral society, despite the underlying literate substrata that infuse the use of computers. The primary mode of communication, e-mail, is written, but, in contrast to traditional literacy, the writing is not formal. Grammatical structures are frequently relaxed, and shorthand and jargon are liberally used. The writing is infused with hieroglyphic signs used to connote feelings and tone and meant to replicate the information that facial gesture and vocal tone convey during face-to-face conversation. Because "wry wit can frequently come across as obnoxious and offensive, humor or irony can be flagged with a 'smiley,' a sideways smile that looks like :-) or :) or a 'grin' that looks like <g>" (Reznick and Taylor 1994, 154).

Discussion Groups on the Internet

A comparison of three types of discussion groups — those of oral society, those of literate society, and those held electronically on the Internet — helps illustrate the point that the Net is an oral medium.

In literate society, aside from informal discussions among friends, a moderator or chairperson always leads the discussion and polices the interaction of the participants, whether the discussion is a political meeting or an academic seminar. In both oral society and Internet society no such structure exists. There is no hierarchy; each participant has an equal voice and is heard.

In oral society, discussions do not have a precise beginning, middle, and end. Whereas in literate society a precise time frame is almost always set for a discussion, in oral society, the discussion goes on until the issue has been dealt with to everyone's satisfaction. No member of the discussion group will call for closure or ask for a vote to determine if the meeting can be terminated. (I have vivid recollections of intense battles in academic forums in which the topic of debate became whether or not to adjourn the meeting.)

On the Net, there need be no end to a discussion; it can go on as long as the participants are willing to participate. Discussions on the

Net are not even limited by biological necessities. Councils were often extended in oral culture by the serving of food during the discourse (the origin of the Symposium, the Passover seder meal, and the banquet) or by having the participants camp together so that they could continue their deliberations after refreshing themselves with a night's sleep. A powwow or council could last several days, but eventually the participants would have to return to their hunting-and-gathering activities to find the food necessary for their daily survival. On the Net, discussions are frozen on the hard drives of the participants and the dialogue entered into at convenient intervals. There is never a biological reason to terminate the discussion group. Only lack of interest can end a session.

Netocracy: Ultimate Participatory Democracy

In a council in the oral tradition, once a speaker has begun an intervention, he or she is allowed to continue uninterrupted. After the speech, there is a period of silence so that the audience can think about what was said. After a short silence, which can seem like an eternity to a literate individual, someone else will begin to speak. In literate society, on the other hand, people are constantly interrupting one another, vying for air time. This behavior is considered boorish by native peoples, who have retained the patterns and rhythms of their oral cultures even after becoming fully literate.

There is no shortage of dispute within oral cultures, but the pattern of dialogue is completely different from that of literate culture. And the dialogue of Net users is not unlike that of tribal people. Net users have their disputes. They may "flame" each other — that is, send a violently argumentative reply — but they are forced by the technology not to interrupt one another's interventions, so that the voice of each participant is heard.

Both oral societies and Net societies practice a form of total direct participatory democracy, while literate society practices a representative form of democracy or, in totalitarian societies, none at all. Absolute monarchies, tyrannies, and totalitarian regimes are produced solely by literate cultures. Although modern literate cultures celebrate the myth that they invented democracy, their triumph is nothing more than a restoration of the democratic practices of preliterate societies.

Totalitarian regimes cannot exist on the Net. The Internet, in fact, is a safeguard of democracy because it cannot be controlled by the state or the wealthy, in contrast to the press or the broadcast media. You cannot buy the Internet or censor it as you can a newspaper. If "freedom of the press belongs to those that own one," freedom of the Internet belongs to those who have access to a computer and can afford an account with an access provider. The appearance of freenets in many cities across North America opens the doors to wider and more democratic participation in Netocracy. As the cost of computing continues to spiral downward, the economic barriers against participation will dwindle.

But cost is less of a barrier than interest. A color television represents a sizable investment, yet its use is universal in both the affluent and the developing world. Only extreme poverty presents a barrier to television usage; the same will eventually be true of the microcomputer and the Internet. Interactive information technology, however, will probably always be used less than television. The fault line between the working class and the computerate class (the electronic middle class) will be a measure of the percentage of Internet and computer use versus that of television use.

Electronic Crime and Punishment

In the oral tradition, when members of society seriously offend the social norms, they are not imprisoned or punished, as they would be in literate society. Instead, they are banished: shut out rather than shut in. The same holds true in the world of the Internet. If users violate the rules and protocols of Internet usage, they are first admonished and warned, usually in the form of a flaming. If the offense continues, they are banned from participation, removed from the discussion group, and their e-mail is ignored.

Tribal Society and Resource-Sharing on the Net

In the computer age, information is not only the principal commodity of exchange, but its very nature has changed. In an electronically configured environment, information is no longer private. The concept of proprietary information, a holdover from the industrial age, is beginning to weaken and is being replaced with the idea of shared information and open systems. The Internet embraces this new notion.

The operating system on which it is based is UNIX, which was originally developed at Bell Laboratories, and is freely available to anyone who wishes to use it — in strong contrast to the operating systems developed by the Apple Corporation and Microsoft. The philosophy underlying the founding of the Internet was the idea that information cannot be hoarded or it becomes useless.

This philosophy parallels that of the sharing of food in tribal societies. The hoarding of food was deemed useless because the food would spoil. Furthermore, sharing it with friends and neighbors put one in a position to receive their surplus in their time of plenty. The strategy of sharing maximizes an individual's or a family's chances of survival.

By and large, users of the Internet have adopted a similar credo. They are willing to share information because they realize that they will be greatly enriched by the process. When information is shared among a group of individuals, their efforts are multiplied. Ten people working together and sharing their information will generate at least ten times as much useful information as an individual working alone. And given that the Internet connects an individual with all its users, the circle of ten can potentially expand to 150 million users. The power of the Internet is not that it puts one in touch with 150 million other users — the network of telephone users, for example, is much greater. The power of the Internet is that built into it are tools allowing individuals with similar interests to make contact with one another and share information. Alternatively, once individuals with a common interest have made contact through some other medium, they then have a medium through which they can collaborate and cultivate a network of others with a similar interest.

(In the course of writing this chapter, I received a telephone call from Jeff Long, director of the Notational Engineering Lab at George Washington University. He had read my previous book, *The Alphabet Effect*, and wanted to invite me to his lab to give a talk and begin a research collaboration. Because we are both Internet users, we did not have to wait the three months until I was able to visit him to begin our work together. We began our collaboration immediately by exchanging papers and commenting on each other's work. The distance between Toronto and Washington, D.C., magically melted away.)

The open sharing of information has been the strategy behind scientific research from its inception, distinguishing it from engineering, where information was often kept secret so as to realize a commercial advantage over potential competitors. Science as a language is built on the foundations of literacy and numeracy, yet it has retained many elements of the oral tradition. The first users of the Internet were scientists who infused the current-day Net with its cultural traditions of open discussions and the full disclosure of information. With the Internet, the circle of research collaborators becomes global. Science has always been a global activity, but with the Internet and other electronic links, collaborations can be carried out in real time because of the instantaneous nature of communications.

With the institution of open discussion groups on the Net, scientific activities have become even more democratic and inclusive. A lack of academic credentials sometimes stood in the way of scholars who had significant contributions to make. This is no longer the case. In electronic discussion groups, ideas are often examined on their own merit, stripped away from the status or expertise of their author. On the Internet, generalists are able to participate in an area of interest to them without the prerequisite of the specialist knowledge required for entry into academic discussions.

Information on the Internet is easily multiplied and communicated to others, with no cost involved in its distribution. Users are, therefore, eager to share and participate in this commerce that enriches all who participate. There is really no such thing as a bad deal when information is being shared. No one ever feels cheated, as is sometimes the case when material goods are exchanged: Nothing can be lost by providing others with information, and there is much to be gained from access to it.

The Internet: Bard and Storyteller

In tribal society, the users of information are also its creators. In the tribal council, every voice is heard and every pair of ears is part of the system. A storyteller's tale would change depending on the mood and reception of the audience (Havelock 1963). Internet participants can do more than just shape a discussion by indicating their mood; they can actually change it by adding their comments. Over time, the story being told becomes their story, a never-ending story. They feel a sense of ownership. Internet participants are expected to participate in the flow of information once they have had time to get the drift of the discussion. "Newbies" — new participants — can follow a discussion for a while without contributing, but if they continue to be passive participants, they are labeled "lurkers," a pejorative for an electronic Peeping Tom or voyeur.

One of the most interesting developments on the Internet has been the emergence of Web sites, through graphical user interfaces such as Netscape or Explorer. Web sites are the corporate bards of the Internet. A Web site is a location on the World Wide Web where Internet users can access information sitting on a host computer. The Web site is accessed via a home page through which other Web pages or sites may be reached through hypertext links. This structure allows users to access the information that best matches their interests and information needs, and to linger over material of particular interest or skip over irrelevant material.

Pages that are linked using hypertext retrieve the patterns of the oral storytellers. Hypertext leads from one story to another, depending on the interest of the user. In the oral tradition, storytellers told one story after another, depending on the interest of the audience. There was no fixed order to how the episodes were related to the audience. Each performance was different, and episodes were told in a different order each time (Havelock 1963). Hypertext is like jazz. Each time the story is told, it is told as an improvisation, one dictated by the users and their needs and not by the producers or source of the information.

The fragmentation inherent in many of the communications and information-processing patterns of today's institutions are holdovers from the industrial age. These forms of fragmentation will begin to disappear as the Internet reintroduces the integrative patterns of oral society. Internet usage is oral and tactile rather than visual and literate; a right-hemisphere rather than left-hemisphere activity; synthetic rather than analytic; nonlinear rather than linear; simultaneous or synchronous rather than sequential; and analogical rather than deductive.

The History of Pre-Electronic Proto-Internets

The discussion group on the Internet can be likened to an electronic dialogue or Symposium similar to the one described by Plato in his Dialogues, but one in which the participants share a common corner of cyberspace rather than sit at a banquet table. The Internet is obviously not the first forum for the sharing of information. The roots of the Internet or information-sharing networks can be traced to the pre-literate storytellers or bards who traveled from settlement to settlement sharing information, carrying news, and relating stories from the past that formed the foundations of their culture. Next came the forums of the city-states, like those of Babylon, which acted as nodes for receiving and sending information.

The subsequent manifestation was the imperial communication systems of Mesopotamia, Egypt, Hellenistic Greece, the Roman empire, and the Roman Catholic Church. In each of these proto-Internets, communications emanated from and were controlled by a central authority (all roads lead to Rome). The information transmitted through these systems was heavily policed, so that only the Imperial political line or the Church dogma received air time. While these closed systems were opposite in spirit from the openness of today's Internet, they did provide global coverage (or at least empirewide coverage) and, relatively speaking, simultaneity. The ancient Roman system of roads and the use of paper documents, with a response time of only a month or two to the farthest outposts of the empire, provided the fastest distribution of information up to the time of the introduction of the railroad and the telegraph.

The proto-Internets of the Renaissance and early industrial age were the trade routes, along which information was carried by traders and merchants. These routes became truly global with the arrival of ocean-traveling ships, which permitted European powers such as England, France, Spain, Holland, and Portugal to set up global trading networks that gathered goods and information from the four corners of the world. The newspapers that emerged in these countries provided readers with news of events from far-off places. With the invention of the telegraph, newspapers were transformed into a global network of correspondents, with the metropolitan newspapers like the London

Times, the *New York Times*, and *Le Monde* serving as nodes. The link between these nodes, where information was collected and disseminated, was the international telegraph system, while the link to end users was daily newspapers, which provided information no more than twenty-four hours old. The next proto-Internets to arise were the broadcasting networks spawned first by radio and then by television.

The feature that all of these proto-Internets lacked was the interactivity of end users, who functioned merely as passive consumers of information.

The Electronification of Information

As McLuhan foresaw, the electrification and then the electronification of information resulted in new patterns of information usage that resemble the oral tradition in many ways. This trend, which began with the introduction of the telegraph and continued with the use of the telephone, radio, and television, is finding its most complete actualization in microcomputers connected through the Internet.

Paradoxically, the bulk of the information being transmitted on the Net is still text. Print as a medium is still holding its own. The sale of books and other forms of reading matter continues to increase. The information now collected in books has been gathered, written, edited, and typeset using electronic media, but the format of print on paper still seems to be the most sensible format for reading. Only the briefest messages, such as e-mail, are read exclusively on a video screen. When lengthy files are transmitted from one computer to another, in most cases, readers will make a hard copy of the document. The reason is simple; reading from a CRT (or video screen) is unnatural because of the way the brain processes video information. Reading is a left-brain activity; viewing video is a right-brain activity. The mosaic pattern of light pulses must be reassembled by the right hemisphere to create an image. There is an inherent conflict in reading directly from a CRT. Thus the book is still a popular medium, and will continue to be so.

Paper-based journals that publish specialized information could easily disappear, however. As archives for information and knowledge, they have long been surpassed by electronic media; with the Internet they have also been surpassed as distribution vehicles. Rather than printing all their articles on paper and mailing them to subscribers, journals can now distribute their material electronically, leaving it to readers to print out those articles they wish to read closely.

But what purpose, then, do electronic journals now serve? Why don't authors simply distribute their articles individually over the Internet? While this does happen, there is still a reason to have a journal, even in an electronic form. First, the journal creates a community, consisting of its readers and its contributors. Second, the editing and vetting of papers by peers can still be maintained. Disputes between editors and authors can be easily resolved by distributing both authorized and unauthorized articles. Readers could enjoy the authority of the publications vetted by an editorial board, and still have the option of reading or ignoring those articles that were not officially approved by the board for formal publication.

The ease with which text can be read is critical to the success of a medium. This principle is illustrated by the different fates of two media that were introduced at approximately the same time, namely, videotext and desktop publishing.

Videotext involved the broadcast of information into the homes of its users, who were able to select what they would view, paying a small fee for each item selected. The service never got off the ground in the U.K. and North America, partly because there was little context to the information provided, but also because the video medium was not conducive to the easy reading of large amounts of data. The fact that information could be kept up to date electronically, and was therefore always more current than printed information, could not overcome the medium's inherent disadvantages. (Another drawback of videotext services, as compared to the Internet, was that the users of videotext couldn't make a contribution to the information hoard being compiled and so felt no sense of ownership of the information. The Internet user, on the other hand, can interact with the online information by adding to it or commenting on it for other users to read. Thus, users are able to shape the overall direction of a newsgroup in which they are participating. They hence develop a sense of ownership of the information, even if it is shared with other users.)

The desktop-publishing medium — based on the rapid and relatively inexpensive production of printed material using laser printers and software packages like PageMaker or Quark — has caused a revolution in the print business. Traditional typesetters who could not adjust to the new medium and learn microcomputer-based typesetting were thrown out of work, and printing houses that did not adopt this new technology soon found themselves out of business. Desktop publishing takes advantage of the mediums of the laser printer, the electronic image setter, and the microcomputer to reduce the cost of production, make short print runs economical, and increase the frequency with which catalogs and newsletters can be updated. At the same time, it retains the advantages of the crispness of the printed page. Material can be copied directly from laser-printer output or sent to an image setter to produce film for phototypesetting. It is even possible now, using computer-to-plate technology, to bypass the film stage and have the computer directly etch the plate.

E-books

A development that will have a major impact on online learning and education is that the electronic book, or e-book. "Electronic books are hand held computerized devices with high-resolution screens, backlighting, and extended-life batteries intended to serve as storage devices for literary works or things like technical manuals that can be digitally distributed easily over the Internet" (Krochmal 1999). Some e-books already exist, but they are not as easy to read as paper-based books. But plans are in progress to create a product with readability superior to that of books in which text appears as ink on paper. The advantages of e-books will be that they are cheaper, more accessible, more available, and more easily searched. They will take up less room, use no paper and, hence, be environmentally friendlier. A number of books and encyclopedias are already available in CD-ROM format, and some business guides are available on Palm Pilots. E-books will only take off when more readable fonts become available. Microsoft is claiming that their prototype font designed for LCD screens, ClearType, will make text more readable on an LCD screen. Microsoft researcher Bill Hill claims, "The next five to 10 years will probably change society as much as the 200 or 300 years that happened after Gutenberg" (Microsoft 1999). This sounds like typical Microsoft hype and bravado, but what if Hill is right? The e-book is clearly a development to keep an eye on.

The Internet, CD-ROM Technology, and Multimedia

The Internet is no longer restricted to text; it is rapidly becoming an important vehicle for the transmission of interactive multimedia data. Multimedia, which combines text, visuals, and audio, owes its current success to the CD-ROM, which has served as both a storage medium and a delivery device for this interactive medium. At one time, the CD-ROM medium totally monopolized the distribution of multimedia products. With the Internet and powerful servers, this no longer holds true. As the bandwidth of modems increases, allowing more data to pass from one user of the Internet to another, multimedia presentations will become more practical.

The Internet has a major advantage over the CD-ROM. The information on a CD-ROM is frozen and cannot be updated, whereas Internet-delivered multimedia information can be updated in real time. By coupling a Web page server with a database server, Web pages can be updated dynamically so that the information being delivered is never out of date.

Multimedia presentations on the Internet are, at the time of this writing, still limited compared to those on CD-ROM, but the capability for more sophisticated material is there; it is only a question of time before the Internet fully supports multimedia.

From the advent of writing on clay tablets to today's Internet, there has been a continuous speedup of the transmission of information. Harold Innis (1950) has documented how the transition from clay to papyrus and then paper speeded up the transmission of information, as did the introduction of the printing press. Word processing on computers, followed by desktop publishing, further increased the speed with which information could be transmitted and the ease with which it could be edited, changed, and updated. The CD-ROM promised to extend this speedy and flexible capability for both textual and non-textual information such as graphics, sound, and music. CD-ROMs have become standard equipment on most microcomputers manufactured today. Despite this, the CD-ROM could be squeezed out as the medium for the active transmission of multimedia by the Internet and survive only as an archiving device.

My guess is that canned packages like entertainment and educational titles will find a natural home in the CD-ROM environment and will be produced and distributed much like books, audio recordings, and videotapes of movies. CD-ROMs are also a useful medium for loading software onto a computer. Information that must be kept current, such as commercial information and catalogs, corporate annual reports, and advertising in the form of infomercials, will likely gravitate to the Internet. On the other hand, with the appearance of recordable CDs and CD burners, the dynamics could change once again: Recordable CDs can be distributed with the most current information, which can be regularly updated through links on the Internet. As in the past, the most likely scenario is some hybrid system that makes use of the best of Internet and CD technologies.

The Information Superhighway

As computers become more versatile at handling different information formats, such as video, graphics, and audio, and as modems or direct digital lines such as ISDN become capable of handling greater amounts of bandwidth or data, the Internet will contain more and more multimedia, and will eventually evolve into the information superhighway that has been the focus of so much recent speculation. The term "information superhighway" is a useful one because it conjures up the image of information traveling quickly from one point to another. A superhighway, however, is a linear system with controlled access, whereas the Internet is a web in which access is not controlled. But there has been so much hype surrounding the term that we are stuck with its use whether it is accurate or not.

Terminology aside, I believe that the Internet will become the information superhighway because, with more then 150 million users and the capability to integrate any other information service into its web, it has too much of a head start for any other initiative to take over as the premier conduit for global information flow. Its ethos of free exchange of information without government interference or the domination of business encompasses the dream of the earlier developers of microcomputers, many of them hackers, who envisioned the unfettered flow of information. (Ironically, some of these early dreamers went on to form some of the largest and perhaps most proprietary and predatory corporations in the microcomputer industry.)

The Electronic Academy

The interactivity of the Internet contributes to its success as an environment for continuous learning. The Internet functions as an educational medium purely by virtue of the fact that its users exchange information with one another and interact actively with that information by reading it and responding to it. The Net is not a medium like television, where the user can be a passive recipient of information, unless the Net is being used simply to download graphics and video. Participants in discussion groups develop new abilities. They develop the skills of electronic or Internet rhetoric, which combine the skills of classical oral rhetoric with those of literacy. Internet use could even create new cognitive structures and aptitudes because the patterns of using and searching for information are so different from those of traditional media.

The Internet is becoming an important tool for schooling and training. One of the first applications of the Internet was as a medium for distance education. It can also be used to deliver online courses, in which class participation and student-teacher interactions take place over the Net. The content of these courses is no different from that of traditional classroom courses. Once again, the content of a new medium is that of an older medium. But as the Internet is used more and more for online courses, its unique format is beginning to color these offerings, and new courses and new forms of education are emerging. Even in those cases where traditional classroom activities are being pursued on the Net, the new medium allows the participation of those who could not attend standard classroom sessions because of distance, scheduling, or physical handicap. The Internet is already changing the nature of education by allowing students to gather information and correspond on a global level.

Ryder considers the Internet an important educational environment, likening it to a library, a publishing house, a school, a community, and a city. The Internet is like a library in that users can access documents containing information they need. Instead of consulting a card catalog, the researcher makes use of a search engine. "Like a library, the Internet affords great potential for research. The processes of information searching are similar, if not identical" (Ryder 1996). The Internet has a number of advantages over the library. Its holdings are more up to date, more extensive, and are always available conveniently on one's desktop. The advantages of the Net as a publishing vehicle are that material can be rapidly disseminated, the author can self-publish without being censored by referees or the publisher, and readers can easily and instantaneously communicate with the author. The Internet is like a school in that there are so many resources available to the student, but, unlike a school, there is no teacher or guide, unless the user belongs to a knowledge network with access to coaches and mentors. The Internet is not just a community but a community of communities and hence, a city where each community pursues its own particular interests. Each listserv and discussion group constitutes a community in which participants exchange ideas and information and come to know each other. The Internet as a city has a global reach, but is a place where individuals for the most part are as friendly and approachable as in a village. The Internet truly does function as a global village. A cliché perhaps, but, as McLuhan claimed, clichés become archetypes.

The traditional classroom environment is changing as more and more teachers recognize the power of the Internet as a teaching and learning tool and demand access to it in their classrooms. "Schools around the country are working on wiring their classrooms, but it's a costly and slow process. In Pennsylvania, for example, the governor has instituted a three-year 'Links To Learn' initiative, now in its second year. When the project is completed, at a cost of $100 million, the state's 1.85 million students will have access to computer networks in every classroom in every school" (Krochmal 1998). Traditional libraries and workplaces are also wired. The Internet is converting all institutions into learning centers and electronic libraries.

Online Training
The Internet and associated intranets are becoming very powerful knowledge-management tools, and the media of choice for the delivery of online training. These media enjoy a number of advantages over

CD-ROM–based multimedia, principally in the ease with which materials can be updated, information distributed, and users networked to share their knowledge. The temporary advantages of CD-ROM–based media, which can deliver more information to a desktop, will soon disappear with the ever-increasing bandwidth of the Internet.

It can also be argued that the more economical approach required to use the smaller bandwidth of the Internet has certain pedagogical advantages in that the emphasis is on the interactivity of the user with the information provided rather than on the visual richness of the information. Educational television provides an example of a medium that had all the bandwidth in the world to operate with but that never succeeded as an educational medium because of its lack of interactivity. Visual richness does not guarantee learning; interactivity does. The low-tech, "less is more" style of creating online courses and learning environments makes use of a minimum amount of memory, which permits rapid access and downloading of the course material.

Another advantage of online training is that it takes place on the user's own desktop and hence is an extension of their work environment. Users can easily make notes and copy pertinent sections onto their hard drives. This advantage does not accrue with the use of a special multimedia CD-ROM–activated computer. Networked users can also easily share their learning experiences and integrate the online training courses into other knowledge-sharing tools such as a casebase forum (a collection of cases that describe the outcomes of projects), an idea pool, or ordinary e-mail. Online courses with two-way communication built in allow students to interact with their instructor to permit coaching and mentoring, and to communicate with other students to take advantage of peer learning and knowledge sharing. The Internet protocol facilitates the networking and sharing essential to the creation of a knowledge community and the emergence of a learning organization.

The Internet and Commerce

When it first impacted on the business community in 1994, the Internet was considered a luxury item that might provide an enterprise with a modest competitive edge. Initially, it was favored by companies that had a particular information dissemination need, such as computer software or chemical companies, whose customers require technical information to use the company's products. Now its use is considered as indispensable to doing business as the telephone, the computer, or the fax machine. In fact, there are already firms that refuse to do business with other firms unless they are connected to the Internet. The Internet is particularly valuable for small- to medium-sized organizations that want to support a worldwide customer base. The importance of the Internet increases as more and more commerce takes place either directly online or through Web sites used to support off-line commerce.

Internet commerce is supported by the sharing of knowledge and experience, which is now much more open than it ever was with traditional media. One of the most interesting phenomena associated with the Internet is electronic discussion groups. These groups focus on topics that can range from an area of research or a professional activity to a shared interest such as a musical form, a hobby, a period of history, or the use of a product, whether it is an automobile or a software package. Discussion groups perform a function similar to that of professional associations, seminar groups, research teams, clubs organized around a shared interest, and so on. But Internet discussion groups are in continuous session and have no geographical barriers: Members can participate at their convenience.

Some of these Internet discussion groups have given rise to informal knowledge communities known as "communities of practice" (COPs) or as "communities of interest." In a COP, people can converse about the common problems they face in their workplaces or in their professional lives. Sometimes COPs are contained within a single organization and sometimes they cross institutional boundaries. A COP does not necessarily have to be transacted solely on the Internet; in fact, the most successful ones often incorporate face-to-face meetings. As good a tool as the Internet is, it can never replace the intimacy and fullness of the communication of individuals in a face-to-face meeting. The importance of the Internet to a COP is that it provides a link between the times when people can get together and hence sustains the group. It also permits a COP to develop among people who are not co-located.

It should come as no surprise that the Internet is, for the most part, currently being used to perform tasks that were previously carried out by telephones, fax machines, courier services, and the post office. The content of any new medium is, after all, some previous medium. But just as the exchange of ideas among academics and hobbyists using the Net is done on the basis of barter, a similar pattern is emerging among commercial users of the Net. The traditional tasks being performed on the Net are already being colored by the Net's information-sharing ethos. Individuals who might ordinarily have customer-supplier relationships in which a fee is charged for the exchange of information are now exchanging information and ideas for free in Internet discussion groups. In fact, the most frequent commercial users of the Net are precisely those individuals from the information and communications sectors who make their living from the exchange of ideas and information. Even among competitors the cooperative spirit of the Internet is easing the cutthroat competition of traditional business. Discussion groups include workers from companies that are in direct competition with each other. These workers are motivated by the desire to solve a mutually shared technical or intellectual problem rather than to secure some advantage for their firms. Their activities, which no doubt benefit society as a whole, have to be a source of concern for the senior managers of their companies. Management is just beginning to realize that the Internet is a difficult force to control. Like the microcomputer that preceded it, the Internet will require a strategic deployment if it is to contribute to a firm's long-term interests.

The Internet is a double-edged sword. At the same time that it is retrieving some of the cooperative patterns of hunting-and-gathering and early Neolithic cultures, when the pace of commerce was considerably slower, it is also accelerating the pace of business by creating the expectation that information can be made available instantaneously. When the postal system broke down and courier systems came into popular use, there was a general speedup of information flow. A similar acceleration occurred with the introduction of the fax machine and then the fax modem card that converted desktop computers into fax transmission centers. With the Internet, the speedup is even greater. With direct desktop-to-desktop communication and no direct costs associated with the transmission of information over long distances, the Internet provides instantaneous communication right across the globe. Physical spaces disappear on the Internet, as does the transmission time of information. The Internet is therefore driving business process reengineering even harder and making the time wasted by unnecessary handoffs intolerable.

The Internet is gaining acceptance in the business world at a phenomenally rapid rate reminiscent of the hold microcomputers took in the early eighties. Like microcomputers, the Internet has been introduced at the grass-roots level in a random manner by individual employees who have discovered that they can enhance their performance at work by using this communication channel. The same chaos that followed the introduction of micros is about to repeat itself with the Internet. Even in those cases where the Internet has been introduced companywide, there are no Internet strategies in place. Companies that adopt the Internet do so largely to realize the cost savings in communications that the use of this technology affords, rather than to realize some overarching organizational objective.

Now that the pioneers have demonstrated its many uses for commerce, the value of the Internet to business is beginning to dawn on the community as a whole. Because the orientation of businesses, whether they are members of the information, service, or manufacturing sectors, is the provision of a greater level of service, communication is a key ingredient for commercial success today. The Internet, which automatically combines communications and computing, contributes to the creative use of communications in business. Some of the uses of the Net include the cost-effective exchange of e-mail and the extensions of wide area networks (WANs) to include isolated co-workers who operate small satellite offices. The Net is used to track standards, conduct technology watches, gather badly needed information, obtain answers to questions, disseminate information, promote products, support customers' use of services and/or products, send and receive all types of documents, and obtain software codes to reduce the cost and time of developing systems software. The Net is particularly useful for conducting customer relations, market research, and product support, as well as for obtaining market feedback.

Analysts often make the mistake of judging the value of the Internet solely in terms of its contribution to direct sales, an increasingly important aspect with the proliferation of e-commerce and portal sites. Direct sales, however, are only one way the Internet can help an organization achieve its goals and hence should not be the only criterion for judging its usefulness. The Internet is probably stronger as a communications, marketing, and customer-support tool than as a sales tool. Its fulfillment of these other functions, however, can increase sales, particularly if its use is guided by an Internet strategy that is aligned with the company's overall objectives. Through the use of such a strategy, other benefits, such as the more efficient operation of different functions of the organization, will also accrue. For instance, companies that spend too much time generating information internally can take advantage of the existing information they can gather on the Net. (The Net must be used wisely, though. It is like a dragnet that pulls everything out of the sea; unless a strategy is in place to filter the data collected, time and effort will be wasted.)

Marketing on the Internet

The Internet is an excellent marketing research tool. "Well informed employees can spot marketing opportunities, the emergence of new competition, unmet customer needs . . . but only if the company has organized its internal information sharing structure to incorporate their insights" (Cronin 1994, 17). With an Internet strategy, firms will be able to take full advantage of the Net. But the strategic use of the Internet requires the cooperation and coordination of the whole organization and hence the reengineering of key business processes, especially those concerned with marketing and customer support, as well as a modest amount of personnel reorganization and training. All levels and aspects of a company's organization can benefit from the use of the Internet.

Individual members of a firm will not be able to spontaneously optimize their organization's use of the Internet by pursuing their own particular interests. Leadership must come from a broadly based group of managers with experience in both marketing and information technology. Responsibility cannot be relegated to MIS departments, which are unable to develop a strategic direction for sales, marketing, and customer support.

As Harvard business professor Michael Porter (Porter and Millar

1991) points out, senior managers and owners of a company can fulfill their managerial responsibilities without becoming directly involved in the management of the information technology in their organization. A champion of the technology within an organization who is not a decision maker should find a way to get members of senior management in front of a computer to discover for themselves the power of the Internet. Once they use it and explore its possibilities, senior managers will discover what a powerful tool it is. Users need a modest investment in time and training to become familiar with the Net, but it is well worth it, as any regular user will attest.

Marketing has proven to be one of the most effective uses of the Internet. The first instinct was to use the Net as an advertising medium — to use the old media of magazines and television as the content for the new medium of the Internet. This approach is not very useful because it does not take advantage of the interactivity that the Net offers. The traditional use of display ads in print media and spots in broadcast media have lost their effectiveness. After almost fifty years of bombardment by rapid-fire sound bites and flashy images, the public has become fairly immune to the effects of traditional advertising. To have an impact today, a superficial hit will not work; potential customers must be *educated* about the advantages of the product or service offered.

Internet marketing that takes advantage of the potential for interactivity can be a powerful strategy. By providing information with which potential customers can interact, companies allow individuals to learn about a product or service on their own terms without feeling that they are being manipulated. Consumers can and will sell themselves on the advantages of a company's products or services. By providing information such as product announcements, newsletters, frequently asked questions (FAQs), corporate profiles, pricing, and product descriptions in an interactive format, a company narrowcasts to potential customers and, at the same time, unobtrusively makes a large amount of data available, allowing individuals to customize the information to suit their needs and interests.

Because the Internet is already segmented into micromarkets, it is now easier to narrowcast one's message with this medium. The challenge of Internet marketing lies in getting consumers to visit a Web site. The ethos of the Internet frowns upon direct advertising and solicitation. Instead, a company must exploit other, more traditional information channels to make potential users aware of its Web site. A telephone is an indispensable part of running a business, but no one would rely on the telephone to inform potential clients of one's telephone number. The same applies to the Internet. But an interesting Web site that has information of relevance to some audience will create word of mouth, and people will soon flock to the site.

Nine Internet Marketing Models

A recent study of life insurance Web sites, sponsored by LIMRA International (Baranoff et al. 1997), identified a number of different models for using the Internet for marketing:

1. **The Traditional Model**, in which the company disseminates information about its products and services.
2. **The Corporate Relations Model**, in which a multinational uses a Web site to link the activities of its various subsidiaries.
3. **The Lead Generation Model**, in which the Web site is used to generate leads, which a sales force then follows up using traditional means of communication such as snail mail or telephone.
4. **The Direct Sales Model**, in which visitors to the site are given the opportunity to buy and/or order a product or service online.
5. **The Personalized User Model**, in which a customer has a personalized folder on the Web site of the provider of a service or a product.
6. **The Corporate Intranet**, in which a supplier is able to place Web pages on a customer's intranet so that employees of the customer can access the supplier's services or products.
7. **The Industry Extranet Model**, in which a group of collaborating organizations coordinate their commercial activities.
8. **The Electronic Commerce Distribution or Portal Site Model**, in which third-party marketing arrangements, through electronic-commerce intermediaries, provide a comprehensive set of related products and services.
9. **The Information Model**, in which an organization, by providing valuable information either through an electronic magazine

(e-zine) or an educational Web site, attracts visitors and is able to introduce their products or services in an unobtrusive manner.

E-Commerce and Direct Sales

Examples of all of the above nine marketing models can now be found on the Internet. The ones causing the most excitement at this early juncture are the direct sales and portal site models. Many organizations are attempting to fulfill sales and find new customers through direct-sale Web pages on their own sites and on portal sites. A portal site focuses on a vertical market niche and offers its visitors the products and services of third parties. These sites are quite successful because the Internet is becoming so large and unwieldy. Surfers prefer to go to a site that focuses on their interests and to search a site that has human scale.

Sales on the Internet started very slowly but they are now threatening to change the nature of commerce. Dell, which has become the number-two seller of microcomputers, distributes its products strictly over the Internet, and is purported to bring in $75 million a day. Auction sites and online garage sales can be found at sites such as ubid.com and ebay.com. Real estate can be bought and apartments rented at sites such as pmrentals.com and rentnet.com. Consumer spending over the Internet during 1998 was estimated at $4.9 billion in the United States and $3.0 billion in Europe (www.rua.ie). And *Internet World* reported on May 10, 1999, that advertisers spent $1.9 billion in 1998 on Internet advertising, versus $1.6 billion on outdoor advertising. Yet as big as business-to-consumer commerce will be on the Internet, it is business-to-business e-commerce that is poised to take off and completely transform business practices.

Alignment: A Strategy for Connectivity and the Use of the Internet

When the microcomputer was introduced, it allowed working groups within an organization to pursue their own information-processing strategies to fulfill the objectives of their particular division. Groups often found themselves in conflict with other working groups and with their MIS department, which lost control of the information-processing activity within the organization. With client-server systems and business process reengineering (BPR), a measure of order and control has been restored so that, by and large, information technology now serves the overall objectives of organizations.

The tools developed to facilitate global communications on the World Wide Web can also be used to set up links between the computer users within an organization. Organizations have a wide variety of interfaces and protocols for retrieving information. The HTML format and HTTP protocol were designed precisely so that users of disparate formats and protocols around the world could communicate with each other. HTML is therefore ideal for use within an organization that is linked by a LAN or WAN, and even in those cases when no network exists. HTML is the *lingua franca* of networked computer users. It supplements e-mail communications by providing graphical interfaces and taking advantage of hypertext links. Individuals can create their own home pages, as well as pages for their working group. Through the use of an intranet, members of an organization become better informed of each others' activities, and can share their knowledge more readily. This connectivity contributes to the coherence of the organization's external communications and the alignment of its operations and activities. The Internet gives an organization the potential to achieve total connectivity with all of its customers and suppliers and hence permits the integration of a number of key business functions, such as marketing, advertising, sales, order fulfillment, distribution, customer support, market research, market feedback, and product design. These activities, to work well together, must be aligned within a strategy that focuses on the overall objectives of the organization. The alignment team should include experts in marketing, communications, and information technology.

Alignment is to the Internet and connectivity what business process reengineering (BPR) is to computing, but alignment takes the process of integration one step further. BPR redesigns business processes to maximize the efficiency of computer use. But the Internet takes these reengineered processes and aligns them, to maximize the flow of information that arises from the connectivity of the Internet, electronic data interchange (EDI), or any other network that connects the firm to its market and suppliers.

Knowledge Management

All large organizations have a strategy for the management of their information but most lack a strategy for the management of their knowledge. Employees of Siemens AG, headquartered in Munich, have been working on the development of an Internet-based knowledge-management strategy for the past three years. They have a saying that succinctly sums up this dilemma: "If Siemens only knew what Siemens knows."

A successful knowledge-management strategy requires the use of information technology, especially the Internet, but the real challenge lies in motivating personnel to participate, share their knowledge, co-create new knowledge, and utilize the knowledge of others.

The Internet and knowledge management, both of which have surfaced only within the past five years, are reconfiguring and transforming communication, learning, and commerce in today's workplace. They are at the vanguard of a shift of emphasis from information to knowledge. The two trends are parallel and support each other's mutual development. They are responsible for the transition from the information age to the knowledge era. Both trends embrace the notion that knowledge is an abundant resource that can be openly shared and co-created and that represents today's principal source of wealth.

In the era before computing and the Internet, when the rate at which knowledge changed was slow, most learning was done by rote. Very little distinction was made between knowledge and information. With the advent of computing and the Internet, the rate of change of knowledge greatly accelerated, along with the speed at which information transmits from one person to another. The ability to access information in today's supercharged environment is no longer sufficient to guarantee survival in the marketplace. Knowledge is much more than just being informed. One must, among other things, be able to cut through the information glut to discern what information is important, and then know how to apply it. The nature of knowledge, and its relation to information and data, has changed due to the impact of information technology. Knowledge and information are often mistaken for one another. It is important to understand the relationship between them, as set out in the definitions formulated in Chapter 6:

Information is data that is structured, adding meaning and context.
Knowledge is the ability to use information strategically to achieve
one's objectives.

Charles Savage's definition of "knowledging" deserves repetition:
"Knowledge is not something that is possessed like a commodity . . .
Known facts can be possessed, but the human process of *'knowledging'*
is a much richer and more dynamic phenomenon . . . *'knowledging'* is
more than just 'knowing', because it suggests an active and continual
process of interrelating patterns" (Savage 1996, 121 — italicization has
been added for emphasis).

Information is a resource to be exploited and knowledge is a tool or
technique that takes advantage of this resource. An understanding of
the relationship between information and knowledge leads to the following definition of knowledge management:

> Knowledge management is the activity of creating an environment,
> both attitudinally and technologically, in which knowledge can be
> accessed, shared, and created in such a way that all of the experi-
> ences and knowledge within an enterprise can be organized to
> achieve its objectives and reinforce its values.

A knowledge-management strategy must embrace the members of
an organization. The application of information can no longer be carried out solely by a small clique of senior managers. When information
and events moved more slowly, owners and managers had time to
absorb all of the information being generated in their commercial
environment, and then make appropriate decisions. But the time for
centralized decision-making is long past. The pace of business has
become so frenzied that decisions must be made on a just-in-time
basis. All of the operations of an organization, from inventory to
training, must mirror this pace.

The only possible way for a company to operate on a just-in-time
basis is for decision-making to be distributed. Distributed decision-
making requires a technological element — the use of an intranet to
allow the rapid dissemination of information — and an organizational
element — the use of knowledge-management techniques to allow

knowledge to be accessed from anywhere within the organization on an as-needed basis.

The optimal way to develop such a knowledge-management strategy in a medium- to large-size organization is to make use of an intranet. The intranet, therefore, plays two roles, first, as a conduit for the rapid distribution of information and then as a tool for the development of a knowledge-management strategy. The intranet becomes a knowledge network with specific tools such as online learning courses, knowledge sharing facilities, a way to identify human resources within the organization, a casebase of projects and best practices, measurement tools, diagnostics tools, a search engine, a help desk, and a directory of coaches and mentors. One such knowledge network, which I have had a hand in developing, is illustrated below. More information can be found at gutenberg.com/~bubble.

The Gutenberg Knowledge Network consists of three principal components: a learning system, a sharing system, and a measurement system.

The Learning System consists of
- diagnostic tools to determine training and/or coaching needs plus a catalog of available learning and training resources;
- online training courses — the basic instructional content of the system;
- a help desk to provide immediate advice;
- coaches and mentors to provide guidance and encouragement;
- a search engine to locate information anywhere within the network; and
- a performance support system, which, by combining the online training courses with a search engine, enables users to access information on a just-in-time basis.

The Sharing System is made up of
- a competence pool — a personal Web site where employees can share their competencies and aspirations;
- an idea pool — an environment for sharing new ideas and useful suggestions;
- best practice examples — a collection of the best practices of the organization;
- a casebase forum — a collection of cases that describe the outcomes of projects; and
- dialogue tools — listservs, chat groups, special interest groups, and support groups.

The Measurement System provides
- testing — as a feature of all online training courses, for the purpose of certification;
- certification — to publicize and record the achievements of employees and track their skills; and
- a skills matrix — a catalog of the skills within an organization.

Another example of a knowledge network that is attempting to serve the collaborative needs of the knowledge-management community can be found at knowledgecreators.com.

Lifelong Learning: Job Security in the Internet Age

One of the key elements of the knowledge-management approach is that all members of an enterprise must engage in lifelong learning and share knowledge that integrates with their role at work. Thirty years ago, Marshall McLuhan described how the electrification of information reversed the fragmented patterns of work and learning characteristic of the industrial age and retrieved many of the holistic patterns of oral society in which learning and work were integrated. The Internet embodies this description. It integrates all forms of media by providing a globally networked medium that accepts any form of information that can be digitized, from text and visual images to audio and music. Information flows from one domain to another and, by so doing, breaks down the barriers between work and learning, entertainment and education, work and leisure, technology and culture, art and science. Computing and the Internet represent a new cultural milieu, a new form of economics, a new way to earn a living by learning a living, and a new way to live.

McLuhan (1964, 346) predicted that automation would end "jobs in the world of work." By the end of jobs, McLuhan did not mean that automation spelled the end of work but, rather, a new way of organizing work. Instead of holding a job, he suggested, an individual would pursue a career and thereby assume a role in society. Consider the position of "secretary," which has, due to the influence of information technology, evolved into the role of "administrative assistant." Secretaries once took dictation, typed documents, and served coffee. They worked from nine to five, at which time they put a cover on their typewriters, went home, and forgot about work. Today's administrative assistants, on the other hand, are junior to middle managers. They make decisions, organize activities, and anticipate problems rather than merely react to them. They stay late and work weekends if required. They are more immersed in their work than the secretaries of yesteryear. They are more likely to learn more about their industry, take courses in their spare time to upgrade their skills, and network socially with colleagues and associates in their field. Like many others in the work force, they are not just earning a living by filling in time, they are pursuing a career and "learning" a living.

During the industrial age, it was common for an individual to work for the same company for an entire lifetime. Today, that is almost unheard of. An individual just entering the work force will probably work for ten or more organizations before retiring, if he or she retires at all. Moreover, companies can go through just as many changes as their employees because of mergers, acquisitions, strategic alliances, and restructurings. Between jobs, many of today's workers do not become unemployed; instead, they become consultants or casual workers. They move in and out of employment and from one company to another, from one project to another, or from one working group to another. The only thing constant is change.

One no longer works at a job; one lives a career. Individuals had better like what they do, because work is no longer a nine-to-five, Monday-to-Friday activity; it is an all-consuming way of life. The meaning of "career" has also changed. It is no longer a linear progression up a hierarchical ladder of increased authority and responsibility based on seniority. Organizations, particularly those in the private sector, are starting to resemble the Internet, where no one is in control anymore. Senior managers are increasingly frustrated that they are not always able to steer their organization in the direction they want. Today's organization, like the tribe or village in oral society, is becoming a self-organizing system. A system of command and control no longer works; inspiration, motivation, and leadership do. And these traits do not necessarily have to come from the top. They can originate from anywhere in the organization.

In an environment where change — technological, economic, structural, and organizational — is pervasive, there is no such thing as job security. The world is changing too rapidly. An individual's only source of security is a set of skills that are up to date and in demand. This store of knowledge can only be achieved through lifelong learning, in which individuals are constantly honing and broadening their skills through reading, training courses, and intensive study. The Internet is a useful ally for those who want to stay current because it facilitates regular monitoring of trends on a global scale and allows easy and instantaneous personal contact with others pursuing a similar career.

The only way to defend against the rapid rate of change that characterizes the information age and the knowledge era is to try to anticipate what is about to take place and then to acquire the knowledge and skills that will be needed to cope with the new conditions, not only for today but for tomorrow and the day after as well. In other words, we all must **learn a living**.

The Emergence of the Computerate Class

The use of computers will create a new social class and a new form of privilege and economic opportunity. Those who are able to exploit the power of computers will have an important advantage over those who cannot, just as those who were literate had an advantage over those who were not. I predict that the middle class will divide into two subsets, one merely literate and the other both literate and computer and Internet savvy.

The new social class that will emerge — the computerate class — will realize a distinct commercial and cultural advantage over those who are not computer literate. The consequences will be extremely important for educational planners. Just as the emergence of literacy affected the patterns of education in literate societies, so too will the need for computer literacy create major changes in and new demands upon our current education system.

Computing is restructuring the way that the existing social classes relate to one another, resulting in a smaller gap between them. It is also changing the role that class structures play in the economics and politics of society as a whole. Computers allow the integration of many different functions and make each individual worker more self-sufficient. Many of the odious and brute-force tasks of the working class are now being performed by robots and other computer-controlled machinery. The percentage of jobs that are unskilled or strictly working-class continues to decrease, while the number of middle-class jobs requiring education, literacy, and computer skills increases. Senior and middle managers are becoming less and less dependent upon support staff.

At the same time, information-age enterprises are much less capital-intensive than industrial-era ones. Often, all that is required to start a major business operation is intellectual capital and a modest amount of cash. A number of middle-class computer whizzes have become multimillionaires in a relatively short time. The middle class is also able to become self-employed and often self-realized in the service sector. While this type of work does not often lead to a glamorous and aristocratic lifestyle, it has indeed done so for a number of entertainers, fashion designers, and restaurateurs.

In the Internet age, we will continue to see a greater merging of the three traditional social classes. The ability to manage one's knowledge and control information, however, will become more and more the key to success and power. Naturally, those who are computer literate will begin to realize tremendous advantages, which could lead to the emergence of a distinct class just when class distinctions seemed to be on the decline. There is no doubt, however, that computers will play an ever more important role in education and educational planning.

Digital Reality: The Sixth Language and Beyond

I am quite comfortable with my assertion that the Internet and the World Wide Web form the sixth language. The question then arises, will this process continue and a seventh and eighth language eventually emerge? Going out on a limb, I suspect that there may be some evidence for two other languages taking shape within the framework of the new digital media — virtual reality (VR) and expert systems could possibly represent the seventh and eighth languages. The evolution of these new languages, their trajectories, and their impacts from a psychological, developmental, and educational perspective are worthy of study and will be a source of dramatic new developments in the months and years to come. The real action right now, however, is the exploration of how to use Internet technology to advance the sharing and co-creation of knowledge. The next ten years will see the refinement of knowledge-management and knowledge-networking techniques so that information technology can be used to help the old dream of increased productivity become a reality.

Albright, W.F. 1957. *From the Stone Age to Christianity*. 2d ed. Garden City, N.Y.: Doubleday Anchor Books.

Anderson, John R. 1980. *Cognitive Psychology and Its Implications*. San Francisco: W.H. Freeman.

Anderson, M.A. 1990. Technology Integration for Mainstreamed Students. *The Computing Teacher* 18 (4).

Ashby, W.R. 1957. *An Introduction to Cybernetics*. 2d ed. New York: J. Wiley.

Aston, M. 1968. *The Fifteenth Century: The Prospect of Europe*. London: Thames and Hudson.

Bain, G., and R. Price. 1972. Who Is a White Collar Employee? *B.J. Industrial Relations* 10.

Bandle, O., H. Klingenberg, and H. Mauer, eds. 1958. Kategorien. *Lehre vom Satz*. Hamburg.

Bank Street College Project in Science and Mathematics Education. 1985. *The Voyage of the Mimi*. New York: Holt, Rinehart & Winston.

Baranoff, R., M. Logan, R. Logan, P. Michalak, and H. Ryan. 1997. *The Strategic Uses of the Internet as a Business Tool*. Hartford: LIMRA International.

Barker, Thomas. 1987. Studies in Word Processing and Writing. *Computers in the Schools* 4 (1).

Baron, N. 1983. *Speech, Writing and Sign*. Bloomington: Indiana Univ. Press.

Becker, Henry Jay. 1991*a*. When Powerful Tools Meet Conventional Beliefs and Institutional Constraints. *The Computing Teacher* 18 (8).

———. 1991*b*. Mathematics and Science Uses of Computers in American Schools. *Journal of Computers in Mathematics and Science Teaching* 10 (4).

Bender, B. 1975. *Farming in Pre-History*. London: J. Baker.

Bitter, G., and R. Camuse. 1984. *Using a Microcomputer in the Classroom*. Reston, Va.: Reston Pub. Co.

Blakenbaker, R. 1987. Databases in the English Class: A Valuable Lesson. *The Computing Teacher* 15 (2).

Blanchard, J. 1989. Hypermedia: Hypertext Implications for Reading Education. *Computers in the Schools* 6 (3/4).

Bledstein, B.J. 1976. *The Culture of Professionalism, the Middle Class and the Development of Higher Education in America*. New York: Norton.

Bloomfield, L. 1933. *Language*. New York: Holt.

Boissenaide, P. 1927. *Life and Work in Medieval Europe*. New York: Knopf.

Bonnington, Paul. 1995. *Internet World* (April).

Bosaquet, E.F. 1930. *English 17th Century Almanacks*. The Library 4th, ser. x.

Boulding, Kenneth. 1961. *The Image*. Ann Arbor: Univ. of Michigan Press.

Bowen, James. 1972. *A History of Western Education*. Vol. 2. London: Methuen.

Brougham (Lord). [1857]. Speeches on Social and Political Subjects. In *History of Education: Socrates to Montessori*, by L. Cole. New York: Holt, Rinehart & Winston, 1950.

Brown, J.S. 1985. Process versus Product: A Perspective on Tools for Communal and Informal Learning Environments. *Journal of Educational Computing Research* 1 (2).

Bruce, B., and A. Rubin. 1984. The Utilization of Technology in the Development of Basic Skills Instruction: Written Communications. Final Report Vol. 1. Tech. Report No. 5766. Bolt, Beranek and Newman.

Bryson, M., P.H. Lindsay, E. Joram, and E. Woodruff. 1985. *Augmented Word Processing: The Influence of Task Characteristics and Mode of Production on Writer's Cognition*. Toronto: Ont. Inst. for Studies in Education.

Burnet, J. 1986. Word Processing as a Tool of an Elementary School Student. Ph.D. diss., Univ. of Maryland. *Dissertation Abstracts International* 47, 1183A.

Carbonnier, G. 1969. *Conversations with Claude Levi-Strauss*. London: J. Cape.

Cole, L. 1950. *History of Education: Socrates to Montessori*. New York: Holt, Rinehart & Winston.

Cole, Sonia. 1970. *The Neolithic Revolution*. London: Trustees of the British Museum.

Coleman, Janet. 1981. *Medieval Readers and Writers*. New York: Hutchinson.

Coulmas, F., and K. Erlich, eds. 1983. *Writing in Focus*. New York: Mouton.

Cronin, Mary. 1994. *Doing Business on the Internet*. New York: Van Nostrand Reinhold.

Czernis, L., and R.K. Logan. 1982. Telidon as Pure Advertising — Implications for Attention Span. Paper presented at Social Impact of Telidon and Other Electronic Technology Workshop, 1–2 March, at Univ. of Toronto, and sponsored by Dept. of Communication, Ottawa, and the Culture and Tech. Seminar, Univ. of Toronto.

Dahrendorf, R. 1959. *Class and Class Conflict in Industrial Society*. London: Routledge & K. Paul.

Daiute, Collette. 1986. Physical and Cognitive Factors in Revising: Insights from Studies with Computers. *Research in the Teaching of English* 20.

Danzig, T. 1968. *Number: The Language of Science*. New York: Greenwood.

Dawkins, Richard. 1976. *The Selfish Gene*. New York: Oxford Univ. Press.

Day Lewis, Cecil. 1947. *The Poetic Image*. London: J. Cape.

Demsky, Aaron. 1972. Scroll. *Encyclopedia Judaica*. Jerusalem.

de Saussure, F. 1967. *Grundfragen der allgemeinen Sprachwissenschaft* (Basic Questions of Linguistics). 2d ed. Berlin.

Dickens, A.G. 1966. *Reformation and Society in 16th Century Europe*. London: Thames and Hudson.

Drazin, N. 1940. *History of Jewish Education 515 BCE to 220 BCE*. Reprint 1979. New York: Arno Press.

Drucker, Peter. 1993. *Post-Capitalist Society*. New York: HarperBusiness.

Duckworth, E. 1964. Piaget Rediscovered. *The Journal of Research in Science Teaching* 2 (3).

Dyrli, O.E. 1986. Electronic Spreadsheets in the Curriculum. *Computers in the Schools* 3 (1).

Edmonson, Munro. 1971. *Lore: An Introduction to the Science of Folklore and Literature*. New York: Holt, Rinehart & Winston.

Eisenstein, E.L. 1979. *The Printing Press as an Agent of Change*. London: Cambridge Univ. Press.

Feeley, J.T., D.S. Strickland, and S.B. Wepner. 1987. Computer as Tool: Classroom Applications for Language Arts. *Computers in the Schools* 4 (1).

Fish, M.C., and S.C. Feldman. 1990. Learning and Teaching in Microcomputer Classrooms: Reconsidering Assumptions. *Computers in the Schools* 7 (3).

Fischer, G., and Scharff, E. 1998. Learning Technologies in Support of Self-Directed Learning. *Journal of Interactive Media in Education* 98 (4) [www-jime.open.ac.uk/98/4].

Fisher, Ernst. 1963. *The Necessity of Art*. Baltimore: Penguin Books.

Fribers, J. 1984. Numbers and Measures in the Earliest Written Records. *Scientific American* 250 (2).

Garrard, J., et al. 1978. *The Middle Class in Politics*. Farnborough, Hents: Saxon House.

Gates, Bill. 1988. Computers in Schools, Today and Tomorrow. *T.H.E. Journal* 16 (12).

Giddens, A. 1981. *The Class Structure of the Advanced Societies*. London: Hutchinson.

Gilman, Daniel. 1906. The Dawn of a University. In *The Launching of a University and Other Papers: A Sheaf of Remembrances*. New York: Dodd, Mead.

Glotz, G. 1926. *Ancient Greece at Work*. New York: Knopf.

Graff, H.J. 1979. *The Literacy Myth*. New York: Academic Press.

Gretton, R.H. 1919. *The English Middle Class*. London: G. Bell and Sons.

Gudschinsky, Sarah. 1968. The Relationship of Language and Linguistics to Reading. In *Literacy: The Growing Influence of Linguistics*, by S. Gudschinsky. The Hague: Mouton, 1976.

Hall, Edward. 1969. *The Hidden Dimension*. Garden City, N.Y.: Anchor Books.

———. 1973. *The Silent Language*. Garden City, N.Y.: Anchor Books.

Hammer, M., and J. Champy. 1993. *Reengineering the Corporation*. New York: HarperBusiness.

Hannifin, M.J., and C.W. Hughes. 1985. *A Framework for Incorporating Orienting Activities in Computer-Based Interactive Video*. (n.p.).

Harkness, John. 1931. *Calvin: The Man and His Ethics*. New York: (n.p.)

Harvey, F.D. 1978. Greeks and Romans Learn to Write. In *Communications Arts in the Ancient World*, ed. E. Havelock and J. Hershbell. New York: Hasting House.

Havelock, Eric. 1963. *Preface to Plato*. Cambridge, Mass.: Howard Univ. Press.

———. 1976. Origin of Western Literacy. Toronto: Ont. Inst. of Studies in Education.

———. 1978. The Alphabetization of Homer. In *Communications Arts in the Ancient World*, ed. E. Havelock and J. Hershbell. New York: Hasting House.

Hawlisher, G. 1987. Word Processing, Revision, and College Freshmen. Cited in Studies in Word Processing and Writing, by Thomas Barker. *Computers in the Schools* 4 (1).

Her Majesty's Inspectors of Schools. 1984. The Content of the Primary Curriculum: Science. In *The Teaching of Primary Science: Policy and Practice*, ed. C. Richards and D. Holford. London: (n.p.)

Hershbell, J. 1978. The Ancient Telegraph: War and Literacy. In *Communications Arts in the Ancient World*, ed. E. Havelock and J. Hershbell. New York: Hasting House.

Hertzler, Joyce. 1965. *A Sociology of Language*. New York: Cooper Sq. Pub.

Hickerson, Nancy. 1980. *Linguistic Anthropology*. New York: Holt, Rinehart & Winston.

Hockett, Charles. 1960. The Origin of Speech. *Scientific American* 203 (3).

The Hulton Press Survey. 1948. London: Hulton Press.

Hunter, B. 1983. *My Students Use Computers*. Reston, Va.: Reston Pub. Co.

Innis, Harold. 1950. *The Bias of Communication*. Toronto: Univ. of Toronto Press.

———. 1972. *Empire and Communications*. Reprint with a foreword by Marshall McLuhan. Toronto: Univ. of Toronto Press. Original edition, Oxford: Oxford University Press, 1951.

Irwin, M.E. 1987. Connections: Young Children, Reading, Writing, and Computers. *Computers in the Schools* 4 (1).

Iserloh, E. 1968. *The Theses Were Not Posted*. Boston: Beacon Press.

Jackson, B., and O. Marsden. 1962. *Education and the Working Class*. New York: Penguin.

Kelman P., N. Roberts, C. Weiner, and P. Coburn. 1985. *Practical Guide to Computers in Education*. 2d ed. Reading, Mass.: Addison-Wesley.

Kenyon, Frederick. 1937. *Books and Readers in Ancient Greece and Rome*. Oxford: Clarendon Press.

King, R., and J. Raynor. 1981. *The Middle Class*. 2d ed. London: Longman.

Kramer, S.N. 1956. *From the Tablets of Sumer*. Indian Hills, Col.: Falcon Press.

———. 1959. *Life Begins at Sumer*. Garden City, N.Y.: Doubleday Anchor Books.

Krochmal, Mo. 1998. Communicating Supplants Computing in Classrooms. TechWeb. [www.techweb.com/wire/story/TWB19980310S0018].

Krochmal, Mo. 1999. E-Book Poised to Eclipse 10,000 Units Sold. TechWeb. [www.techweb.com/wire/story/TWB19990219S0025].

Kuhn, T.S. 1972. *The Structure of Scientific Revolutions*. Chicago: Univ. of Chicago Press.

Kurland, D.M., and L.C. Kurland. 1987. Computer Applications in Education: A Historical Overview. *Annual Reviews of Computer Science* 2:319–20.

Labbett, Beverley. 1988. Skillful Neglect. In *Breaking into the Curriculum*, ed. J. Schostak. London: Methuen.

Lepper, M.R., and R.W. Chabay. 1985. Intrinsic Motivation and Instruction: Conflicting Views on the Role of Motivational Processes in Computer-Based Education. *Educational Psychologist* 20 (4).

Levin, J.A., M. Riel, N. Miyake, and M. Cohen. 1987. Education on the Electronic Frontier: Teleapprentices in Globally Distributed Educational Context. *Contemporary Educational Psychology* 12.

Lewis, R., and A. Maude. 1949. *The English Middle Class*. London: Phoenix House.

Lieberman, Philip. 1975. *On the Origins of Language*. New York: Macmillan.

Litchfield, B., and S. Mattson. 1989. The Interactive Media Science Project. *Journal of Computers in Mathematics and Science Teaching* 9 (1).

Logan, Robert K. 1979. The Mystery of the Discovery of Zero. *Etcetera* 36.

———. 1982. Five Technological Breakthroughs. Cited at Telidon in the Total Information-Communications Environment Workshop, 1–2 March, in proceedings of the Dept. of Communication Workshop on Social Psychological Issues in Videotext Development. Seminar, Univ. of Toronto.

———. 1986a. *The Alphabet Effect*. New York: William Morrow.

———. 1986b. The Use of Computers in Primary and Junior Science Education: A Guide for Classroom Teachers, Consultants and Software Developers. Ont. Min. of Ed. Report (December).

Logan, Robert K., S. Padro, L. Miller, R. Ragsdale, E. Sullivan, J. Brine, E.M. Johnston, B. McKelvey, and H. Wideman. 1983. Research Questions on the Impact of Computers in the Classroom. Ont. Min. of Education. Ed. and Tech. Ser. ONO 4268.

Ludwig, O. 1983. Writing Systems and Written Language. In *Focus*, ed. F. Coulmas and K. Erlich. New York: Mouton.

Lusseyran, Jacques. 1963. *And There Was Light*. Boston: Little Brown.

Maddux, C.D. 1988. Preface to Assessing the Impact of Computer-Based Instruction. *Computers in the Schools* 5.

Malone, T.W. 1981. Toward a Theory of Intrinsically Motivating Instruction. *Cognitive Science* 4.

Mandinach, E. 1989. Model Building and Use of Computer Simulation of Dynamic Systems. *Journal of Educational Computing Research* 5 (2).

Manzelli, J. 1986. New Curriculum Soundings on a Voyage of the Mimi. *Computers in the Schools* 3 (1).

Marchand, Philip. 1989. *Marshall McLuhan: The Medium and the Messenger*. Toronto: Random House.

Marshack, A. 1964. *Science* 146.

Marx, Karl, 1954. *Das Kapital*. Moscow: Progress Publishers.

Marx, Karl, and F. Engels. 1940. *The Communist Manifesto*. Toronto: Progress Books.

McLuhan, Marshall. 1962. *The Gutenberg Galaxy: The Making of Typographic Man*. Toronto: Univ. of Toronto Press.

———. 1964. *Understanding Media*. New York: McGraw Hill.

———. 1967. *The Medium Is the Massage*. New York: Bantam Books.

———. 1972. Foreword to *Empire and Communications*, by Harold Innis. Reprint. Toronto: Univ. of Toronto Press.

———. 1977. Letter to Kaj Spenser, 8 November. In *Marshall McLuhan: The Medium and the Messenger*, by Philip Marchand. Toronto: Random House, 1989.

———. 1988. Media and the Inflation Crowd. *The Antigonish Review*, nos. 74/75 (summer/autumn).

McLuhan, Marshall, and R.K. Logan. 1977. Alphabet, Mother of Invention. *Etcetera* 34 (December).

McLuhan, Marshall, and Eric McLuhan. 1988. *Laws of the Media: The New Science*. Toronto: Univ. of Toronto Press.

McLuhan, Marshall, and Barrington Nevitt. 1972. *Take Today: The Executive as Dropout*. Don Mills, Ontario: Longman.

Mehan, H. 1989. Microcomputers in Classrooms: Educational Technology or Social Practice. *Education and Anthropology Quarterly* 20 (1).

Mersich, D. 1982. *Canadian Datasystems* 14 (10).

Meyers, E. 1960. *Education in the Perspective of History*. New York: Harper.

Microsoft. 1999. Microsoft Researcher Bill Hill Spearheads the Transition from Reading on Paper to Reading on the Computer Screen. [www.asia.microsoft.com/presspass/features/1999/07-07ebooks.htm].

Mill, James. 1969. *James Mill on Education*. London: Cambridge Univ. Press.

Montague, Marjorie. 1990. Computers and Writing Process Instruction. *Computers in the Schools* 7 (3).

Moore, M. 1987. The Effect of Word Processing Technology in a Developmental Writing Program on Writing Quality, Attitudes Towards Composing, and Revision Strategies of 4th and 5th Grade Students. Ph.D. diss., Univ. of South Florida. *Dissertation Abstracts International* 48, 635A.

Moravcsik, Julius. 1967. Aristotle's Theory of Categories. In *Aristotle: A Collection of Critical Essays*, ed. J. Moravcsik. Garden City, N.Y.: Anchor Books.

Morocco, C., and S. Newman. n.d. Word Processors and the Acquisition of Writing Strategies. *Journal of Learning Disabilities* 19.

Naisbitt, John, and Patricia Aburdene. 1985. *Reinventing the Corporation*. New York: Warner Books.

Nonaka, I., and H. Takeuchi. 1995. *The Knowledge Creation Company*. New York: Oxford Univ. Press.

Olds, H.F. 1986. Information Management: A New Tool for a New Curriculum. *Computers in the Schools* 3 (1).

Olson, John. 1988. *Schoolworlds/Microworlds*. Oxford: Oxford Univ. Press.

Ong, Walter. 1977. *Interfaces of the Word*. Ithaca and London: Cornell Univ. Press.

———. 1982. *Orality and Literacy: The Technologizing of the Word*. London and New York: Methuen.

Osborne, David, and Ted Gaebler. 1992. *Reinventing Government*. Reading, Mass.: Addison-Wesley.

Paivio, A., and I. Begg. 1981. *Psychology of Language*. Englewood Cliffs, N.J.: Prentice-Hall.

Palm, F.C. 1936. *The Middle Class Then and Now*. New York: Macmillan.

Pankey, Robert B. 1998. Piloting Exercise Physiology in the Web-Based Environment. [www.thejournal.com/magazine/98/dec/feat06.html].

Papert, S. 1980. *Mindstorms: Children, Computers and Powerful Ideas*. New York: Basic Books.

Pea, R., and R.D. Kurland. 1986. Cognitive Technologies for Writing. *Review of Research in Education* 13.

Perkin, H. 1969. *The Origin of Modern English Society*. London: Routledge and K. Paul.

Piaget, Jean. 1950. *Introduction à l'epistomologie génétique*. Paris: Presses Universitaires de France.

Pitschka, R. 1984. Little CAI in Hollister. In *The Intelligent Schoolhouse*, ed. D. Peterson. Reston, Va.: Reston Pub. Co.

Pfeiffer, John. 1977. *The Emergence of Society*. New York: McGraw Hill.

Polin, Linda. 1990*a*. Computer Environments and the Organization of Classroom Tasks. *The Computing Teacher* 18 (2).

———. 1990*b*. Young Children, Literacy and Computers. *The Computing Teacher* 18 (3).

———. 1990*c*. Computers for Student Writing: The Relationship between Writer, Machine, and Text. *The Computing Teacher* 18 (7).

————. 1991. Current Thinking about Critical Thinking: Implications for Technology Use. *The Computing Teacher* 19 (5).

Porter, M., and V. Millar. 1991. How Information Gives You Competitive Advantage. In *Revolution in Real Time: Managing IT in the 1990s*. Cambridge, Mass.: Harvard Business Review.

Poulantzas, N. 1978. *Classes in Contemporary Capitalism*. London: Verso.

Power, E. 1970. *Main Currents in the History of Education*. 2d ed. New York: McGraw Hill.

Prigogine, Ilya, and Isabelle Stengers. 1984. *Order Out of Chaos*. New York: Bantam Books.

Putnam, George. 1962. *Books and Their Makers during the Middle Ages*. New York: Hillary House.

Reznick, R., and D. Taylor. 1994. *The Internet Business*. Indianapolis: (n.p.).

Riel, M. 1991–1992. Approaching the Study of Networks. *The Computing Teacher* (December/January).

Roberts, K., et al. 1977. *The Fragmentary Class Structure*. London: Heinemann.

Rohman, G. 1965. Pre-writing: The Stage of Discovery in the Writing Process. *College Composition and Communication* 16.

Rondo, Cameron. 1993. *A Concise History of the World*. New York and Oxford: Oxford Univ. Press.

Ryder, Martin. 1996. Affordances and Constraints of the Internet for Learning and Instruction. Educational Communications Technology Conference. Indianapolis (14–18 February). [www.cudenver.edu/~mryder/aect_96.html].

Sahlins, M. 1968. Notes on the Original Affluent Society. In *Man, the Hunter*, ed. R. Lee and I. Devore. Chicago: Aldine Pub. Co.

Sapir, Edward. 1921. *Language*. New York: Harcourt, Brace.

Savage, Charles. 1996. *Fifth Generation Management*. Boston: Butterworth-Heinemann.

Schickel, Richard. 1965. Marshall McLuhan: Canada's Intellectual Comet. *Harper's* (November).

Schmandt-Besserat, D. 1978. The Earliest Precursor of Writing. *Scientific American* 238.

————. 1979. An Archaic Recording System in the Uruk-Jemdet Nasr Period. *American Journal of Archeology* 83.

————. 1980. The Envelopes That Bear the First Writing. *Technology and Culture* 21 (3).

————. 1981. From Tokens to Tablets: A Re-evaluation of the So-Called Numerical Tablets. *Visible Language* 15.

——. 1984*a*. Before Numerals. *Visible Language* 18.

——. 1984*b*. The Use of Clay before Pottery in the Zagros. *Expedition* 16 (2).

——. 1985. Clay Symbols for Data Storage in the VIII Millennium BC. In *Studi di Palentologia in onore di Salvatore M. Puglisi*. La Spaienza: Universita di Roma.

——. 1986*a*. An Ancient Token System: The Precursors to Numerals and Writing. *Archeology* 39 (6).

——. 1986*b*. The Origins of Writing. *Written Communication* 13.

——. 1986*c*. Tokens at Susa. *Oriens Antiquus* 25 (1/2).

——. 1987. Oneness, Twoness, Threeness. *The Sciences*. New York Academy of Sciences.

——. 1988*a*. Quantification and Social Structure. In *Communication and Social Structure*, ed. D.R. Maines and C.J. Couch. Springfield, Ill.: C.C. Thomas.

——. 1988*b*. Tokens at Uruk. *Bagdader Mitteilungen* 19.

——. 1992. Before Writing: Vol. 1. *From Counting to Cuneiform*. Houston: Univ. of Texas Press.

Schostak, John. 1988*a*. Impact on the Curriculum. In *Breaking into the Curriculum*, ed. J. Schostak. London: Methuen.

——. 1988*b*. Intelligence Communities. In *Breaking into the Curriculum*, ed. J. Schostak. London: Methuen.

——. 1988*c*. Introduction to *Breaking into the Curriculum*, ed. J. Schostak. London: Methuen.

Schwartz, E. 1991. At This High Tech School "Gum" Is a Requirement. *Business Week* (11 November).

Schwartz, Joel. 1989. Implementing Computer Literacy in Our Schools: What We Have Learned. *Computers in the Schools* 6 (1/2).

Science Council of Canada. 1984. Science for Every Student: Educating Canadians for Tomorrow's World. Report 36. Ottawa.

Senge, Peter. 1993. *The Fifth Discipline*. New York: Doubleday.

Shibles, Warren A. 1971. *Metaphor, An Annotated Bibliography and History*. Whitewater, Wis.: Language Press.

Sloan, D. 1985. Introduction to *The Computer in Education*, ed. D. Sloan. New York: Teachers College Press.

Smith, F. 1982. *Writing and the Writer*. New York: Holt, Rinehart & Winston.

Smith, Ken. 1991. Hypermedia in Education: Implications for Cognition and Curriculum. An unpublished paper submitted as a term paper to the author in a course on media and computers, given in the Dept. of Measurement, Evaluation and Computer Applications at the Ont. Inst. for Studies in Educ., Toronto.

Smith, W. 1955. *Ancient Education*. New York: Philosophical Library.

Stebbins, B. 1990. HyperCard: The Tool for the Classrooms of Tomorrow. *Computers in the Schools* 7 (4).

Steinberg, S.H. 1955. *Five Hundred Years of Printing*. Middlesex: Penguin Books.

Stevenson, Ken. 1999. Laptop Computers and Their Impact on Sixth-Grade Learning. [horizon.unc.edu/TS/cases/1999-03.asp].

Strickland, A.W., and T. Hoffer. 1989. Databases, Problem Solving and Laboratory Experience. *Journal of Computers in Mathematics and Science Technology* 9 (1).

———. 1990–1991. Integrating Computer Databases with Laboratory Problems. *The Computing Teacher* (December/January).

Stubbs, Michael. 1980. *Language and Literacy*. London: Routledge & K. Paul.

———. 1982. Written Language and Society. In *What Writers Know*, ed. M. Nystrand. New York: Academic Press.

Sullivan, E., P. Olson, N. Watson, D. Bors, H. Wideman, J. Zimmerman, and R.K. Logan. 1986. The Development of Policy and Research Projections for Computers in Education: A Comparative Ethnography. Project No. 499-83-0017. Study funded by Social Science and Humanities Research Council of Canada and carried out at Ont. Inst. for Studies in Educ., Toronto.

Sveiby, Karl Erik. 1997. *The New Organizational Wealth: Managing and Measuring Knowledge-Based Assets*. San Francisco: Berrett-Koehler.

Tapscott, D., and A. Caston. 1993. *Paradigm Shift*. New York: McGraw Hill.

Taylor, R.P., ed. 1980. *The Computer in the School: Tutor, Tool, Tutee*. New York: Teachers College Press.

Teale, W., and E. Sulzby, eds. 1986. *Emergent Literacy: Writing and Reading*. Norwood, N.J.: Ablex Publishing Corp.

Thorpe, Ronald. 1999. Can Computers Change the System? [www.edweek.org/ew/ewstory.cfm?slug=08thorpe.h19].

Tierney, R. 1989. Student Thinking Process. ACOT Report 3. Apple Computer Inc. ERIC document No. 316-201.

Toffler, Alvin. 1980. *The Third Wave*. New York: William Morrow.

———. 1990. *Powershift*. New York: Bantam Books.

Vygotsky, L.S. 1962. *Thought and Language*. Cambridge, Mass.: M.I.T. Press.

Weber, M. 1946. *Essays in Sociology*. Trans. H. Gerth and C. Wright Mills. Oxford: Oxford Univ. Press.

———. 1948. *The Protestant Ethic and the Spirit of Capitalism*. Trans. T. Parsons. London: Allen and Unwin.

Whorf, Benjamin Lee. 1964. *Language, Thought and Reality: Selected Writings*. Cambridge, Mass.: M.I.T. Press.

Wilson, Peter. 1988. *The Domestication of the Human Species*. New Haven: Yale Univ. Press.

Young, M., and P. Willmot. 1973. London: Routledge and K. Paul.

as language, 5–6, 62, 66, 77, 120, 124, 261
conceptualization, 69–71, 227
content. *See specific media*; media
content analysis, 18–19
cooperation. *See* sharing
counting, 83–84, 86. *See also* computing;
   mathematics; tallies; tokens
creativity, 27, 184, 257
"A Critical Review" (Innis), 57–58
Cronin, Mary, 265
Crusades, 151
curriculum, 8–9, 221
   and computers, 237–38
   guidelines for, 194, 234–37
   historical, 137–41, 150
   industrial model of, 8–9, 234
   and modes of language, 238–41
   need for integration of, 194–95, 222
   and new media, 24, 237–43
   planning, 236–43
cybernetics, 128–29, 211. *See also*
   computers
   and theorem of requisite variety, 72, 74

data, 169, 228
databases, 50, 77, 137–38, 166, 200, 251,
   276. *See also* hypertext
   in education, 180, 196, 246–47
   software for managing, 19, 173
Dawkins, Richard, 21
decentralization, 290–91. *See also*
   centralization
decoding, 36
democracy, 127
   class structure in, 148, 155, 158
   and computers, 171–73, 193–95, 203–4
   and the Internet, 267–68
desktop publishing, 166, 274–75, 276
   software for, 167, 173
discussion groups, 266–67, 270–71, 272,
   274, 279, 281, 292. *See also* listservs;
   oral tradition; World Wide Web
Doing Business on the Internet (Cronin),
   265
Drucker, Peter, 211, 213, 216, 217, 265
dyslexia, 173, 233. *See also* education,
   special

e-books, 275
e-commerce, 20, 34, 78, 122, 280–87
education, 6–13, 18, 44, 54–55, 63,
   114–15, 133, 190, 196. *See also*
   curriculum; learning; literacy; schools;
   training
   alternative, 196–98, 247–50
   art, 57, 239–40, 248–49
   and cognitive skills, 230–32
   and computing, 18, 29, 31, 115, 132,
   179–98

effects of electric media on, 35, 46,
   132–33, 262–63
goals of, 220–21, 229–30
history of, 11, 35, 131, 137–41, 149–51,
   153, 156–57, 233
integration with work of, 10–12, 220–26
and the Internet, 132, 168, 262–63,
   278–80
knowledge and, 59, 289–95
and nationalism, 156–57
in preliterate societies, 134, 233
special, 185–86, 197, 248–49 (*see also*
   dyslexia)
and technology, 6–7, 200–202, 232–34
universal, 158–59
and work, 6–7, 200–202
educational psychology, 234–35
Egypt, ancient, 34, 272
   education in, 35, 138–39, 140
   science in, 116–17
   social structures of, 44, 59, 148
   and writing, 81, 105, 127
electric information. *See* information,
   electric
electricity, 6, 26–27, 48, 52
   and education, 160–62
   and information flow, 59, 272–73
electronic cottage, 52, 201
electronics, 38, 40
e-mail, 20, 24, 56, 78, 253, 273, 283, 288
   emoticons (smiley faces) in, 25, 266
   flaming in, 267, 268
   and learning, 202, 280
Empire and Communications (Innis), 14,
   33
ENIAC, 40
envelopes. *See under* tokens, accounting
equivalence, 31
Europe, 287. *See also* Industrial
   Revolution; Middle Ages; Renaissance
   electric media in, 54, 272
   history of literacy in, 82, 137, 149–50,
   153, 156–58, 237
   industrialization of, 11
   political change in, 216–17
extranets, 78

farming. *See* agriculture
feudal system, 149–50
field theory, 21
The Fifth Discipline (Senge), 219–20
figure-ground relationship, 22, 56
Fisher, Ernst, 64
folktales, 80. *See also* storytelling
Ford, Henry, 27–28
fragmentation, 7, 213–14, 271, 293. *See
   also* centralization; integration
   and literacy, 43–45, 47
freenets, 268

and computers, 164–68
and the middle class, 145
information sharing, 49–50, 133
and computers, 18, 31–32, 200
and the Internet, 42, 47, 60, 268–72,
277–78, 281
information storage, 38, 53, 80
electronic, 39, 40–41, 165, 275–77
evolution of, 39, 70
the Internet and, 42, 165, 278–79
information superhighway. See Internet
information technology, 10, 30. See also
computers; hybrid systems
and knowledge monopolies, 59–60
social context of, 252
transitions in, 172–78
and work, 6–8
Innis, Harold, 14–17, 21, 26, 27, 35. See
also McLuhan, Marshall; Toronto
School of Communications
The Bias of Communication, 56
on communications, 34, 43, 47–49,
53–58, 252
"A Critical Review," 57–58
Empire and Communications, 14, 33
on media, 17, 44, 276
Minerva's Owl, 14
integration, 271
of communications and technology, 31,
128–29, 172–73
in curriculum design, 241, 248–49
of information, 166–69, 195–96, 204
of knowledge and work, 10–12, 221–26,
263, 280, 287–88
of work groups, 218
intelligence, artificial, 164–65
interaction, social. See also sharing
in schools, 191–93
in the workplace, 202
interactivity. See also multimedia
of books, 184
of computers, 181, 183–85, 200
and the Internet, 185, 261–62, 278–86
Internet, 50, 121–24, 172, 259–60, 277–78.
See also discussion groups; e-mail;
WebTV; World Wide Web
and collaboration, 18, 42, 268–80
in curriculum, 239, 240
in education, 9, 31, 182, 183, 187–90,
193, 197–98, 249, 278–80
effects of, 24–25, 29–30, 168–69, 260,
264–66
as general systems approach, 42, 129
and information overload, 72–73
interactivity of, 185, 261–62, 278–86
and knowledge monopolies, 60
as language, 5–6, 20, 56, 62, 66–67,
77–78, 122, 261
marketing on, 283–84, 286–87

as medium, 24–26, 29–30, 42, 169
socioeconomic impacts of, 5–6, 33–34,
35, 53
and work, 31, 199–204, 260
Internet Explorer, 122, 253, 271
Internet literacy, 253–54
intranets, 78, 122, 165, 174–75, 263,
279–80, 288, 290–91

Java scripting, 253

knowledge
as basis for wealth, 6, 7, 49–50, 212–13,
219
defined, 169, 290
explicit, 226–28
and information, 290
management of, 226–28, 289–92
monopolies of, 59–60
tacit, 60, 226–28, 230
knowledge community, 227–28, 261–62
The Knowledge Creation Company
(Nonaka and Takeuchi), 226–27
knowledge era, 7, 42, 212–20, 289
knowledge networks, 227–28, 263, 279,
291. See also sharing
Kuhn, Thomas, 19, 23, 51, 55

language, 1–2, 62–64, 66. See also
computing; Internet; mathematics;
science; speech; writing
and abstraction, 70–72
as communication, 3, 63, 68
definitions of, 63–64
evolutionary chain of, 3–4, 62, 119,
126–29
evolution of, 69–73, 238
and evolution of thought, 67–68, 70–71
and informatics, 3, 63, 68–70
modes of, 61–67, 238–41
physical tools of, 123–24
and social context, 252
syntax of, 73–78
verbal, 3, 63, 74–75
LANs. See local area networks (LANs)
law, in ancient world, 36, 52, 108, 126
Laws of the Media (McLuhan), 28–32
learning, 17
and computers, 181
individualized, 29–30, 181, 188–90,
201–2, 249–50, 262–63
in industrial age, 289
and the Internet, 202
lifelong, 12, 219, 262–64, 293–95
self-directed, 180, 181, 188–90, 201–2,
234–35, 243, 262–63
learning a living, 6, 293–95
learning disabilities, 247–49. See also
dyslexia; education, special

learning organizations, 219–26, 263–65
Levi-Strauss, Claude, 146
linguistics, 61, 63–66, 73, 83, 100, 116
links. *See* HTML; Web pages
listservs, 78, 253, 279, 292
literacy, 2, 6, 43–45, 114. *See also*
    computer literacy; Internet literacy
  alphabetic, 47, 112, 121, 151
  and class structure, 131–32, 135–36,
    142, 144–49, 152–53, 156–59
  and curriculum, 237, 239
  defined, 250
  and education, 135–41
  evolution of, 34, 135–36, 147–60
  and fragmentation, 43–45
  role of computers in, 186, 200–201,
    248
  and television, 26
  visual bias in, 17, 45
literate societies, compared to preliterate
    societies, 17, 53–54, 227, 267
local area networks (LANs), 168, 171,
    174, 288
Logan, Robert K., 2–3, 36, 103, 108, 183
logic
  analog, 227
  binary, 255
logic, deductive, 227
  development of, 52, 109, 117, 127
  and mathematics, 76
  as new medium, 24, 37
  and visual bias, 53
LOGO, 180, 185, 244, 254
logograms, 88–89, 94–103. *See also*
    writing, logographic
Lusseyran, Jacques, 55

mainframe computers. *See under*
    computers
management information systems. *See*
    MIS (management information
    systems) departments
managers, 8, 72, 131, 147, 293. *See also*
    knowledge, management of
  in industrial era, 220–21, 223, 290
  in information age, 294–96
  and information technology, 176, 204–5,
    284–85
  in learning organizations, 220
  as middle class, 143, 152
marketing, Internet, 284–87
markup languages, 20, 122, 253, 288
Marshack, Alexander, 82
Marx, Karl, 144
mass media, 35, 272–73
mass production, 43–45, 52, 158, 211
mathematical notation, 3, 81–83. *See also*
    counting; numerals, abstract
  evolution of, 108–13

mathematics, 37, 52–53. *See also* counting
  and abstraction, 76, 83–88, 90, 113–14,
    144, 246
  and computers, 248
  evolution of, 70–72, 255–56
  as language, 66, 76, 110–11
  and logic, 76
  origins of, 3, 66, 81
McLuhan, Marshall, 4, 6, 7, 13, 16, 26,
    56–58, 211–12. *See also* global village;
    Innis, Harold; Toronto School of
    Communications
  "Alphabet, Mother of Invention" (with
    Robert K. Logan), 36
  author's collaboration with, 2–3, 36,
    103, 108, 183
  on business-process reengineering,
    214–15
  catchphrases of, 58
  on centralization, 47–49, 264
  on education, 6, 195–96, 219
  on electric information, 26, 37–39, 43,
    211, 218, 273, 293
  on fragmentation, 45, 195–96, 204, 293
  on globalization, 216–17
  The Gutenberg Galaxy, 15, 37
  on history, 33, 34–36
  on information and media, 21, 26, 27,
    31, 43, 44, 50
  on Innis, Harold, 15, 23, 26, 33
  Laws of the Media, 28–32
  on media, 16–17, 31–32, 35, 195, 252
  on oral tradition, 53, 57–58, 216
  predictions of, 212–13
  on specialization, 54, 58, 194–95
  on technology, 16–17, 32, 39
  on television and radio, 26, 48–49, 54
  Understanding Media, 211–12, 226
  on work, 6, 204, 213, 221, 264–65, 293
  on writing, 44–45, 108, 252
media. *See also specific types of media* ;
    communication; mass media;
    technology
  analysis of, 18–19, 26, 33
  cultural impacts of, 17, 24, 27–29, 33–34
  history of, 34–36
  Laws of (McLuhan), 28–32
  as staples, 33–34
  as tools, 30
  understanding, 31–32
media, electric, 43, 48, 132, 160–62, 194
  bias of, 53–54
  compared to electronic media, 35–36,
    273
  effects on education of, 35, 46
  evolution of, 34, 37–42, 272–73
media, electronic, 17, 26, 29
  compared to electric media, 35–36,
    272–73

and computers, 295–96
social interaction, 18, 191–93
software, 52, 77, 119, 167–68, 251. *See also specific types of software*
  educational, 180, 183
  evolution of, 172–73, 177–78
  versus hardware, 38, 49–50
special education. *See* education, special
specialization, 45, 54, 103
  and computers, 29
  in curriculum, 8–9, 44, 195–96
  in industrial age, 128, 263
speech, 67. *See also* oral tradition
  and children, 67–68, 137
  in curriculum, 239
  evolution of, 69, 99
  as language, 64, 66, 79, 80
  relationship to writing of, 64, 98–99
spreadsheets, 166, 251
  in education, 180, 196, 246–47
  software for, 19, 119, 173
  in the workplace, 200
storytelling, 134, 270–72
The Structure of Scientific Revolutions (Kuhn), 55
Stubbs, Michael, 65
Sumer. *See also* Mesopotamia
  education in, 131
  origins of mathematics in, 66, 71–72, 81, 87–89, 126
  origins of writing in, 103–5, 126
  science in, 115–16
  social structure of, 135–36
Sveiby, Karl Erik, 228
syllabic systems, 74, 103–5
syntax, 73–78, 85–86, 95
systems
  computer, 168, 171–78, 200, 204–5, 287–88
  expert, 296

Takeuchi, H., 226–27
tallies, 61, 81–83, 87–88, 90, 91, 93, 126
Talmud, 139
Tapscott, Dan, 170, 172–73, 211, 217–18, 265
Tartaglia, Niccolo, 156
taxonomy, 77
Taylor, R.P., 180, 243
TCP/IP, 122, 174
teaching
  and computers, 181, 185, 188–89, 191–94
  peer, 192–93
technology, 5, 8, 62, 82, 156, 170, 172–73, 198, 208. *See also* computers; industrialization; Industrial Revolution; Internet; media
  breakthroughs in, 37–42, 51–52

defined, 30
and education, 10, 232–35
evolution of, 123–29
explosion of, 27
as extensions, 31–32
impacts of, 12, 21, 27–29, 151
as medium, 30–31
and work, 10
telecommunications, 8, 35. *See also* global village
  development of, 38–39, 42–43
  impact of, 46, 53
telegraph, 38–39, 43, 161, 272–73. *See also* telecommunications
telephone, 161, 273, 282
  and decentralization, 48–49
  user as content of, 56
television, 18–20, 26, 29, 48–49, 260, 273
  versus computers, 181, 183, 184, 198–99
  impact on education of, 132, 160–62, 180, 194, 263, 280
  McLuhan on, 26, 48–49, 54
  negative effects of, 162, 186
textbooks. *See* books
Thales, 116, 140
theorem of requisite variety, 72, 74
The Third Wave (Toffler), 52, 212, 215
Thorpe, Ronald, 192
thought, 67–68, 73, 82, 255. *See also* conceptualization
Thought and Language (Vygotsky), 67–68
Toffler, Alvin, 158–59, 201, 210, 211, 265
  Future Shock, 216
  Powershift, 212–13, 222, 224–25
  The Third Wave, 52, 212, 215
tokens, accounting, 3, 61, 81–83, 87–89
  cognitive impact of, 85–88
  envelopes for, 85, 88–89
  evolution of, 96–103, 126
  origins of mathematics in, 66, 81
  origins of writing in, 90–103
Torah, 139
Toronto School of Communications, 15–16, 18, 22–23, 26, 33, 52–53. *See also* Innis, Harold; McLuhan, Marshall
trade unions, 155–56
training. *See also* education; schools
  apprenticeship, 11–12, 134, 151
  benefits of, 223–24
  computer, 199
  online, 201–2, 262, 278–80, 291–92
  vocational, 242, 294
  workplace, 10–12, 206–7, 222–26
tribal societies, 267, 269. *See also* oral tradition
  and communication, 54, 270–72
  evolution of, 131–32, 134, 266
  versus individualism, 46
Turing, Alan, 256–57